# THE LAST LOG OF THE
# TITANIC

Nothing . . . shall exonerate any vessel, or the owner, master or crew thereof, from the consequence of . . . the neglect of any precaution which may be required by the ordinary practice of seamen.

INTERNATIONAL RULES OF THE ROAD

# THE LAST LOG OF THE
# TITANIC

David G. Brown

INTERNATIONAL MARINE / McGRAW-HILL

Camden, Maine • New York • San Francisco • Washington, D.C. • Auckland • Bogotá •
Caracas • Lisbon • London • Madrid • Mexico City • Milan • Montreal • New Delhi •
San Juan • Singapore • Sydney • Tokyo • Toronto

*International Marine*
A Division of The *McGraw·Hill* Companies

2 4 6 8 10 9 7 5 3 1

Copyright © 2001 David G. Brown
All rights reserved. The name "International Marine" and the
International Marine logo are trademarks of The McGraw-Hill Companies.
Printed in the United States of America.

*Library of Congress Cataloging-in-Publication Data*

Brown, David G. (David Geren), 1944–
The last log of the Titanic / David G. Brown.
p.    cm.
Includes bibliographical references (p.     ).
ISBN 0-07-136447-1
1. Titanic (Steamship) 2. Shipwrecks—North Atlantic Ocean—Chronology. I. Title.
G530.T6 B755 2000
910'.91634—dc21          00-057569

This book is printed on 55 lb. Sebago by
R.R. Donnelley & Sons, Crawfordsville, IN
Design by Dennis Anderson
Production by Dan Kirchoff and UG / GGS Information Services, Inc.
Edited by Jonathan Eaton, Charlie Doane, and Shana Harrington

To the reader: Notes are keyed to the text by page number
and by the relevant text phrase. Notes begin on page 211.

To the families whose loved
ones sail forever aboard *Titanic*.
History owes them the truth.

# CONTENTS

# INTRODUCTION

*T*ITANIC ran over the iceberg because the berg was in its path. It sank because the hull filled with water. These are the two certainties of the tragedy. The ultimate simplicity of the sinking was demonstrated by a humorous exchange between Second Officer Charles H. Lightoller and a pompous Senator Duncan U. Fletcher during the U.S. Senate hearings into the disaster.

> SENATOR FLETCHER: I will get you to state, not only from your actual knowledge of the immediate effect, but also from your experience as a navigator and seaman, what the effect of that collision was on the ship, beginning with the first effect, the immediate effect; how it listed the ship, if it did; what effect it had then, and what in your opinion was the effect on the ship that resulted from that collision.
>
> MR. LIGHTOLLER: The result was she sank.

A spectacular Hollywood movie named after the ship has recently triggered a short flurry of public interest in the tragic sinking. Unfortunately, this flurry has been concerned more with period costumes and a fictional romance than with historical fact. Despite millions of dollars spent on authentic movie sets and colorful books, nearly everything the average person knows about history's most famous shipwreck is based on inaccurate myths and legends.

Some myths surrounding the *Titanic* story are harmless, such as the band playing the hymn *Nearer My God to Thee*. This charming story is a romantic fiction. Other fictions, such as the single left turn to avoid the iceberg, serve only to mask the truth. Myths die harder than ships. It took *Titanic* two hours and forty minutes to founder, yet for almost ninety years a collection of half-truths has obscured what happened that April night.

A key *Titanic* myth concerns the weather. It was clear, cold, and still on the night of the disaster. Each of these conditions is rare on the stormy North Atlantic, but to have all three occur simultaneously was unusual enough to allow the ship's second officer to concoct his "everything was against us" myth. Usually, favorable weather makes it easier for ships to avoid dangers like icebergs, but

Lightoller portrayed *Titanic* as the helpless victim of circumstances beyond human control. In effect, he claimed that good weather made the iceberg virtually impossible to see until it was too late. Historians and moviemakers continue to repeat this claim (with emphasis on the unusually good weather) even though the facts show Lightoller was wrong. The clear, calm conditions allowed the lookouts to spot the deadly berg several minutes before the accident.

In reality, those calm conditions were the indicators of mortal danger threatening the ship. Ice navigation texts state flatly that the absence of swell (wave motion) is an indicator that a ship is approaching pack ice. Also, an oily look to the surface of frigid water is produced by the formation of spicules, or *frazil* ice. Frazil is the first stage in the development of new sea ice. Its formation would have been expected once the temperature of the seawater dipped below the freezing point. (Seawater freezes at a lower temperature than does freshwater.)

Based on the conditions reported by Lightoller and the other surviving officers, *Titanic* must have been steaming through patches of ice and dodging occasional bergs for several hours at the time of the accident. There was plenty of time to set extra lookouts, slow down, and alter course more to the south. All three of these prudent actions should have been taken. Yet, despite overwhelming evidence to the contrary, Lightoller's "everything against us" version of the story continues to be repeated in books, TV documentaries, and feature films:

> we know now the extraordinary combination of circumstances that existed at that time which you would not meet again in 100 years; that they should all have existed just on that particular night shows, of course, that everything was against us.

Although the story is untrue, the public has always sympathized with a ship that had "everything against it." This explains why the mythical *Titanic* created by Lightoller remains such a strong subject for popular entertainments. The second officer transformed a ship of steel and steam into Greek tragedy on a colossal scale: a star-crossed floating hotel taking rich and poor alike to certain doom. Lightoller's "everything against us" theory provided the perfect backdrop for the human drama played out on the decks of the sinking ship. His argument remains seductive today because it is superficially believable and it is romantic. To his credit, Lightoller never misled himself. In his 1935 autobiography, he admitted:

> in London it was very necessary to keep one's hand on the whitewash brush.
>
> Sharp questions needed careful answers if one was to avoid a pitfall, carefully and subtly dug, leading to a pinning down of blame to someone's luckless shoulders. . . .
>
> A washing of dirty linen would help no one. The Board of Trade had passed that ship as in all respects fit for sea, in every sense of the word, with sufficient margin of safety for everyone on board. Now, the Board of Trade was holding an inquiry into the loss of that ship—hence the whitewash brush.

Such whitewash applied by Lightoller and others during the two formal investigations into the sinking continues to obscure the truth. Sorting reality from the myths surrounding *Titanic* would be much easier if we had a detailed log of every event during the ship's last hours. We need the tape from a modern electronic "black box," which records the final moments of an aircraft disaster. Of course, electronics was in its infancy in 1912. Aircraft-style recorders would not exist for another half century. The closest thing to a flight recorder aboard *Titanic* was fallible human memory.

Unlike electronic recordings made on indestructible metallic belts, human memories die with their owners. That is why the official record of the *Titanic* disaster contains nothing from key witnesses like Captain Edward J. Smith, shipbuilder Thomas Andrews, or First Officer William M. Murdoch. These men died with the ship. Fortunately, however, important memories of other survivors were carefully preserved by two government inquiries conducted in 1912, one by the U.S. Senate and the other by a British Wreck Commission convened by the British Board of Trade. Other recollections of survivors were published in newspaper interviews and magazine accounts.

In the United States, Senator William Alden Smith (no relation to *Titanic*'s Captain E. J. Smith) moved with speed seldom seen in government to organize a probe into the sinking. He had himself appointed chairman of a Senate subcommittee on April 17, just two days after the sinking and one day before *Carpathia* arrived in New York with *Titanic* survivors. Smith put his first question to J. Bruce Ismay before the week was out, at 10:30 A.M. on Friday, April 19. The

3

British inquiry was delayed somewhat by Smith's hearings. It began on May 2 and continued intermittently through July 30. The hasty organization of both inquiries is evident in the random order in which witnesses were called. In the end, however, the rapid convening of both probes benefitted future historians because the memories of the tragedy were still fresh in the minds of the survivors.

These preserved memories can be studied in much the same way as can "black box" recordings recovered from the wreckage of modern airplane crashes. Testimony transcribed from the 1912 hearings contains important clues that might help identify the causes of the disaster. Just as modern "black box" recordings must be played back accurately to learn the details they contain, historic testimony must be quoted exactly as it was spoken. Often this means presenting the questions as well as the responses, because the full import of an oral statement sometimes can be recognized only in context. The questions often contain the germ of truth that the witnesses may have attempted to avoid. Written documents also must be reproduced faithfully, complete with mistakes in fact, grammar, and syntax.

Building a detailed log of *Titanic's* final hours turned out to be more difficult than anticipated. Many cherished beliefs about the disaster are based on myths or incomplete news accounts that arose in the aftermath of the disaster. Even sworn testimony was not always true, because witnesses sometimes lied outright or twisted the truth to suit their needs. Newspaper reports are notorious for factual errors. Books were often published more to satisfy the author's vanity than to provide dependable history. The only reliable test for accuracy is to compare what was printed or said to the provable facts. Accounts that fit the facts can be presumed true; the rest are subject to doubt.

Unfortunately, much testimony from both the ship's officers and officials of the White Star Line, the owner of *Titanic*, fails this simple test of historical accuracy. For instance, Lightoller, Third Officer Herbert J. Pitman, and others claimed the ship did not break apart on the surface that fateful night. Their description of *Titanic* plunging intact to the bottom became the standard version of the story, even though it was false.

The ship's breakup became obvious when Robert D. Ballard of Woods Hole Oceanographic Institution discovered the wreck. His underwater photographs show that *Titanic* probably separated into two large pieces either at or near the surface. Once the ship split apart, the bow and stern sections suffered distinctly different fates on their way to the bottom. The new photographs would not have surprised seamen Frank Osman and Edward J. Buley, who witnessed the breakup from their lifeboats and later described it in exact detail at the U.S. Senate hearings.

It is easy to surmise why the surviving officers were often less than candid in their testimonies. They had all participated in numerous violations of the Rule of Good Seamanship, which is taught to aspiring deck officers. Their ship was speeding through a known ice field, yet the officers failed to post extra lookouts and failed to warn the engineers to be ready for emergency engine orders from the bridge. Heavy field ice known to be across *Titanic*'s path had already claimed two other ships, yet no one dared to suggest taking a more southerly course. After the accident, the ship resumed making way even though the full extent of the damage had not been determined. Considering these mistakes in seamanship, it is no surprise that *Titanic*'s surviving officers reached for Lightoller's metaphorical whitewash brush.

Even truthful eyewitness testimony suffers from the vagaries of human memory. It was not uncommon for a witness to remember specific details but jumble their order or duration. This seems to have happened to quartermaster Alfred Olliver, who was quite specific about the actions on the bridge during the accident, but whose memory compressed time so that separate events seemed to happen simultaneously.

*Titanic*'s real log book may still lie deep within the wreckage discovered by Ballard. This document was not cataloged among artifacts found in the lifeboats, and no one has reported seeing it since the accident. The book probably remained in the chart room just behind the wheelhouse until the bow finally submerged. Most likely, the real book was trapped in wreckage after funnel #1 collapsed. Both the wheelhouse and the starboard bridge wing must have been damaged by the tons of steel in the falling funnel. Once the bow started its freefall to the bottom, the book would have been swept along with other parts of the bridge structure.

Because the real book is unavailable, it was necessary to create log entries based on the events of the tragic voyage. These reconstructed log entries should not be read as absolute fact. Rather, they are

intended to guide the reader through the events and actions surrounding *Titanic*'s accident and foundering. In all likelihood, the log
presented here is more detailed than the actual book that went down
with the ship. *Titanic*'s real log may someday be found in good
condition, but it will likely be a disappointment to historians. The
actual log probably contains little more than a brief mention of the
accident and nothing of events beyond midnight.

The method sailors use to record a voyage explains why the actual
book would have few entries after 11:30 P.M. Information is usually
noted in a "rough log" first and then is later transcribed into the formal book. Considering the confusion during the sinking, it is doubtful anything was transcribed into the official book after midnight,
when ordinary ship's business was put aside in favor of launching
lifeboats. For this reason, the number and complexity of entries in
this rebuilt log decrease as the ship sinks. Written entries cease after
the first boat is launched. By then, *Titanic* was little more than floating wreckage, and the bridge was deserted except for a lonely Captain Smith.

The hardest part of rebuilding *Titanic*'s missing log was to create
an accurate chronology. Establishing this chronology required that
one event be fixed arbitrarily in time to serve as a reference point
around which the evening's other events could be arranged. Without
this fixed reference point, it would have been impossible to properly
order thousands of eyewitness memories of events that unfolded at
night on the decks of a sinking ship. No one had the opportunity to
write down the exact instant each event took place or its duration.
Confusion over the chronological order of events was inevitable.
This problem also plagued investigators in 1912.

> The later stages of the sinking cannot be stated with any precision,
> owing to the confusion of the times which was natural under the cir-
> cumstances.

To make sense of this jumble, I assigned an arbitrary time to the
instant Frederick Fleet rang the crow's nest alarm bell three times
and reported "Iceberg right ahead." The time I chose for this event is
11:40 P.M. Investigators in 1912 were unable to be any more accurate. The British proceedings placed this alarm at "a little before
11:40," while the U.S. Senate investigation fixed it at 11:45 P.M. Any
of these estimates could have been used as the starting point for re-

constructing the ship's log. The exact moment of the alarm is less important than the correct order of events is.

Times were assigned to individual events based on their relationships to other events that took place earlier or later. This sorting process required a series of experiments with the actions of major characters in the story. Often what seemed a logical arrangement during one sequence of events placed individuals in the wrong place later that night. New insights became clear as the web untangled. Details like the late arrival by *Titanic*'s builder, Thomas Andrews, on the bridge explained themselves. What up to now had been considered a chance meeting of Fourth Officer Joseph G. Boxhall and carpenter John Hutchinson became a pivotal event in the unfolding drama.

Since eyewitnesses were incapable of pinning events down to the second, it is presumptuous to think that a researcher can do it with accuracy at a distance of nearly ninety years. Thus, times given for specific events in this chronology are not meant to represent actual o'clock times. Rather, they are intended only as temporal dividers so that events can be presented in the most logical order of their occurrence. Thus, a few seconds' difference in the times of two events is not meant to convey the actual length of time that passed between them. It indicates, instead, only the sequence in which the events occurred.

Ordering events required making educated guesses about how long each event lasted. By its nature, this process relied on estimates. For example, many histories have Fourth Officer Boxhall running back and forth to the damaged areas of the bow in record times. Even a young man in good physical condition must have taken several minutes to descend seven flights of stairs, run a couple hundred feet horizontally, then return following the same circuitous route. All too often, histories have given durations of "a few minutes" or "about ten minutes" for events that must have taken either longer or shorter periods of time.

Nowhere is the problem of chronology more acute than during the minute before and the minute after the impact. Events on the ship's bridge during that span must correlate with those taking place in the stokeholds and engine room. Everything must occur within the bounds of reality as defined by an 882-foot steamship. First Officer Murdoch was undoubtedly moving at adrenaline speed during the moments before the accident. He had a lot of work to do: shift the helm, ring down for "all stop" on the engines, and order the watertight doors closed. Still, human beings can accomplish only so much during a given period of time. Seconds did not get any longer just because Murdoch needed more time to analyze the situation and react properly.

As with any moving object, time is intertwined with speed aboard *Titanic.* Establishing a chronology forced the selection of a speed for the ship during the period from 5:20 P.M. April 14 until the instant of impact with the berg. Speed estimates ranging from 20.5 to 22.25 knots have been suggested by various authors. J. (Joseph) Bruce Ismay, chairman of the White Star Line, and the surviving officers believed their ship was making 22.5 knots at the time of the accident. This speed seems to be confirmed by the few pieces of reliable navigational data that survive, so it has been used throughout this book.

Sorting through the events of April 1912 produced several surprises. Why Captain Smith handed J. Bruce Ismay the wireless message received from *Baltic* has always been controversial. For ninety years this message has wrongly been called an "ice warning" when it actually warned of a more immediate danger to the ship's safety. Probing *Titanic*'s enigmatic Halifax connection uncovered information on the effectiveness of the ship's bilge pumps.

The most exciting surprise was Ismay's off-the-cuff remark about Chief Engineer Joseph G. Bell's assessment of damage from the iceberg. This remark to the U.S. Senate investigation directly contradicted Ismay's carefully contrived story of how the ship sank. Yet, Ismay freely testified that, more than ten minutes after the impact with the iceberg and several minutes after the engines began pushing the damaged ship northward, Bell did not think *Titanic* was sinking. (The restarting of *Titanic*'s engines was not mentioned in either official report on the sinking, but it was documented by survivor after survivor.)

In writing these reconstructed log entries, I used only testimony or published documents from 1912 in order to avoid people on the ship "knowing" something not discovered until the 1980s or later. All information for the log came from the testimony of people on the ship that night. Newly reported details about the wreckage from Ballard and other recent visitors to the broken hulk have been excluded from the reconstruction to ensure a realistic record of what people on the ship experienced. After all, they are the ones who would have written the log.

This does not mean that information arising from modern visits to the wreck site has been ignored. Photographs of the hulk and scientific analysis of the ship's steel give us a better understanding of the 1912 testimony. We now know what happened to the ship after it disappeared below the surface. However, modern expeditions to the wreck have offered very little information about the events surrounding the sinking. Photos of twisted metal tell us nothing of Captain Smith's reasoning for not slowing the ship or taking an alternate route away from the ice. Nor have the trips to the bottom revealed anything about the fatal ice damage, because that part of the ship remains hidden from view. Almost without exception, the new "discoveries" are not new information but are only confirmation of testimony recorded by the two government investigations in 1912.

Forensic investigators of airplane crashes have found that "accidents" are almost always caused in part or in whole by human error, and that there is seldom one specific error that can be singled out as the cause of a particular accident. The final mistake made at the instant of disaster is usually just the last link in a chain of errors made by the people in command. Often, none of these errors in itself is significant enough to have caused the crash. But, taken together, this chain explains why trained and skilled people doing their best can still be caught in a disaster.

*Titanic's* fatal chain of events started in 1889 when Captain Edward J. Smith grounded the liner *Republic* off Sandy Hook. Two years later he repeated this performance by running the steamer *Coptic* aground off Rio de Janeiro. Finally, in November of 1909, Smith grounded the liner *Adriatic* in Ambrose Channel near New York. No one was injured in any of these groundings, nor was serious damage done to any of the ships. The real impact of these three incidents was made on Captain Smith, who learned that groundings (in those smaller ships) were not always serious events.

*Titanic* was roughly ten times the size of *Adriatic*. Smith's education in the School of Hard Knocks did not apply to *Titanic's* iceberg incident, but he did not know that. His experience told him (erroneously) that the ship may not have been seriously damaged. Based on his experience, Smith seems to have downplayed any evidence to the contrary prior to midnight on April 14, 1912.

Another link in the chain of disaster was Captain Smith's failure to understand the profound differences between handling the smaller liners of the nineteenth century and the huge, Olympic-class ships—named for the *Olympic*, the first vessel of that blueprint—that ushered in the twentieth. In 1911 the *Olympic*, whose younger sister *Titanic* was a virtual duplicate, was under Smith's command when it was involved in a collision with the HMS *Hawke*, a much smaller British navy vessel. Captain Smith allowed his gleaming new liner to flash too close past the ram-bowed navy ship. When sailors on *Hawke* felt their ship drawn toward the huge passenger liner, they naturally attempted to turn away from danger, but suction between the two vessels proved too much for the steering gear of the warship. *Hawke* succumbed and suddenly swerved into *Olympic*'s starboard side.

Smith was still proclaiming his innocence at the time of his death. After all, everyone could see that the navy ship had run into *Olympic* and not the other way round. In the end, however, Smith was judged to be at fault by the maritime community. He had disobeyed not a law of the sea but one of physics: Bernoulli's Principle (see the chapter titled Cool Hand Murdoch). However, the captain's statements about this incident, coupled with his unquestioning confidence in Olympic-class vessels, demonstrated the feeling of invincibility he felt striding the bridge of *Titanic*.

In short, Captain Smith was overconfident.

Overconfidence may be the single biggest cause of accidents in all types of transportation. During World War II, the U.S. Army Air Corps claimed it lost more pilots to overconfidence than to enemy action. In fact, the condition was so common that it was given a name. An overconfident pilot was dubbed "fat, dumb, and happy."

That sobriquet may well be applied retroactively not only to Captain Smith but also to the officers who shared *Titanic*'s bridge with him. To some degree, all of the ship's officers felt the same sense of mastery over nature. None gave serious thought to changing course or reducing speed after 8:30 P.M. despite the ice surrounding the ship. As late as 11:30 P.M. on the night of the accident, the officers who controlled *Titanic* viewed ice as a mere inconvenience, not an extreme danger.

Perfunctory sea trials on April 2, 1912, were another link in the chain of tragedy. No two vessels are ever exactly alike, even when built side-by-side from the same set of blueprints. Each has its own particular handling quirks that must be mastered before going to sea with paying passengers. No one today knows the handling character-istics of *Titanic*. Sadly, First Officer Murdoch had had precious little experience with the ship in 1912 during his moment of trial. Perhaps he could have avoided the berg if the ship had made a few more test maneuvers during its sea trials. We will never know.

Captain Smith forged the master link in *Titanic's* disaster chain by allowing Ismay to encroach on the master's authority. Smith lost mastery over his ship, though this loss of command authority was not obvious. The other officers still reported to him and obeyed his orders, but Smith could not provide genuine leadership when the sit-uation demanded it. A two-man committee composed of Captain Smith and J. Bruce Ismay made critical command decisions that were Smith's responsibility alone. In the end, Ismay's demands ap-pear to have overridden Smith's years of experience at sea.

*Titanic's* fatal chain of disaster always comes back to Captain Smith's feeling of invincibility aboard his giant liner. Any danger from the sea seemed so trivial when one stood 60 feet off the water, surrounded by tons of steel. *Titanic* gave a sense of permanence and safety that persisted even as it was dying. "I cannot conceive of any vital disaster happening to this vessel" the captain once said of the liner *Adriatic*. "Modern shipbuilding has gone beyond all that."

## CONVENTIONS

**Bearings** and **courses** are always expressed in degrees true from north (000°) unless otherwise specified. This follows current navigational practice. In 1912, bearings and courses were expressed in degrees east or west of north or south. Thus, today's 266° would have been "south 86 west" in 1912 parlance.

**Distances** are given in nautical miles. One nautical mile is equiv-alent to 1 minute of latitude, or approximately 2,000 yards or 6,000 feet (actual distance: 6,076.1 feet). One nautical mile is about 1.15 statute miles on land.

**Speeds** are expressed in nautical miles per hour (knots).

**Temperatures** are given in degrees Fahrenheit.

**Times** are given in the A.M.-P.M. system as kept aboard *Titanic* un-less otherwise specified. In 1912, each ship kept its own time, based on local apparent noon for the longitude in which it was sailing. Clocks on two ships in sight of each other usually agreed as to hour but not as to minutes, because each had been reset at a different longitude. Standard practice was to adjust clocks at midnight for the next day's anticipated noon longitude. *Titanic*'s clocks were scheduled to be retarded by twenty-two minutes at midnight, but it is uncertain whether this was done. Testimony by First Officer Lightoller, radio operator Harold Bride, and Fourth Officer Boxhall reveals some confusion regarding this twenty-two minute discrepancy. At the time of the accident, the clocks on *Titanic* were apparently one hour and fifty-five minutes ahead of Eastern Standard Time in New York City.

## *TITANIC* ROLL

The following individuals are closely associated with *Titanic*'s story and are referred to throughout this book.

ANDREWS, THOMAS—Head of the delegation from Harland and Wolff, *Titanic*'s shipbuilding firm. He had overseen the construction of *Titanic* and was aboard with eight other Harland and Wolff employees attending to the normal problems encountered with a new ship on its first voyage.

BALLARD, DR. ROBERT D.—Oceanographer from the Woods Hole Oceanographic Institution. He discovered *Titanic*'s wreckage in 1987.

BARRETT, FREDERICK—Stoker. He described water coming through an opening 2 feet off the deck in boiler room #5 just after the accident.

BELL, JOSEPH G.—Chief engineer. He at first thought the pumps were keeping *Titanic* afloat.

BOXHALL, JOSEPH G.—Fourth officer. He was responsible for establishing the ship's final position for the distress calls.

BRIDE, HAROLD—Junior wireless operator. He was an employee of Marconi's Wireless Telegraph Company Limited, the owner of *Titanic*'s wireless equipment.

FLEET, FREDERICK—Lookout. He rang the alarm bell and reported the iceberg to the bridge.

HITCHENS, ROBERT—Quartermaster. He was on duty at *Titanic*'s wheel during and after the collision.

ISMAY, J. BRUCE—President of International Mercantile Marine, the company that owned the White Star Line, which in turn owned *Titanic*. He was also general manager of White Star.

LIGHTOLLER, CHARLES HERBERT—Second officer. He launched the lifeboats on the port side. He was the senior surviving officer and became the spokesman for White Star during the two investigations.

LORD, STANLEY—Master of the single-screw freighter *Californian*, which was trapped by ice and probably witnessed *Titanic*'s sinking.

LOWE, HAROLD G.—Fifth officer. He assisted in loading lifeboats and later admitted firing warning shots from his pistol.

MERSEY, JOHN CHARLES BIGHAM, LORD—Wreck commissioner. He headed the British inquiry into *Titanic*'s sinking.

MOODY, JAMES—Sixth officer. He was on duty with Murdoch at the time of the accident.

MURDOCH, WILLIAM M.—First officer. In charge at the time of the accident, he tried in vain to avoid the deadly iceberg.

OLLIVER, ALFRED—Quartermaster. He was returning to the bridge at the time of the accident.

PHILLIPS, JOHN ("JACK")—Senior wireless operator. He was an employee of Marconi's Wireless Telegraph Company Limited.

PIRRIE, WILLIAM JAMES, LORD—Head of the Harland and Wolff shipyard at the time the Olympic-class vessels were planned. He retired during the construction of *Titanic* but remained active in shipping.

PITMAN, HERBERT J.—Third officer. He came on duty at midnight and assisted in launching the lifeboats.

ROSTRON, ARTHUR H., CAPTAIN—Master of *Carpathia*, the ship that came to the aid of *Titanic*'s passengers.

SMITH, EDWARD J., CAPTAIN—Master of *Titanic*. He was also the de facto commodore of the White Star Line.

SMITH, WILLIAM ALDEN, SENATOR—Head of the U.S. Senate probe of the sinking (no relation to Captain Smith).

13

WILDE, HENRY F.—Chief officer of *Titanic*.

WILDING, EDWARD—Naval architect. He was an employee of Harland and Wolff and helped design and build *Titanic*.

## *Titanic* Watch Schedule
### Sunday, April 14, and Monday, April 15, 1912

Captain Smith as master did not stand regular watches. He was considered on duty at all times.

Senior deck officers Wilde, Murdoch, and Lightoller: four hours on duty, eight hours off duty, in rotation.

Junior officers Pitman, Boxhall, Lowe, and Moody: four hours on duty, four hours off duty, in rotation.

| Crew Name | 6 P.M. | 7 P.M. | 8 P.M. | 9 P.M. | 10 P.M. | 11 P.M. | 12 A.M. | 1 A.M. | 2 A.M. |
|---|---|---|---|---|---|---|---|---|---|
| Chief Officer H. Wilde | | | | | | | | | Senior Watch Officer |
| 1st Officer W. Murdoch | | | | | Senior Watch Officer | Senior Watch Officer | Senior Watch Officer | Senior Watch Officer | |
| 2nd Officer C. Lightoller | Senior Watch Officer | Senior Watch Officer | Senior Watch Officer | Senior Watch Officer | | | | | |
| 3rd Officer H. Pitman | Bridge Watch | Bridge Watch | | | | | Bridge Watch | Bridge Watch | Bridge Watch |
| 4th Officer J. Boxhall | | | Bridge Watch | Bridge Watch | Bridge Watch | Bridge Watch | | | |
| 5th Officer H. Lowe | Bridge Watch | Bridge Watch | | | | | Bridge Watch | Bridge Watch | Bridge Watch |
| 6th Officer J. Moody | | | Bridge Watch | Bridge Watch | Bridge Watch | Bridge Watch | | | |
| Q'master R. Hitchens | | | Relief Q'mst | Relief Q'mst | Wheel | Wheel | | | |
| Q'master A. Olliver | | | Wheel | Wheel | Relief Q'mstr | Relief Q'mstr | | | |
| Lookouts in crow's nest | Hogg & Evans | Hogg & Evans | Symons & Jewell | Symons & Jewell | Fleet & Lee | Fleet & Lee | Hogg & Evans | Hogg & Evans | Symons & Jewel |

# COAL AND ICE

Sunday, April 14, 1912

**1:30 P.M. to 8:50 P.M.**

**1:30 P.M.** Sea calm, weather fair. Engines turning 75 revolutions for 22.25 knots. Fuel burn 650 tons per day. Remaining coal is just sufficient for three days' steaming. Per Mr. Ismay's request, all boilers except five single-ended units in boiler room #1 have been fired. Engines are running smoothly, but the heat in some second-class cabins is not functioning properly. Andrews will address this problem later. —E. J. SMITH, Master

*T*ITANIC was short of coal.

This fuel shortage had nagged Captain Edward J. Smith since the beginning of the voyage. His ship needed a lot of coal at its current speed of 75 revolutions of the engines, or about 22.25 knots. Sweaty stokers had to sling 650 tons of fuel into the furnaces every twenty-four hours to keep up the pace. This was a normal expenditure of fuel for a ship the size of *Titanic*, but when the ship had sailed from Southampton on April 10, 1912, the bunkers had been less than half full due to a coal strike. British Board of Trade records show *Titanic* had only enough coal to make New York at 22 knots, given a minimal 10 percent margin for safety.

The White Star Line, the company that owned the new liner, gathered fuel for *Titanic* by "stealing" it from the bunkers of other company ships. Some American coal had been hauled from New York by *Titanic*'s older sister ship, *Olympic,* specifically for this maiden crossing. Transferring dusty coal from ship to ship was a dirty job involving shovels, wheelbarrows, and canvas sacks. It is doubtful that anyone actually weighed every ton. Men doing this backbreaking work could be excused if they occasionally counted a phantom ton or two. Aboard *Titanic,* the total was probably estimated simply by eyeballing the level in the bunkers.

That original store of fuel was reduced somewhat while the ship was docked in Southampton because it took about 400 tons to provide heat and electricity while taking aboard last-minute supplies, mail, and passengers. When the ship departed, it likely had no more than 5,400 tons of bunkered coal. Captain Smith surely would have wanted to arrive in New York with a prudent 10 percent of fuel in re-serve. Subtracting the reserve meant that 4,900 tons were available, the exact amount required for seven and a half days of steaming at 22 knots.

The fuel problem was complicated by a fire that had been smol-dering in the forward bunker of boiler room #5. The existence of this fire had been hidden from the ship's passengers as well as from offi-cials of the British Board of Trade. Bunker fires were relatively com-mon in 1912, before oil-fed engines became the preferred energy sources for moving ships. Coal carried as fuel by steamships was subject to spontaneous combustion, especially when compressed under its own weight in the confined space of a bunker.

The only unusual aspect of *Titanic*'s bunker fire was that it burned for at least ten days. Sailors have always feared fire at sea more than other emergencies, so standard practice was to extinguish bunkers quickly by pulling coal out of the bunker and jettisoning as much as necessary until the smoldering fuel could be removed. *Ti-tanic*'s fire may have been allowed to burn because the ship was so woefully short of fuel. The officers may have assumed that the glow-ing hot spot would consume less coal than would have been lost dur-ing the laborious process of extinguishing the fire.

A more believable reason for letting the fire burn was to prevent the ship's maiden voyage from being delayed by Board of Trade in-spectors, who would have demanded that repairs be made to the over-heated bulkhead between boiler rooms #5 and #6. Removing the dis-torted metal and replacing it with new steel could have delayed the maiden voyage by a fortnight or longer. Eventually, on Saturday, April 14, the smoldering fuel was shoveled out of the bunker and fed to the furnaces to provide steam. The bulkhead cooled and was oiled, although stoker Frederick Barrett said later that the half-inch thick metal remained distorted as a result of the heat. This distortion is the basis for assumptions that heat weakened the metal of the bulkhead.

Barrett testified at the British Wreck Commissioner hearings that the last of the burning coal had been removed from the bunker by backbreaking work on Saturday, April 13. "The Chief Engineer, Mr. Bell, gave me orders, 'Builder's men wanted to inspect that bulk-head,'" he told the wreck commissioner, John Charles Bigham, Lord Mersey. "The bottom of the watertight compartment was dinged [sic] aft, and the other part was dinged forward."

One person aboard *Titanic* who did not appear to be worried by the coal shortage was the chairman of the White Star Line, J. Bruce Ismay. Effectively the owner of the ship, Ismay had discussed with Chief Engineer Joseph G. Bell a plan to increase speed throughout the voyage. On Thursday, April 11, while *Titanic* was embarking passengers in Queenstown (now Cobh, Ireland), Ismay had explained to Bell how the engine revolutions would be gradually built up during the maiden voyage. On the Sunday of the iceberg accident, it was Ismay who allegedly had asked for the engines to turn 75 revolutions for an estimated speed of 22.25 knots.

That a clearly defined commander was lacking would become a major factor in the *Titanic* disaster. Captain Smith was the legal master of the ship, but throughout the ill-fated maiden voyage J. Bruce Ismay acted as an independent cocaptain despite his lack of formal training or experience for such an important position. It was widely known aboard ship that Ismay wanted *Titanic* to come to full speed on Monday in order to make a dramatic arrival in New York the next day.

Buried inside the Monday, April 15, 1912, edition of the *New York Times* was a small shipping announcement placed by Ismay on behalf of the White Star Line saying that *Titanic* would arrive at 4:00 P.M. on Tuesday April 16, which establishes the shipboard scuttlebutt as fact. Ismay told a bald-faced lie to U.S. investigators when he testified that the ship was not due in port until the morning of Wednesday, April 17. Wednesday was the ship's official arrival date based on White Star's *published* schedule, but the *Times* announcement proves Ismay intended to beat the official schedule on *Titanic*'s maiden voyage. Why Ismay was not trapped in this obvious perjury is one mystery surrounding the disaster investigations.

A rumor circulated among passengers on Sunday that the White Star chairman planned a 24-knot dash for the following day, Monday, April 15. Earlier on Sunday, the last of the ship's twenty-four double-ended boilers had been fired to allow an overnight buildup of steam power. Fuel consumption by these additional boilers was about to dig deeply into the 10 percent ration of coal reserved by Captain Smith for contingencies. That worried Smith, and the potential for disaster would only worsen if the rumored burst of speed on Monday also required firing the remaining five single-ended boilers, putting all twenty-nine boilers on line.

Except for an encounter with one iceberg, the ship should have reached New York by 4:00 P.M. on April 16, as Ismay hoped. Doing so would have required approximately fifty-four hours of steaming at 22 knots, from the ship's 5:45 P.M. position on April 14 when it made a planned course change for the approach to New York. There would have been no need for Ismay to increase speed on Monday to meet his self-imposed goal of a Tuesday arrival.

The purpose of Ismay's planned Monday speed run must have been a convoluted publicity stunt. He apparently wanted *Titanic* to make a surprise appearance in New York several hours ahead of the 4:00 P.M. Tuesday arrival time that he had published in the *New York Times.* That would have been nearly a day ahead of the White Star Line's own official schedule and faster than *Olympic*'s best trans-Atlantic run. Ismay's scheme would have given the impression that *Titanic* was faster than *Olympic* and almost equal to the Cunard competition (the Cunard liners, in fact, were much faster). His goal must have been to fool the public into thinking that the world's largest ship was also the world's fastest liner, even though the only speed record it would have broken was a meaningless arrival time set by its owner for publicity purposes.

Four days after the ship sank, the planned speed run became more than a shipboard rumor when Ismay took the witness stand in New York to testify before a U.S. Senate subcommittee investigating the tragedy. Ismay was well aware of the anger directed at the White Star Line by the public and the press. Most people believed *Titanic* hit an iceberg because it was recklessly speeding hell-bent across an ice-strewn ocean.

Chairman of the subcommittee that investigated the sinking of *Titanic,* Senator William Alden Smith of Michigan seemed to want to embarrass the ship, its late captain, and the White Star Line. Knowing the importance of Smith's line of questioning, Ismay chose his words carefully when he explained the ship's speed to Senator Smith. The White Star chairman did not want to feed rumors of his plan to set a speed record on the ill-fated maiden voyage. Still, he was obviously proud of the fast passage the ship had been making.

MR. ISMAY: I understand it has been stated that the ship was going full speed. The ship never had been at full speed. The full speed of the ship is 78 revolutions. She works up to 80. So far as I am aware, she never exceeded 75 revolutions. She had not all her boilers on. None of the single-ended boilers were on.

It was our intention, if we had fine weather on Monday afternoon or Tuesday, to drive the ship at full speed. That, owing to the unfortunate catastrophe, never eventuated.

On the afternoon prior to the accident, Captain Smith had been concerned by Ismay's intent to "drive the ship at full speed." Sustained high speed could have caused *Titanic* to run short of coal within sight of New York Harbor. The captain knew that Ismay was ignoring the simple relationship between speed and fuel consumption. The faster the ship goes, the greater the fuel consumed per nautical mile, so increased speed can never compensate for spent fuel. The result is a substantial decrease in range (the distance a ship can travel before running out of fuel) for only modest increases in speed. The faster *Titanic* steamed, the more fuel it would burn.

Warming the extra boilers for Monday's planned high-speed dash was already threatening coal reserved by Captain Smith for such contingencies as heavy weather. Although the sea was calm on the night of the tragedy, storms lay ahead. (The rescue ship *Carpathia* encountered heavy weather as it took survivors to New York after the disaster.) Smith's legal and moral responsibility for the safety of the ship forced him to oppose his superior's high-speed plans.

On that Sunday evening, *Titanic* had not started to use its 10 percent reserve of fuel. There was still enough coal in the bunkers to reach New York safely because the ship's speed had been gradually increased during the voyage as the engines were "run in." Lower speeds early in the trip would have reduced consumption somewhat. It was not deemed appropriate to run new engines at full speed until the bearings and piston rings had seated themselves properly. The process of running in a new marine steam engine was not unlike that of breaking in the small gasoline engine of a 1912 automobile. The gradual increase in speed is shown in the following table.

### Average Speeds of *Titanic*

| Date | Day of Voyage | Miles Steamed | Average Speed |
|------|---------------|---------------|---------------|
| 12 April | One | 464 | 19.3 |
| 13 April | Two | 519 | 21.6 |
| 14 April | Three | 546 | 22.8 |
| 15 April | Four | n/s | 22.25 (estimated) |

Coal saved by operating at 19 or 21 knots during the first two days of the voyage was still in the bunkers and would have been available for use on the fifth and sixth days. Ismay was likely counting on this unburned coal to fuel the high-speed dash he planned for Monday. Even so, his plan was a gamble with a brand-new ship carrying more than 2,200 people. Despite the ship's fuel savings on the first two days, Captain Smith was correct in his attempt to persuade Ismay against increasing speed beyond 22.25 knots for the remainder of the voyage. Their ship did not have enough fuel aboard for such publicity stunts.

It is one of history's curious footnotes that, except for an unfortunate encounter with an iceberg, *Titanic* might have earned fame for a different ignominy. Ismay's plan would have depleted the ship's supply of coal before it arrived in New York Harbor, possibly leaving it a helpless, drifting hulk. If that had happened, the entry of the world's largest liner into New York would have been at the end of a salvage ship's towing hawser.

**1:42 P.M.** Warning of "not under command" oiltank steamer *Deutschland* received by Marconi from *Baltic*. Captain says derelict ship appears safely south of present course. Mr. Ismay asked to keep this message for the afternoon, agreeing to have it back before we reach the ice this evening. Message also contained information about that ice.　　—W. M. MURDOCH, First Officer

*Titanic* was equipped with the best radio transmitting and receiving equipment available in 1912. Unlike modern practice, this equipment was owned by Marconi's Wireless Telegraph Company Limited, which also employed the two operators. Much of the time, the ship's radio equipment was used to send messages from wealthy passengers to friends ashore. These messages were called Marconigrams. The importance of radio communication to navigation was not totally ignored. Marconi operators were supposed to carry any messages concerning the safety of the ship to the bridge immediately.

J. Bruce Ismay does not appear to have accepted criticism gracefully from anyone, especially from one of his employees. Just before *Titanic*'s departure, he actually changed the status of the ship's orchestra from "crew" to "second-class passengers" rather than capitulate to demands of the Musicians Union. Like any other White Star employee, Captain Smith would not have risked a direct confrontation with this sort of employer. Rather, Smith sought a tactful way to cajole Ismay into voluntarily canceling his planned high-speed run. The captain found an opportunity in a wireless message about another unfortunate ship, *Baltic,* which had actually run out of coal. Smith used this message to correct his superior gently without offending him. Considering the shortage of fuel, the implications for *Titanic* of the warning message sent by *Baltic* were obvious.

Historians have consistently misinterpreted the contents of the 1:42 P.M. *Baltic* wireless message by viewing it as only a warning of ice ahead. In reality, the more important danger to other ships was *Deutschland,* a derelict vessel drifting in the shipping lane.

**1:42 P.M.—From *Baltic*:** HAVE HAD MODERATE, VARIABLE WINDS AND CLEAR, FINE WEATHER SINCE LEAVING. GREEK STEAMER *ATHENAI* REPORTS PASSING ICEBERGS AND LARGE QUANTITIES OF FIELD ICE TODAY IN LAT 41°51' N LONG 49°52' W. LAST NIGHT WE SPOKE GERMAN OILTANK STEAMER *DEUTSCHLAND* STETTIN [sic] TO PHILADELPHIA, NOT UNDER CONTROL, SHORT OF COAL, LAT 40°42' N LON 55°11' W. WISHES TO BE REPORTED TO NEW YORK AND OTHER STEAMERS. WISH YOU AND *TITANIC* ALL SUCCESS. COMMANDER.

Understanding the importance of this wireless message requires comprehension of the nautical parlance of 1912. The phrase "not under control" means that *Deutschland* was out of fuel and could not maneuver on its own to avoid collision with another ship. For practical purposes, the tankship was derelict in the middle of busy shipping lanes. It was a hazard to navigation similar to that of a stalled car blocking a crowded lane of an expressway.

This drifting vessel was a far more immediate threat to shipping than ice was because it was an unexpected danger directly in the paths of other vessels. Recognizing his predicament, *Deutschland*'s master had shouted a request to *Baltic*'s captain to report his helpless ship to other vessels traveling the North Atlantic shipping lanes. "Speaking" another ship in 1912 meant to come close enough to shout back and forth between the two vessels. The captain of the disabled ship did not want to be run down by a speeding liner.

The ice mentioned in the *Baltic* message was much less of an immediate threat to *Titanic* because it was already known to lie across the liner's path. Captain Smith and his officers had known there would be ice in their ship's path even before they had sailed from Southampton. If anything, Smith would have been comforted

21

by a report that the ice was still exactly where he expected to encounter it.

This wireless transmission, or Marconigram, has become famous as the supposed "ice warning" handed by Captain Smith to J. Bruce Ismay on the afternoon prior to the iceberg accident. Ismay reportedly showed it to several first-class passengers later that day. He eventually returned the message to the captain, who posted it in the chart room behind the wheelhouse. Did the misfortune of *Deutschland* convince Ismay that his proposed speed run would squander the precious stock of fuel? Only the events of the next day would have told, but for *Titanic*, that day never dawned.

Understanding that Captain Smith used the *Baltic* message as a warning to Ismay not to waste precious coal dispels one popular myth about *Titanic*'s maiden voyage. Legend holds that Ismay pocketed not just any ice warning, but the specific warning that should have saved the ship. In fact, the contents of this famous wireless were far more important than merely a repetition of already-known ice information.

The first person to surmise a deeper meaning of *Baltic*'s message and its impact upon Captain Smith's actions was solicitor Clement Edwards. Speaking to the British inquiry on behalf of the Dock, Wharf, Riverside and General Workers Union in May 1912, Edwards suggested that Ismay pocketed the message in hopes the captain would forget its ice warning. Edwards claimed Ismay's actions were proof that he was sailing as far more than an ordinary first-class passenger. On this point, there can be no doubt. Ismay was de facto co-captain of *Titanic*. The only person who never seemed to admit his role in the tragedy was Ismay himself.

> During the voyage I was a passenger and exercised no greater rights or privileges than any other passenger. I was not consulted by the commander about the ship, the course, speed, navigation or conduct at sea. All these matters were under the exclusive control of the Captain.

In one sense, Ismay was right. He was not consulted by the captain about the conduct of the voyage. Smith did not need Ismay's assistance in the day-to-day routine of navigating across the North Atlantic, known as the "Western Ocean" to British mariners. However, by his own admission, Ismay did instruct the chief engineer about the ship's speed at various points in the voyage.

**5:20 P.M.** Air temperature 43° and dropping. Otherwise, weather remains fair. Engines turning 75 revolutions for 22.25 knots. Captain Smith orders delay in making turn from great circle route to rhumb line course for Nantucket Shoal lightship. Ship on course 242°.     —H. F. WILDE, Chief Officer

*Titanic*'s intended track followed a great circle route from Fastnet Light off the tip of Ireland to a spot of empty ocean in latitude 42° N, longitude 47° W, known to sailors as "the Corner." From there the ship was to turn right to meet a rhumb line course for the Nantucket Shoal lightship off the Massachusetts coast. This route was the recognized westbound shipping lane of 1912. *Titanic* was due to make a 24-degree course change at the Corner at 5:20 P.M. However, in the night order book, Captain Smith instructed Chief Officer Henry F. Wilde to delay turning for nearly half an hour. The captain never explained why he made this request.

The only plausible reason for delaying the turn was to take the ship a bit to the south, where presumably there would be less ice. If so, delaying the course change by only half an hour was not a particularly effective safety measure. *Titanic*'s new course was still far enough north to run through areas the captain knew to be ice covered. The only known danger other than icebergs that night was the derelict tankship. However, that ship lay well south of the liner's intended track and was not a threat.

By delaying the turn, Smith could have been setting up an alibi in case his ship ran into ice. All captains know they are always to blame in an accident unless they can prove otherwise. Usually, there is no excuse for a shipping casualty. However, official sanctions may be reduced or avoided if the guilty captain shows he made an attempt to avoid the danger. Captain Smith did not survive to defend himself, so we will never learn his reason for delaying the turn. He may have ordered the delayed turn as proof that he took action to avoid the ice danger that night. Then, if something did go wrong, he could be accused not of doing nothing, but only of not doing enough. Such slight differences are often sufficient to allow a mariner to keep his license and avoid large fines.

Except to avoid impassable ice, Captain Smith would not have wanted to delay the turn more than half an hour. Delaying too long would have increased the distance the ship would need to steam to reach New York. *Titanic*'s meager stock of bunker coal did not allow for extending the route by any appreciable amount.

**5:45 P.M.** Position 41°55′ N, 47°11′ W. Per captain, turn at "the Corner" delayed until now. New heading 266°. Engines turning 75 revolutions. Sea calm and weather fair.     —H. F. WILDE, Chief Officer

Quartermaster George T. Rowe was at *Titanic*'s wheel when Chief Officer Wilde ordered the delayed turn. Rowe recalled the event for Assistant Attorney General Butler Aspinall during the British hearings, saying that the turn was made at 5:45 P.M. "We always make a practice of what we call 'rounding the Corner,'" Rowe explained. "The man at the wheel generally takes notice of it." Rowe had been steering "South 85 West" (265°) before the turn. After the turn, he settled the steering compass on a new course of "North 71 West" (289°). *Titanic* has traveled 9.6 miles past the Corner at the time of the delayed turn. It was now 5 miles south of its intended track.

This calculated speed made good should not be confused with the ship's actual speed of advance through the water. There are too many potential sources for error in the data used in the computation. Not only are the geographic positions little more than guesses, but the effects of surface currents on the ship or of underwater currents on the wreckage have been ignored. This calculated speed, however, does indicate that *Titanic* was making in excess of 21 knots.

**6:00 P.M.** Second Officer Charles H. Lightoller has properly relieved me as officer of the watch. Commencing rounds.     —H. F. WILDE, Chief Officer

Mr. Wilde is relieved. Heading 266°. Engines making 75 revolutions. Seas calm, weather fair.     —C. H. LIGHTOLLER, Second Officer

Although the ship was new, everything else about the routine of standing watches was familiar to the officers of *Titanic*. They followed a routine of four-hour watches that was as old as seafaring. The junior officers (Herbert J. Pitman, Joseph G. Boxhall, Harold G. Lowe, and James Moody) alternated four hours on duty with four hours off. The senior officers (Wilde, William M. Murdoch, and Lightoller) stood four-hour watches with eight hours off duty. As master, Captain Smith had no assigned watch. By tradition, the captain is considered on watch at all times, even when he is not present on the bridge.

Second Officer Lightoller came on duty at 6:00 P.M., relieving Chief Officer Wilde, who then began *rounds,* a tramp taking him the full length of the ship to both the bow and stern on various decks. Rounds were required to be performed by every senior watch officer upon being relieved of duty on the bridge. By the time he joined First Officer Murdoch for dinner at 6:30 P.M., Wilde had walked the ship's 880-foot length several times.

Far below the ship's waterline, *Titanic's* licensed engineers rotated watches, eating, and sleeping in the same manner as the deck officers on the bridge. Like the captain, Chief Engineer Bell was considered on watch at all times. Two of the six second engineers were also on duty during each watch, one supervising the engines while the other handled the boilers. Additional junior engineers brought the total number of licensed men on duty to seven (compared to three licensed deck officers on duty).

The seven engineers supervised the work of more than ninety firemen (or *stokers*), trimmers, and greasers per watch. Known as the "black gang" for their inevitable coating of black coal dust, these men were not supposed to be seen by passengers. They lived in barracks-style quarters on D, E, F, and G decks, which were tucked into the bow of the ship. A spiral staircase descended through their berthing areas to the level of the boiler rooms. From there, a special passage took the black gang through holds #2 and #3. This route allowed them to travel to and from the stokeholds without meeting passengers. Work in the stokeholds (*Titanic* had two per boiler room) was so hot and dusty that shipping companies were required to provide an open air "promenade" for these men. This space was incongruously in full sight of the first- and second-class promenades on the boat deck.

**7:00 P.M.** I have temporarily relieved Mr. Lightoller for his dinner. Heading 266°. Engines making 75 revolutions. Seas calm, weather fair.

—W. M. MURDOCH, First Officer

According to Second Officer Lightoller, at 7:00 P.M. First Officer Murdoch offered to help Lightoller get away from the bridge for a moment to eat. The second officer had the misfortune of standing watch while dinner was served in the officers' dining room. Lightoller could have ordered his meal delivered to the bridge or could have requested that it be held until he came off watch. Instead, his close friend Murdoch voluntarily took temporary command while Lightoller hurried off to dinner.

**7:03 P.M.** All officers please note *Baltic* message pinned to the board in the chart room on which I have written the word "ice." We will need extra vigilance tonight. —E. J. SMITH, Master

Captain Smith also departed the bridge for dinner, but not to eat in the tiny officers' dining room. His was a more formal affair with the Widners, who were sailing as first-class passengers. Smith entertained passengers well, making him popular with White Star's wealthy clients. His ability to charm the ladies and jolly along the gentlemen was part of his rise to de facto commodore of the White Star Line.

**7:10 P.M.** Captain Smith is off the bridge. He is to be called if anything unusual develops. Heading 266°. Seas calm, weather fair. 75 revolutions. —W. M. MURDOCH, First Officer

Murdoch and the other officers and sailors on deck watch probably squinted a bit as the ship's westerly course forced them to look into the sunset. Twilight gathered rapidly after the sun went down at 6:42 P.M., but one spot on the foredeck did not grow darker. It was an open hatch through which light spilled onto the forecastle head. That hatch would have to be closed because its light would dazzle the eyes of the lookouts after dark.

**7:15 P.M.** Light from forecastle hatch is interfering with lookouts. Lamp trimmer Hemming agrees to close hatch on his way forward. He reports all navigation lights are burning brightly. Temperature is still dropping. —W. M. MURDOCH, First Officer

Lamp trimmer Samuel Hemming reported to Murdoch that the lamps had been properly placed for the evening, and then he started to leave the bridge. Although *Titanic* had electric lights throughout the passenger accommodations, it still relied on a few traditional oil lamps to provide illumination for its steering compasses.

"I was walking aft of the bridge, and he called me back," Hemming later recalled of Murdoch. "He said, 'Hemming, when you go forward get the fore scuttle hatch closed. There is a glow left from that. As we are in the vicinity of ice, I want everything dark before the bridge.' " Hemming closed the hatch himself.

**7:25 P.M.** Ship's wireless operators intercept message from *Californian* to *Antillian* reporting ice in Lat 42°3′ N, Lon 49°9′ W. Marconi operator Bride delivered this information to bridge. —W. M. MURDOCH, First Officer

**7:35 P.M.** Resumed watch from Mr. Murdoch after shooting a round of star sights to fix the ship's position. Sights given to Fourth Officer Boxhall for computation. The outside air temperature is now 33°.

—C. H. LIGHTOLLER, Second Officer

By 7:25 P.M., Lightoller was back on the bridge with a sextant to "shoot" the evening round of star sights. Later, these sights would be resolved by Fourth Officer Boxhall and checked by Captain Smith. In 1912, star sights during morning and evening twilight were the most accurate method of establishing a ship's location at sea. Several stars would be shot at a time by the senior officer of the watch using a sextant to measure the angle of each above the horizon. Lightoller apparently observed six stars that evening. Each sight increased the accuracy of the celestial position thus obtained.

Nautical twilight existed from sunset until about 7:40 P.M. that night. Twilight starts when the sun goes down, and it extends as long as there is enough light to see the horizon. It is necessary to have a visible horizon to obtain star sights with a sextant. Lightoller had waited until the stars were twinkling brightly near the end of nautical twilight to make his sights.

Between 7:00 P.M. and 7:30 P.M., Lightoller noticed a 4-degree drop in air temperature. "When Mr. Murdoch mentioned it to me, as far as I recollect it had fallen from 43 degrees to 39," the second officer told the British inquiry. As a precaution, Lightoller asked the relief quartermaster to read the thermometer at regular intervals and report the temperature.

**8:00 P.M.** I calculate we should be seeing first ice any time, certainly no later than 9:30 P.M. Sixth Officer Moody anticipates the ship will reach the ice around 11:00 P.M. —C. H. LIGHTOLLER, Second Officer

The air temperature was now down to 33 degrees. This was close enough to freezing to prompt action from Lightoller. "I sent word down to the carpenter about nine o'clock," he later told John Charles Bigham, Lord Mersey, at the British hearings. "It was then 33 degrees, and I sent word to the carpenter and to the engine room—for the carpenter to look after his fresh water; that is to say, he has to drain it off to prevent the pipes from freezing—and to the engine room for them to take the necessary precautions for the winches." Lightoller did not want any problems from ice on his watch.

Small day tanks located in a house on the boat deck between the third and fourth funnels supplied the potable water system. Gravity created pressure in the system because the day tanks were higher than the spigots. Engineers pumped drinking water from larger tanks deep in the hull to the day tanks on the boat deck as needed. Large U-shaped loops of piping, which are clearly visible in photographs of the funnels, were part of the plumbing system. Clearly, these pipes were exposed to the freezing night air—hence the need for the carpenter to attend to them.

**8:50 P.M.** Air temperature 33 degrees. Ship's carpenter instructed to protect the freshwater supply and pipes from freezing. Engine room is reminded of possibility of freezing.          —C. H. LIGHTOLLER, Second Officer

At the hearings in London after the sinking, Antarctic explorer Sir Ernest Shackleton was asked by Lord Mersey to comment on the sudden drop in temperature that April night. Shackleton had first-hand experience navigating through icebergs and was a national hero whose comments carried weight with the British public. "If there was no wind and the temperature fell abnormally for the time of the year," the explorer testified, "I would consider that I was approaching an area which might have ice in it."

# PARALLEL TRACKS

Sunday, April 14, 1912

**8:50 P.M. to 11:25 P.M.**

**8:50 P.M.** Heading 266°. Engines turning 75 revolutions. Weather fair. Sea becoming extremely calm.                    —J. MOODY, Sixth Officer

TWO ships were heading for close encounters with North Atlantic ice on this particular evening. One, a giant liner, was bound for New York. The other, a stodgy cargo ship, was looking for freight in Boston. Their intended destinations were so close on the North American continent that their westbound paths this far offshore were nearly parallel. Men on both ships were aware that dangerous ice lay across their paths. Captain Stanley Lord, master of the single-screw freighter *Californian,* was concerned enough to post extra lookouts. A seaman shivered on the forecastle where his deck-level position, well below the crow's nest, gave the best chance of spotting ice against the horizon.

*Titanic* was behind and slightly to *Californian*'s south but was rapidly catching up to the slower freighter. On the liner, Captain Smith was also becoming concerned about the ice. Although less worried than his fellow captain, Smith decided it would be prudent to break off a dinner engagement with passengers and visit his bridge.

**8:55 P.M.** Captain Smith on bridge to discuss ice situation with Mr. Lightoller. Some ice has already been spotted well away from ship. Heading 266°. Engines making 75 revolutions. Seas calm, weather fair.   —J. MOODY, Sixth Officer

*Titanic* was approaching the 49th meridian, which would mark its entrance into a zone known to contain dangerous amounts of ice. It was here that the French liner *Niagara* had smashed its nose against an iceberg during dinner on the previous Thursday evening. *Titanic*'s officers recognized the potential for experiencing a similar fate, which led to Captain Smith's reappearance on the bridge, having ended his dessert coffee earlier than expected. Second Officer Charles H. Lightoller later provided a detailed account of their matter-of-fact conversation to the British inquiry.

"It's getting cold," remarked the captain.

"Yes, it is very cold, sir. Only a degree above freezing. I've sent word down to the carpenter and rung up the engine room and told them it is freezing, or will be during the night," Lightoller responded.

"Not much wind."

"No, it is a flat calm, as a matter of fact."

"A flat calm."

"Yes, quite flat. There is no wind. It's a pity we don't have a breeze while going through the ice," Lightoller said. Both men knew that without a breeze there would be no breaking waves against the bases of floating icebergs. The lack of foam from breakers would make the bergs harder to spot.

"It seems quite clear," said the captain.

"Yes, perfectly clear."

The two officers continued talking as their liner hurtled through the night at 22.25 knots. Despite the signs of ice around the ship, neither man spoke of reducing speed. Captain Smith ended the conversation by saying, "If it becomes at all doubtful, let me know at once. I will be just inside." With that, he stepped into the wheelhouse for a visit to the chart room.

There is reason to question whether Captain Smith really visited the bridge at 8:55 P.M. During the U.S. hearings into the sinking, a first-class passenger from Wisconsin, Daisy Minahan, sent an affidavit to Senator William Alden Smith that contained a disturbing claim. She said the captain was in the à la carte café with Sir Cosmo Duff-Gordon, Duff-Gordon's wife, and several friends at the same time that Lightoller claimed the master was on the bridge.

> I had read testimony before your committee saying that Capt. Smith had talked to an officer on the bridge from 8:45 to 9:25. This is positively untrue, as he was having coffee with these people during this time. I was seated so close to them that I could hear bits of their conversation.

Lightoller was somewhat free with the truth regarding other instances, so it is possible that he concocted the story of the captain's bridge appearance. It is unlikely in this case, however, because of the implications raised by the captain's discussion of ice during his visit. Lightoller's version adds fuel to the argument that *Titanic* was recklessly speeding into ice despite the fact that its captain and officers knew of the danger, a situation contrary to the impression of careful navigation the second officer wanted to present, so it is unlikely that Lightoller fabricated the story of the captain's visit to the bridge.

It is probable, however, that Daisy Minahan and Lightoller both told the truth as they saw it. This seems to be a case of time confusion so common within the story. If Minahan's watch was still set to the time based on the ship's longitude of the previous day, it might well have read 9:30 while the official ship's time had already been set back because of *Titanic*'s westward progress, making it 8:30 P.M. on the bridge. Still, what Ms. Minahan said cannot be dismissed out of hand. If true, her story provides evidence that the captain took ice danger far too lightly—the same conclusion that may be drawn from Lightoller's testimony.

Time confusion of this type is easy to understand. Depending upon their intended use, clocks aboard *Titanic* showed three different times. A chronometer in the chart room carried Greenwich mean time for navigation, and its hands were never reset during a voyage. Most clocks on the ship, including the famous one in the grand stairway, showed Apparent Ship's Time (AST), which was based on local longitude. These public clocks were reset daily to reflect the ship's passage. When they remembered, passengers would reset their watches to match the public clocks. *Titanic*'s clocks were scheduled to be set back twenty-two minutes at midnight on the night of the accident, but no one could say for sure if that occurred. Finally, a special clock in the wireless room was kept on New York time for coordinating communication with American ground stations.

**9:30 P.M.** Per Captain—reduce speed if it becomes even slightly hazy. Call him if it becomes at all doubtful. Lookouts instructed to be especially wary of growlers.                                    —C. H. LIGHTOLLER, Second Officer

Captain Smith's conversation was still fresh on his mind when Lightoller asked Sixth Officer James Moody to telephone the lookouts in the crow's nest, which was located 90 feet off the water on the ship's foremast. "Keep a sharp lookout for ice, particularly small ice," Moody told George Symons and Archie Jewell, the two seamen on lookout duty in the crow's nest. Not satisfied with these directions, Lightoller told Moody to ring up the lookouts a second time and specifically mention "growlers." Growlers are small bergs that are particularly difficult to spot at night, often because they have recently upended and show only their smooth, dark undersides. The second officer told the British proceedings that he always sent this message to the lookouts when the ship was approaching ice. He denied any connection between this warning to the lookouts and his conversation with Captain Smith.

An unsolvable mystery of the sinking is Captain Smith's failure to increase the number of lookouts even though he knew that his ship was approaching an area of known ice. In 1912 (as now), it was the ordinary practice of seamen to add additional lookouts as low and as far forward on the bow as possible when conditions warranted. No one would have complained if either Lightoller or First Officer William M. Murdoch had called out extra lookouts in response to the increasing amount of ice.

The failure of Smith (and to a lesser extent of the senior officers, Wilding, Murdoch, and Lightoller) to increase the lookout by placing a trained sailor on the forecastle head was not the result of difficulty communicating from bridge to bow. The Harland and Wolff designers had envisioned the need to place additional lookouts at times, so they had provided *Titanic*'s officers with direct telephone communication between the bridge and the forecastle. This phone line should have been used to pass information from a lookout stationed on the ship's prow. Unfortunately, there was no one at the far end to make a warning call to the bridge.

Even the few officers and sailors present on the bridge that night were not used efficiently. Relief quartermaster Alfred Olliver was away performing inconsequential duties just when his eyes were needed for the ship's safety. Sixth Officer Moody seems to have been in a poor location—inside the wheelhouse behind two sets of windows—to keep lookout. First Officer Murdoch was on the open captain's bridge, but his duties as officer of the watch prevented him from being an effective lookout (an opinion traditionally held by seamen regarding watch officers).

Fourth Officer Joseph G. Boxhall was also on duty that night, but his primary concern seems to have been resolving Lightoller's star sights and doing the other work required for navigation. From the chart room, Boxhall was unable to see anything outside the ship— even though he was "on watch." He was forced later to patiently explain watchkeeping aboard *Titanic* to the London proceedings. His inquisitor, Thomas Scanlan, had difficulty understanding how this witness could have been "on watch" without also being a designated "lookout."

MR. SCANLAN: Is it [lookout] part of the duty you were told to do?

MR. BOXHALL: No, I was not told to do it.

MR. SCANLAN: Were you told to watch at all that night?

MR. BOXHALL: No, I was not.

MR. SCANLAN: In point of fact, you were not on watch that night?

MR. BOXHALL: I was on watch. I was on duty, but I was not on the bridge. I was not on the lookout, if that is what you mean.

MR. SCANLAN: That is exactly what I want to know. At no time that night were you keeping the lookout on the bridge?

MR. BOXHALL: No.

MR. SCANLAN: Who besides Mr. Murdoch was keeping the lookout on the bridge?

MR. BOXHALL: Nobody, Mr. Murdoch was keeping the lookout himself.

MR. SCANLAN: And there were no extra lookouts?

MR. BOXHALL: Not that I know of. I did not hear of any.

In the Marconi room behind the bridge, senior wireless operator **9:40 P.M.** John ("Jack") Phillips copied down a string of Morse code being sent by a nearby ship, *Mesaba*. It was yet another ice message. He handed it to his assistant, Harold Bride, to read. Neither man recognized the importance of what was written on that paper.

**From *Mesaba* to *Titanic* and all east-bound ships:** ICE REPORT IN LAT. 42° N TO 41°25′ N, LONG. 49° TO LONG. 50°30′ W. SAW MUCH HEAVY PACK ICE AND GREAT NUMBER LARGE ICEBERGS. ALSO FIELD ICE. WEATHER GOOD, CLEAR.

According to Lightoller, this message was placed under a paperweight in the Marconi office while Phillips continued communicating with the land station at Cape Race. In his autobiography, the second officer claimed, "That delay proved fatal and was the main contributory cause to the loss of that magnificent ship and hundreds of lives." In fact, *Titanic* was already steaming through the outskirts of the deadly mix of bergs, field ice, and pack ice described by this message. Although there is no excuse for the failure of the two Marconi operators to carry this message to the bridge, it is unlikely that anything would have changed had they shown it to Lightoller, Smith, or any other officer.

In 1912 the route to New York between January 15 and August 14 was called the *Outward Southern Track*. North Atlantic routing charts of the era show this track as passing only 25 miles south of an area known for field ice between March and July. This 1912 track was well inside a zone where icebergs are regularly seen between April and June. Based on the routing charts, Captain Smith should have expected to find ice on his course whether he received any warnings from other ships or not. Ice was always encountered on the Outward Southern Track at this time of year.

In addition to routing charts, *Titanic* carried pilot books printed by the Hydrographic Office of the British Admiralty. Captain Smith (and the ship's other officers) had available the 1909 edition of *United States (East Coast)*, which warned

> one of the chief dangers in crossing the Atlantic lies in the probability of encountering masses of ice, both in the form of bergs and of extensive fields of solid compact ice, released at the breaking up of winter in the Arctic regions and drifted down by the Labrador Current across their direct route. Ice is more likely to be encountered in this route between April and August, both months inclusive.

The Hydrographic Office went into great detail, describing the nature of the icebergs ships would certainly encounter:

> the specific gravity of fresh-water ice, of which these bergs are composed, is about seven-eighths that of sea water; so that, however vast the berg may appear to the eye of the observer, he can in reality see one-eighth of its bulk, the remaining seven-eighths being submerged.

Captain Smith also knew from firsthand experience that icebergs do not respect shipping routes. During 1903, 1904, and 1905 he and other North Atlantic captains had been forced to move the Outward Southern Track about 60 miles farther south than usual because of ice conditions. The winter of the disaster (1911–12) produced an excess of ice because of warmer than normal weather that resulted in an unusually high number of bergs breaking off the Greenland ice cap.

Even before the ship left Southampton, the captain knew there would be considerably more icebergs and fields of ice than usual floating across his route to New York. This ice information was also available to investigators in 1912. Both probes could have confirmed that conditions around *Titanic* were warnings of mortal danger. Instead, the officers ignored the deadly implications of strangely calm seas in the usually turbulent North Atlantic.

While we do not know why additional lookouts were not posted, there is little doubt as to why *Titanic* did not slow down as it approached the ice danger zone. Passengers in 1912 (as today) voted for speed over safety by purchasing tickets on ships that arrived "on time every time" regardless of weather or ice conditions. Captains were compelled by public expectation to "crack on," or maintain speed and course under virtually all weather and sea conditions. Slowing for fog or ice may have been prudent, but it was not popular among ticket buyers. Passengers did not want to spend more than a week traveling between the Old and New Worlds. Ismay understood the impact on profits of the public's desire for fast passages, and this is probably what motivated his plan to arrive early in New York City.

Profit-minded ship owners demanded increasingly faster ships. Due to the dynamics of fluids, the easiest way to increase speed is to make ships larger and longer. There had been a tenfold increase in the size of passenger ships from the late nineteenth to the early twentieth century. To command these behemoths, owners promoted those captains who kept to the published schedules. No one believed that high speed was the safest way to cross the Atlantic; however, it was simply necessary to attract large numbers of passengers.

The paradox of satisfying public demand for speed while operating within acceptable safety limits was explored—tentatively at best—by both investigations. In London, Second Officer Lightoller skillfully, if not convincingly, handled questions on this subject from interrogator Thomas Scanlan.

> MR. SCANLAN: In view of the abnormal conditions and of the fact that you were nearing ice at ten o'clock, was there not a very obvious reason for going slower?
>
> MR. LIGHTOLLER: Well, I can only quote you my experience throughout the last twenty-four years, that I have been crossing the Atlantic most of the time, that I have never seen the speed reduced.

Lightoller's own testimony about the unusual weather and sea conditions that night put him in a most uncomfortable position. He could not argue both that the ship was operating at a safe speed *and* that conditions were such that "everything was against us," so he sidestepped this paradox in the time-honored method of children who argue that "everybody else does it." Scanlan brushed Lightoller aside with a question aimed at the heart of the matter, but the second officer could not be lured from his somewhat childish argument.

> MR. SCANLAN: Is it not quite clear that the most obvious way to avoid it is by slackening speed?
> MR. LIGHTOLLER: Not necessarily the most obvious.
> MR. SCANLAN: Well is it one way?
> MR. LIGHTOLLER: It is one way. Naturally, if you stop the ship you will not collide with anything.
> MR. SCANLAN: What I want to suggest to you is that it was recklessness, utter recklessness, in view of the conditions which you have described as abnormal, and in view of the knowledge you had from various sources that ice was in your immediate vicinity, to proceed at twenty-one and one-half knots?
> MR. LIGHTOLLER: Then, all I can say is that recklessness applies to practically every commander and every ship crossing the Atlantic Ocean.

Scanlan was not to be deterred. An accomplished verbal boxer, he wanted to put Lightoller on the ropes. The interrogator's roundhouse of questions was aimed at obtaining an admission that *Titanic*'s speed was tantamount to reckless operation. Lightoller proved a worthy opponent in this verbal bout.

> MR. SCANLAN: I am not disputing that with you, but can you describe it yourself as other than recklessness?
> MR. LIGHTOLLER: Yes.
> MR. SCANLAN: Is it careful navigation in your view?
> MR. LIGHTOLLER: It is ordinary navigation, which embodies careful navigation.

Lightoller was supported by testimony from Gerhard C. Affeld, marine superintendent of the Red Star Line. An experienced captain with thirty-nine years at sea, Affeld testified in London that he never slowed down for ice when crossing the North Atlantic. "I only slow down in the case of fog or thick weather," the veteran navigator said. He was questioned about Red Star ships operating in the vicinity of *Titanic* on the night of the disaster. He recalled at least four and possibly five company ships that happened upon ice in that region. One Red Star ship successfully navigated in field ice for some time before slowing down to protect its running gear.

MR. ROWLATT: Did they change their course or their speed?

MR. AFFELD: Absolutely not. The Manitou slowed down after she entered the ice field. She went into field ice at full speed for about an hour and then the ice field became thick, heavy lumps amongst it, and her Captain slowed her down for about an hour. He reduced speed for fear of damaging the propeller.

Affeld was right in saying there was nothing unusual about a passenger liner speeding across the North Atlantic despite obvious danger. His acceptance of this situation may not have reflected the opinions of all 1912-era sailors, however. Affeld's employer, the Red Star Line, also happened to be owned by International Mercantile Marine (IMM), the conglomerate that controlled White Star Line. As president of IMM (as well as chairman of White Star Line), J. Bruce Ismay was Affeld's ultimate boss. It was no surprise that Affeld drove home the point that captains employed by IMM on North Atlantic passenger routes were paid to be bold seamen.

MR. FINLAY: You have told us the practice is not to reduce speed. Is that the practice of all your captains of the Red Star line?

MR. AFFELD: Yes, all of them.

MR. FINLAY: And, as far as you know, in other lines too?

MR. AFFELD: I believe every captain will give you the same answer; they will not slow down unless it becomes thick or hazy.

First Officer Murdoch adjusted his cap as he closed the door to his **9:45 P.M.** cabin on the port side of the officers' quarters. He turned and walked forward along the corridor that led past the chief officer's cabin and into *Titanic*'s wheelhouse. Polite "good evenings" were exchanged with Quartermaster Alfred Olliver standing to the ship's steering wheel. In keeping with nautical tradition, Murdoch arrived fifteen minutes early for the 10:00 P.M. change of watch to get a feel for the situation before assuming the responsibility of conning the ship for the next four hours.

Like every other officer coming on watch, Murdoch first checked the chart room behind the quartermaster for new information, in this case the *Baltic* warning. He must have noticed the captain's handwritten notation, "ice," on this message. The captain was still in the chart room with Fourth Officer Joseph G. Boxhall, so the *Baltic* message was probably discussed. The night order book, in which Murdoch had initialed the instructions that the master should be called if anything unusual developed, was also in the chart room.

Murdoch remained unaware of the 9:40 P.M. message from *Mesaba* warning of heavy pack ice and icebergs with field ice located west of latitude 49°00′ W. If the track of *Titanic* is plotted backward from the point of impact with the iceberg, it shows the ship crossed the danger meridian slightly before 9:30 P.M., about fifteen minutes before Murdoch came on duty.

Stepping back through the wheelhouse, Murdoch emerged into the freezing night air of the semiprotected captain's bridge. He knew he was facing four cold hours on duty as he joined Second Officer Lightoller on the raised footbridge behind the open bulwark of the bridge wing. Murdoch expected to encounter bergs on his watch, so ice was the natural topic of conversation between the two officers. Their discussion echoed what Lightoller and Captain Smith had said a few minutes earlier.

"It's pretty cold," Murdoch observed.

"Yes," Lightoller answered, "it's freezing."

"And quiet, too."

"Too quiet."

Although not what the order book meant as an "unusual situation," the weather surrounding *Titanic* bothered both men. It was too quiet for the North Atlantic. The sky was crystal clear, and the sea was becoming what sailors call "oily calm." There was danger in this calm. Lightoller commented on the conditions during their brief conversation. "No wind, no waves tonight," Lightoller had said. "We won't be able to spot bergs by foam around their bases." On a normal night, waves crashing against the ice would have reflected starlight. Bergs were often seen in rough seas by light reflected from their beards of white foam. Tonight, the North Atlantic was as quiet as a baptismal font.

While the two officers were speaking on the footplate, Captain Smith used dividers to, in Fourth Officer Boxhall's words, "prick off" the ship's 7:30 P.M. celestial fix obtained by Lightoller. Boxhall had done the math resolving the sights, so it was only a few moments' work for the captain to plot the ship's location at the time the sights were taken. By this time, *Titanic* had steamed about 45 miles west of its 7:30 P.M. location, which the captain neatly marked on the chart.

**10:00 P.M.** First Officer William M. Murdoch has properly relieved me as officer of the watch. Commencing rounds.

—C. H. LIGHTOLLER, Second Officer

Mr. Lightoller is relieved. Heading 266°. Engines making 75 revolutions. Seas calm, weather fair. Air temperature has dropped to 31°. Heading: 266°.

—W. M. MURDOCH, First Officer

### Range to iceberg: 76,874 yards (38.4 nautical miles)

The ship's bell rang four times in two groups of two strokes each—four bells, or 10 P.M.—immediately followed by a cry of "all's well" from the crow's nest. "I have the bridge. You are relieved, Mr. Lightoller," Murdoch said. "Thank you," the other officer responded, "I am relieved." The words sounded excessively formal even to the two friends who spoke them, but both officers understood their importance. "Don't forget to call the captain if it's the least bit hazy," Lightoller reminded his relief. With that exchange, the immediate responsibility for the safety of *Titanic* and the 2,200 people on board transferred from Lightoller to Murdoch. Despite the formality, this was a routine event for these two longtime friends and shipmates.

Lightoller was headed for bed, but not until he finished the ritual of rounds. "First of all I had to do rounds," he wrote in his autobiography. "And in a ship of that size it meant a mile or more of deck, not including a few hundred feet of ladders, staircases, etc. . . . then back to my warm cabin."

Overhead, the tiny crow's nest was temporarily busy as lookouts Symons and Jewell were replaced by Frederick Fleet and Reginald Lee. The two men going off duty reminded their replacements to keep a sharp eye for icebergs and especially for those hard-to-spot growlers. With that reminder, Symons and Jewell disappeared down the ladder inside the foremast leading to the deck. Fleet and Lee settled in for two hours of cold duty.

Boxhall and Smith spoke for a moment in the doorway of the captain's suite before the ship's commander disappeared into his private quarters. The master of *Titanic* enjoyed a suite on the starboard side of the officers' quarters, just behind the bridge. A doorway from the wheelhouse led to the captain's navigation room—a cross between a ship's office and a private chart room. Behind that were a sitting room, a bedroom, and a private lavatory. A window on the

10:05 P.M.

front side of his navigation room allowed the captain a view of the bridge.

10:15 P.M.  Of all the captains, mates, and seamen on the North Atlantic that night, only one took positive action to prevent the *Titanic*'s maiden voyage disaster. He was Captain Stanley Lord, master of *Californian*. On this Sunday evening, his ship was 15 or 20 miles to the north, also heading westward on a track nearly parallel to *Titanic*'s. At 6:30 P.M. it passed several large icebergs (reported to *Titanic* at 7:25 P.M.) floating about 5 miles to the south.

Sighting these bergs in the dusk made Captain Lord concerned for his ship's safety. As noted earlier in this chapter, he increased his lookout by putting a seaman right in the bow of the ship on the forecastle head. Extra eyes were needed to navigate safely through the bits and pieces of ice floating east of 49°50′ W longitude. Although *Californian* was slightly north of *Titanic*'s track, the two ships experienced almost identical conditions that night; identical down to the fact that both ran into the ice.

"We doubled the lookout from the crew, put a man on the forecastle head—that is, right at the bow of the ship," Lord later told Senator Smith in the U.S. Senate hearings. "I was on the bridge myself with an officer which I would not have been under ordinary conditions."

Lord fingered his binoculars. He tried using his glasses to spot danger ahead, but he later testified that he was dissatisfied with the way they confined his vision in the darkness. The "seeing" conditions were disconcerting tonight because the horizon was somehow different. He explained this difference to the British proceedings in London.

MR. EDWARDS: You have said there was no haze that night.
MR. LORD: Yes.
MR. EDWARDS: Did you tell the American Court of Inquiry that the light that night was very extraordinary, the conditions were deceiving?
MR. LORD: I told them it was a very strange night. It was hard to define where the sky ended and the water commenced. There was what you call a soft horizon. I was sometimes mistaking the stars low down on the horizon for steamers' lights.
MR. EDWARDS: What is that condition of things due to, if not due to haze?
MR. LORD: I do not know. Just a flash, that is all.

10:21 P.M.  At 10:21 P.M. Captain Lord became the first of two men to drive a ship into the ice that night. Somebody on *Californian*'s bridge noticed something dead ahead. Third Officer Charles V. Groves later took credit for this spotting, although he admitted that he first thought the ice was a school of playful dolphin. "Ice, that's ice!" the dreaded word was shouted. A low-lying line of white seemed to stretch from the north to south horizon in front of the ship.

"All back emergency!" yelled Captain Lord. A crash stop with the ship's engine straining in reverse was his instant reaction to impending disaster. Full reverse power seemed to have little effect. The bow raced ever closer to this seemingly impenetrable wall of ice. The single propeller shook the stern as it tried in vain to check the freighter's forward momentum. There was not enough distance between *Californian* and the ice for an emergency stop to prevent possible disaster.

In a last-second effort to dodge the inevitable, Lord ordered a turn to the right. It was futile. The ice was too close, and reverse thrust from the propeller reduced the effect of the rudder. *Californian*'s commander watched helplessly as his ship pushed smaller bits aside and drove into the field of closely packed ice. With right rudder, the ship's path through the floating ice resembled a huge question mark. Almost as soon as it was made, the curving wake began to disappear as pieces of ice closed in behind. The bow continued rotating to the right until the freighter was pointed east-northeast after it came to a stop.

It was time to breathe again. Captain Lord quickly determined his vessel was miraculously undamaged by its half-sideways rush into the ice field. The shaken captain asked Groves to check the spinning propeller of the patent log, which normally trailed astern to measure the distance the ship traveled. *Californian*'s spinner was gone, cut by the ice. In the dark, it was impossible to judge the amount of ice surrounding the ship, but to Lord it seemed endless. There was little doubt in his mind that he was trapped until sunrise, when there would be enough light to pick his way through the ice.

**10:30 P.M.** Growlers and bergs becoming more common. Sea temperature is now 31 degrees. Surface has "oily calm" appearance. Heading: 266°. Revolutions 75. —J. MOODY, Sixth Officer

**Range to berg: 54,074 yards (27.0 nautical miles)**

*Titanic*'s motion was unusually quiet as it sliced through the North Atlantic. Ice littering the sea around the ship was beginning to calm the surface by damping wave action. This damping action would become more pronounced over the next seventy minutes, as the ship steamed deeper into the mass of floating ice. The air temperature was now at freezing. During Lightoller's watch, the sea temperature had dropped to a degree colder than freezing. Murdoch undoubtedly was grateful that the ship's carpenter had been instructed to protect the freshwater supply from freezing. It was one less thing for Murdoch to worry about.

Frederick Fleet, one of *Titanic*'s lookouts, later testified that he noticed the same "seeing" conditions encountered by Captain Lord earlier that night. The horizon ahead of the speeding liner was no longer clear and distinct. Fleet thought it was developing haze and remarked to his fellow lookout, "Well, if we can see through that we will be lucky." Reginald Lee, who shared the crow's nest, agreed. There seemed to be a light haze on the water, which had been hardly noticeable when the two men went on watch at 10:00 P.M. but which seemed to become thicker as time passed. The stars overhead twinkled brightly, a common occurrence when low-lying haze or fog circulates on an otherwise clear night.

10:42 P.M.   The sea around *Titanic* must have become increasingly crowded with ice as the liner entered the region that *Athenai* reported by radio to *Baltic*. This is the ice mentioned in the wireless message pocketed by Ismay, so its appearance should not have surprised Murdoch. That warning had been posted in the chart room since early in Lightoller's watch. Lightoller even reminded Murdoch of this particular warning during their conversation at change of watch. If anything, the first officer was comforted by the appearance of this danger exactly when and where it was expected. Unexpected dangers are feared the most.

The breath of twenty-four-year-old lookout Fleet formed clouds of steam that were immediately torn apart by wind from the ship's forward speed. Fleet and his fellow lookout, Lee, crouched inside *Titanic*'s small crow's nest 95 feet above the water, trying to escape the numbing wind. As was their custom throughout the voyage, Fleet was in the port side of their perch while Lee occupied the starboard. From time to time, both men must have knuckled wind tears from their eyes.

Neither lookout saw or felt the electromagnetic signals speeding to and from their ship through the cold night air. Wireless communication was a new invention in 1912. Sailors were as entranced by radio as everyone else was, but they had not fully accepted its practicality. By dawn, however, more than seven hundred *Titanic* survivors would owe their quick rescues to the ship's powerful Marconi equipment. At the time, wireless was a commercial undertaking that was intended primarily as an amusement for wealthy passengers and only secondarily as an aid to navigation. Unseen and unheard by the lookouts, a warning was about to flash into *Titanic*'s wireless office from a nearby freighter.

**10:55 P.M.** Heading: 266°, 75 revolutions. Lookouts warned again to keep a sharp lookout for growlers. —W. M. MURDOCH, First Officer

**Range to berg: 35,074 yards (17.5 nautical miles)**

On *Californian*, Captain Lord recognized his responsibility to warn other mariners of the field ice in which he was trapped. He went to his ship's tiny Marconi office to speak with operator Cyril Evans. "I asked him what ships he had. He said, 'nothing, only the *Titanic*,'" Lord told the British inquiry. He asked Evans to warn *Titanic* as a courtesy of the impassable ice conditions. Lord's ice warning should have precluded any books or motion pictures about a 1912 *Titanic* disaster. If Lord's warning had been carried to the liner's bridge, there should have been no accident, no sinking, no loss of life. A few words written on a slip of paper would have warned Murdoch about the deadly mixture of floating ice. Captain Smith would have been notified, and *Titanic* could have been steered around the danger. That didn't happen because *Californian*'s radio operator used the wrong salutation when he started to key the warning message.

"Say, old man, we are stopped and surrounded by ice," *Californian*'s wireless operator, Evans, tapped in Morse code. "Old man" was—and still is—a conventional salutation in code to another wireless operator of any age. It is a simple string of dashes representing the letters "O" and "M." Dash-dash-dash, dash-dash. However, Evans should have started his message with "Captain *Californian* to Captain *Titanic*." This formal wording would have indicated the importance of the warning. Instead, he chose the informal "old man" reserved for casual chatter among radio operators.

"Shut up . . . DDD . . . DDD . . . I'm working Cape Race," snapped back Jack Phillips, *Titanic*'s senior operator. "You are jamming me." (DDD, dash-dot-dot, is telegraph shorthand for "shut up.")

Miffed by the big liner's rebuff, Evans slipped off his earphones and shut down his equipment for the night. Aboard *Titanic,* Phillips had reason to be testy. The previous day, his 5-kilowatt Marconi wireless transmitter had broken down. He and his assistant, Harold Bride, had worked without sleep to repair their equipment. It was fixed by 5:00 A.M. Sunday, the day of the accident. The transmitter breakdown had left a huge backlog of mostly frivolous messages to be sent on behalf of first-class passengers. Dead tired, Phillips simply did not have time for more discussion about icebergs. He had been sending ice warnings to the bridge all day. One more seemed meaningless. Everyone knew there was ice around the speeding liner.

*Californian*'s rebuffed ice warning contained specific information about the density of pack ice directly across the speeding liner's path. Existence of this pack was already known on *Titanic*'s bridge, but no one suspected it had become a nearly impassable band of field ice, perhaps 3 miles wide and studded with icebergs, looming less than forty minutes ahead. We can only speculate what Captain Smith would have done if he had received this warning. Instead, this critical message was cut short and never delivered to Murdoch.

By failing to convey the importance of this warning to Evans, Captain Lord played an unwitting role in having his own message cut off. Had he known, Evans would have started out by saying the warning was a personal message from one captain to another instead of starting with "OM," the usual greeting among fellow radio operators. Also, Evans would have used the international one-letter marine signal code for his warning. Had he telegraphed the letter "U" several times, Phillips would undoubtedly have recognized the importance of the message. In the international code of signals between merchant ships, the single letter "U" means, "You are standing into danger."

Phillips likely never knew he prevented Evans from describing the unusual density of the pack ice that had forced *Californian* to halt. The density of this pack (bergy bits, growlers, and full-sized bergs bumping together) would quickly become the key factor in events aboard *Titanic.* The senior radio operator knew none of this as he tapped "DDD . . . DDD . . . DDD." He also never knew that cutting short this ice warning may have been the most costly peacetime error (in terms of human life) in maritime radio history. Fate challenged Jack Phillips with an opportunity to prevent the impending catastrophe, and he failed.

Having done his duty to alert his fellow sailors of their danger, Captain Lord stretched out on a settee in the chart room beneath *Californian*'s open bridge. The fact that he chose the settee instead of his bed, which was only 15 feet away, and that he remained dressed ("all standing," in sailor talk) indicates the freighter captain did not expect uninterrupted rest. Captain Lord anticipated being called to his bridge that night.

The magnificent floating hotel was now less than 19 miles from that impassable wall of ice. In front of that tightly packed line of ice was an iceberg. Not just any iceberg, but The Iceberg. Oblivious of its fate, *Titanic* was navigating around an increasing number of ghostly bergs and growlers. In the calm inky black sea, the pieces of ice must have appeared to glide past the liner, rather than the opposite.

# A DARK MASS

Sunday, April 14, 1912

**11:25 P.M. to 11:40 P.M.**

**11:25 P.M.** Course generally 266°, although we are swinging around ice. Air temperature down to 28°. 75 revolutions. —W. M. MURDOCH, First Officer

**Range to berg: 12,274 yards (6.1 nautical miles)**

I T was bitterly cold in *Titanic*'s crow's nest, an environment made worse by freezing wind, a result of the ship's forward motion. Lookouts Frederick Fleet and Reginald Lee were still trying to identify the thin line that appeared to be haze on the horizon ahead of the ship. To make their duty less painful, the two men probably took turns peering over the protective forward wall of their tiny enclosure, which was perched 95 feet above the water.

Fleet and Lee both claimed that *Californian* was not visible from the crow's nest at this hour. Yet, men on the small freighter were sure they spotted the huge liner. This discrepancy is not surprising. Lookouts on the passenger ship would have been most concerned about spotting ice around their vessel, not about searching for tiny specks of light several miles to the north that did not signify danger. The same was not true for *Californian*'s deck watch. Those men had little to do but scan the horizon and wait until dawn, when their ship would presumably begin moving again. Spotting the lights of the world's largest ship would have been a pleasant diversion for the freighter's crew.

**11:30 P.M.** Seven bells and all's well. Navigation lights burning brightly. Heading centered on 266°; 75 revolutions. —J. MOODY, SIXTH Officer

Ding-ding . . . ding-ding . . . ding-ding . . . ding.

The ship's bell rang seven times, marking 11:30 P.M. in ship's time. *Titanic*'s lookouts had been on duty for ninety minutes, and cold air had saturated their heavy sailor's clothing. The White Star Line employed professional seamen who understood the importance of their jobs as lookouts. This night, the two on duty were performing as well as possible under the conditions. Second Officer Charles H. Lightoller's warning at 9:30 P.M. had been passed to them by the previous shift of lookouts when Fleet and Lee came on duty at 10:00 P.M. The men knew what they were to do.

One task not expected of the lookouts was to analyze what they saw. They were just to report it. "We are only up there to report anything we see," Fleet later explained his duties to the U.S. Senate hearings. "A ship or anything."

Due to a mixup in Southampton, neither lookout had binoculars. "We had none this time. We had nothing at all, only our own eyes to look out," Fleet recalled during the U.S. hearings. Normally White Star provided a pair of binoculars to the lookouts. There was even a special box to contain them built into the crow's nest. "We asked them in Southampton, and they said there was none for us. We asked Mr. Lightoller, the second officer." Unlike the lookouts, the officers working on *Titanic*'s bridge did have binoculars.

Responding to a direct question about whether the lack of binoculars contributed to the disaster, Fleet said simply, "We might have seen it a bit sooner." He almost certainly oversimplified the situation. Glasses (as sailors call binoculars) of 1912 vintage would not have helped spot the berg sooner. While their optics were sharp and their magnification powerful, pre–World War I binoculars lacked the modern coated lenses that actually "gather" and thereby increase the amount of light seen by the observer. The optically inefficient glasses available to Fleet and Lee would have "seen" less light than the human eye alone.

Even with binoculars strapped around his neck, Fleet probably would have used his unaided eyes to scan the dark waters ahead. Trained lookouts did not then (or now) use binoculars alone to spot dangers. Magnification restricts the field of view, so wide scanning with the unaided eye often works better for initial spotting. Glasses are best for identifying objects after they are spotted. Fleet's own testimony proved that the lack of binoculars was not a factor in spotting the berg early enough to have avoided disaster. What most likely blinded the lookouts that night was the air rushing past the crow's nest, which brought tears to their unprotected eyes.

If binoculars might have made a difference that night, it would have been with the actual identification of the berg. Fleet and Lee saw the "dark mass" early enough, but they failed to report it correctly—possibly for want of glasses that might have allowed them to recognize the dark spot as an iceberg. That would have allowed the lookouts to make a correct report several minutes before the actual iceberg alarm. Presumably, there might have been enough time to turn or stop the ship.

With or without binoculars, the lookouts still spotted and reported dangers around the ship. They apparently sent the bridge at least one warning of something ahead of the ship during the critical ten-minute period immediately prior to the accident. In particular, the lookouts notified the bridge of a "dark mass" looming directly ahead of the ship. Fleet used the direct telephone to the wheelhouse for this warning. He remembered making that call at "just after seven bells" (11:30 P.M. land time).

**11:33:40 P.M.** Lookouts report "dark mass" on horizon ahead of ship. Mr. Murdoch acknowledges and requests lookouts make regular reports of what they see. Heading: centered on 266°; speed 22.25 knots.

—J. MOODY, Sixth Officer

**Range to berg: 5,700 yards (2.9 nautical miles)**

During their first call to the bridge about the dark spot, neither Fleet nor Lee knew what it represented. It was just an undefined dark area against the horizon. Several days later, at the U.S. Senate hearings, Fleet knew for certain what he had seen that night: the iceberg. Yet he corrected himself when he said "iceberg" during his testimony by reverting back to calling it a "black mass."

SENATOR SMITH: Did you keep a sharp lookout for ice?
MR. FLEET: Yes, Sir.
SENATOR SMITH: Tell what you did.
MR. FLEET: Well, I reported an iceberg right ahead, a black mass.
SENATOR SMITH: When did you report that?
MR. FLEET: I could not tell you the time. [In other testimony, Fleet said he did not wear a watch.]
SENATOR SMITH: About what time?
MR. FLEET: Just after seven bells.

By the time Fleet arrived in London after the U.S. Senate hearings, his story had undergone a transformation. The "black mass" had evaporated from his account. Instead, everything was haze in front of the ship, "about three points on each side." The lookout also said he continued to perceive haze right up until the instant of the accident. Apparently, none of the questioners in London thought to ask the lookout why he did not report so much "haze" to the bridge. Haze was the one threat that Captain Smith admitted to Lightoller would have forced slowing *Titanic* or changing its course. Smith even specifically mentioned "haze" in his verbal orders because he knew that reduced visibility would make dodging icebergs extremely difficult. One word from the lookouts—"haze"—in just one report to the bridge, and history would have been forever altered. Instead, the seamen in the crow's nest mentioned only a "dark mass."

Survivors, including Fleet and Lee, testified that the ship contacted the ice at just past 11:40 P.M., nearly ten minutes after the "dark mass" report. The length of this delay between the first mention of what proved to be the fatal iceberg and the actual accident makes credible claims by *Titanic* historian George Behe that Murdoch received not one, but several, ice warnings. Talking to author Leslie Reade some fifty years after the sinking, Fleet reconfirmed his New York testimony. The lookout told Reade that he and Lee had watched and talked about the dark mass for several minutes before recognizing it as an iceberg.

In London, Lee flatly contradicted Fleet's testimony to the U.S. Senate hearings that nearly ten minutes elapsed between the first report of the "dark mass" and the final warning of "iceberg right ahead." Lee was adamant that the first and only report of the deadly iceberg was sent to the bridge just seconds before impact. However, this claim of only one warning immediately prior to impact could have been true only if there had been a solitary berg on the glassy surface of the Atlantic Ocean that night.

THE ATTORNEY-GENERAL: Before half-past eleven on that watch, that is seven bells, had you reported anything at all? Do you remember?

MR. LEE: There was nothing to be reported.

THE ATTORNEY-GENERAL: Then what was the first thing you did report?

MR. LEE: The first thing that was reported was after seven bells struck. It was some minutes, it might have been nine or ten minutes afterward. Three bells were struck by Fleet, warning "right ahead." And, immediately he rung the telephone up on the bridge, "Iceberg right ahead." The reply came back from the bridge, "Thank you."

THE COMMISSIONER: This would be about 11:40?

THE ATTORNEY-GENERAL: That is right my Lord, ten minutes after seven bells.

There was no solitary iceberg. Ice conditions encountered by *Californian* prior to *Titanic*'s accident, and *Carpathia*'s pell-mell run through icebergs during her rescue dash, are proof that the sea through which the doomed liner steamed was littered with ice. The fatal berg was only one among hundreds. Fleet and Lee must have been busy throughout their watch reporting ice to the bridge, so Lee's claim of nothing to report does not stand up. There had been plenty of ice to report throughout his watch.

Strictly speaking, however, Lee was not lying. It can be said that only one true iceberg warning preceded the accident. The first report sometime after 11:30 P.M. was of a "dark mass" that they did not recognize. It was not identified as an iceberg until 11:40 P.M., when Fleet banged the warning bell and reported, "iceberg right ahead."

In his New York testimony (and years later to author Reade), Fleet most likely provided a glimpse at the truth: the first "dark mass" warning went to the bridge at about 11:33 P.M., just after seven bells. Beyond that, neither lookout ever provided much useful information about the true ice conditions that night. In fact, Fleet became an extremely uncooperative witness when Senator Smith pressed for a specific assessment of the time between the first warning and the accident. Fleet's short answers are typical of someone who has been coached by a lawyer in how not to reveal incriminating evidence while giving every pretense of cooperating with the questioner.

SENATOR SMITH: Would you be willing to say that you reported the presence of this iceberg an hour before the collision?
MR. FLEET: No, sir.
SENATOR SMITH: Forty-five minutes?
MR. FLEET: No, sir.
SENATOR SMITH: A half-hour before?
MR. FLEET: No, sir.
SENATOR SMITH: Fifteen minutes before?
MR. FLEET: No, sir.
SENATOR SMITH: Ten minutes before?
MR. FLEET: No, sir.

Fleet's and Lee's performances between 11:30 P.M. and 11:40 P.M. were imperfect, due in part to the previously mentioned lack of binoculars in *Titanic*'s crow's nest. Although they probably would not have helped the men see the dark mass any sooner, the missing binoculars seem to have changed the men's attitudes toward their job. Fleet's testimony implied considerable resentment over being rebuffed when he asked Lightoller for the missing equipment. That resentment went into the crow's nest with him. He and Lee may not have spotted the deadly iceberg any sooner without binoculars, but they might have responded more positively when that danger did appear. They might have been more aggressive in calling the officer of the watch, or they could have been more accurate in their description of the danger ahead.

*Titanic's* huge size also may have made it more difficult for the lookouts to sort out the ice conditions ahead of the ship. The bridge was more than 60 feet off the water, and the crow's nest was 35 feet above that. This height gave the lookouts a greater distance to the horizon, but horizon distance is not what they needed on the night of the accident. Antarctic explorer Sir Ernest Shackleton explained in London that "from a height it [ice] is not so easily seen; it blends with the ocean if you are looking down at an angle like that. If you are on the sea level it may loom up."

The bridge watch that fatal night consisted of seven people: two lookouts in the crow's nest, two quartermasters, and three officers. Robert Hitchens was the quartermaster actually standing behind the ship's primary steering wheel in the wheelhouse. His relief, Alfred Olliver, was away attending the ship's standard compass, located on a platform between the second and third funnels. Sixth Officer James Moody was junior watch officer, while First Officer William M. Murdoch was in charge. Fourth Officer Joseph G. Boxhall was also on duty, but departed the bridge for the officers' quarters.

The physical layout of *Titanic's* control center also played a part in events that night. The control center consisted of a semienclosed center section (called the *captain's bridge*) and two bridge wing enclosures. Open walkways with head-high bulwarks connected the center with both wings. Windows gave weather protection to the center bridge and both wing enclosures. The window sills were lower than the bulwarks to enable those on watch to look forward through the windows while standing on the deck. Except for these windows, all three enclosures were open to the cold night air.

Grouped inside the captain's bridge were sets of engine order telegraphs, a compass binnacle, and an auxiliary steering wheel. The ship's primary steering wheel was located in an enclosed wheelhouse at the back of the captain's bridge. Placement of the primary steering wheel inside a wheelhouse separate from the bridge was typical for British ships of the era. _Titanic's_ wheelhouse allowed the quartermaster to work in relative comfort, even during freezing weather—like the weather that April night. More important, it isolated him from outside distractions. "Iron Mike," as automatic steering devices would later be known, was not fitted in _Titanic_ (the British Royal Navy would get its first such device in late 1914, two years after _Titanic's_ demise), so only a quartermaster's human skill kept the ship on course. Undivided attention to the compass was needed to produce a straight wake. The enclosed wheelhouse also gave protection for telephones and other electrical equipment.

The two steering wheels on _Titanic's_ bridge were connected by an overhead system of rods and gears. Either wheel could control the ship's course. During docking or other close-quarters maneuvers, the quartermaster stood to the auxiliary wheel, but the ship was steered from inside the wheelhouse when at sea. The telemotor to which the primary wheel was attached is still standing in place on the wreck, although the wheelhouse that surrounded it, the auxiliary wheel, and the engine room telegraphs on the captain's bridge are missing. _Titanic_ had yet a third steering wheel, reserved for emergencies only, located on the docking bridge above the fantail.

Sixth Officer Moody was inside the wheelhouse, where he could answer the lookouts' phone messages about ice ahead of the ship, including the one about the "dark mass." He apparently stayed near the telephone instrument in the wheelhouse after passing this information to Murdoch, possibly to await more details from the crow's nest. Because he was inside a room inside the bridge, Moody was twice removed from the outside world. Standing next to the telephone, he was unable to provide effective service as a lookout.

First Officer Murdoch remained alone on the captain's bridge. In the cold weather, he probably stepped onto the raised footplate for only moments at a time, returning often to the shelter offered by the bridge windows. The glass in these windows would have shielded Murdoch's eyes from the wind created by the ship's forward motion. This shelter, coupled with his lower position, may have given the first officer a better view of ice in front of the ship than the one available to the lookouts. However, his other duties as officer of the watch prevented him from giving his undivided attention to looking ahead.

The locations of the seven men on watch at 11:36 P.M. on April 14 meant that *Titanic* had only two men in the crow's nest who were specifically assigned to spot danger. When Fleet and Lee hunkered down from the cold, blinding wind to wipe their tearing eyes, the ship may well have been steaming blindly through ice-infested waters at 22.25 knots. This lack of proper lookout did not escape the attention of the British proceedings.

> THE ATTORNEY-GENERAL: We have no evidence of anybody who was watching, except these two men [Fleet and Lee]; I mean there is no officer who has been able to give evidence as to this, no officer was actually looking or watching at the time.
>
> THE COMMISSIONER: Or, seeing?
>
> THE ATTORNEY-GENERAL: Or seeing. Of course, I mean who have been called before you. I am speaking of evidence. The only evidence we have got of persons who were actually looking out is the evidence of Lee and this witness [Fleet].

First Officer Murdoch chose not to alert Captain Smith of the lookouts' "dark mass" report just after seven bells, in seeming contradiction of the direct order given to Second Officer Lightoller by the captain at 9:30 P.M.: "If it becomes at all doubtful, let me know at once." Smith had instructed with a particular mention of haze, and Lightoller had passed this order to Murdoch at the 10:00 P.M. change of watch.

Murdoch did not alert the captain between 11:32 and 11:40 P.M., apparently because the lookouts' warnings did not contain the specific word *haze*. Of course, Murdoch was wrong. The situation was extremely doubtful from 11:30 P.M. onward, with ice around the ship, an unusual appearance to the horizon, and a menacing "dark mass." Notifying the captain anytime an uncertainty arises for any reason is the first lesson that every young officer learns. On most ships, instructions to this effect are written in the night order book. *Titanic*'s tragic end was the result of a series of human errors, one of which was Murdoch's failure to call the captain.

Two hours after *Titanic* foundered, the rescue ship *Carpathia* raced safely at high speed through the same mass of floating ice that had claimed the giant liner. The difference between Captain Smith's failure to get through the ice and Captain Arthur H. Rostron's success was vigilance. Both men knew there was danger, but only one captain took effective action to prevent disaster.

MR. ROSTRON: I knew the Titanic had struck ice. Therefore, I was prepared to be in the vicinity of ice when I was getting near him, because if he had struck a berg and I was going to his position I knew very well that there must be ice about. I went full speed, all we could—

SENATOR SMITH: You went full speed?

MR. ROSTRON: I did, and doubled my lookouts, and took extra precautions and exerted extra vigilance. Every possible care was taken. We were all on the qui vive.

SENATOR SMITH: You had a smaller ship, however, and it would respond more readily to a signal?

MR. ROSTRON: No.

SENATOR SMITH: Would it not?

MR. ROSTRON: No sir, it would not. I do not maintain that for one moment.

SENATOR SMITH: How many men were on the bridge, on lookout, so to speak, in that situation, on your ship?

MR. ROSTRON: There were three officers with me: a quartermaster, one man in the crow's nest, and two men in the eyes of the ship—that is, right forward on the deck nearer to the water than the crow's nest.

SENATOR SMITH: Was that the ordinary complement, or did you put them there because of the danger?

MR. ROSTRON: I put an extra lookout on forward.

SENATOR SMITH: An extra lookout?

MR. ROSTRON: Yes, and the officer came up extra with me. I had another officer up with me, extra. He came up voluntarily.

SENATOR SMITH: What would be the ordinary complement?

MR. ROSTRON: The ordinary complement of a night lookout, two men. We keep one in the crow's nest and one in the eyes—that is right forward.

Contrast Rostron's eight pairs of trained eyes searching for icebergs with *Titanic*'s lookout of two men in the crow's nest and the senior watch officer on the open bridge. It does not appear that Captain Smith or his officers fully appreciated the seriousness of the ice threat. Admiralty law has a phrase describing *Titanic* that night: "It had not a proper look-out." Even Lord Mersey's final report grudgingly admitted that

it is not considered that the look-out was sufficient. An extra look-out should, under the circumstances, have been placed at the stemhead, and a sharp look-out should have been kept from both sides of the bridge by an officer.

**11:37 P.M.** More ice around the ship. Mr. Murdoch gives frequent helm orders to avoid ice. Heading centered on 266°; speed 22.25 knots.

—J. MOODY, Sixth Officer

### Range to berg: 3,154 yards (1.6 nautical miles)

Neither the lookouts nor Murdoch had actually seen the fatal iceberg yet. All experienced marine observers, they watched a dark spot against a ghostly white line on the horizon in front of the ship. It could have been a silhouette of a dark object, or it could have represented a gap in the field ice. At first Fleet thought the "dark mass" was no larger than two tables pushed together. As the ship drew nearer, he changed his estimate to the size of a small cottage. Only when they were dangerously close did the "haze" reveal itself to be densely packed ice and the dark spot to be an iceberg. For the moment, though, the lookouts saw only an innocuous dark spot against a wispy horizon.

In his book *Voyage of the Iceberg*, Richard Brown attempted to give the life story of "the berg that sank the *Titanic*." He made an excellent case that the deadly berg was calved in Greenland's Jakobshavn ice fiord. Brown theorized that, before it broke away from its mother glacier, it picked up a "smear of coal" from the underlying ground. The ice floated down into the ship's path, rolling over several times. Brown claimed that on this night the berg's "black side" faced the speeding liner.

Based on the ship's speed, the fatal berg was about 3 nautical miles ahead of *Titanic* at the time of the initial "dark mass" sighting. Seeing anything on a dark night at such a distance is an impressive feat. On a flat calm night like April 14, the lookouts should not have detected the deadly ice until it was within a quarter mile (500 yards) of the ship. Even in rough seas, the lookouts would not have been expected to see the deadly berg at a distance of much more than a mile. But this night there was the band of "haze" silhouetting the berg. It made all the difference.

Richard Brown's "black smear" theory, while interesting, is probably misleading. Certainly a black berg would have been extremely hard to spot against the North Atlantic on a moonless night under normal conditions, but conditions that night were not normal. What Fleet, Lee, and Murdoch saw was the berg's silhouette against a light band of "haze." Given these circumstances, a black side might have made the ice easier to see that night, not harder.

THE ATTORNEY-GENERAL: What sort of a night was it?

MR. LEE: A clear, starry night overhead, but at the time of the accident there was a haze right ahead.

THE ATTORNEY-GENERAL: At the time of the accident a haze right ahead?

MR. LEE: A haze right ahead. In fact, it was extending more or less round the horizon. There was no moon. . . .

THE ATTORNEY-GENERAL: Did you notice this haze which you said extended on the horizon when you first came on the lookout, or did it come later?

MR. LEE: It was not so distinct then, not to be noticed. You did not really notice it then, not on going on watch, but we had all our work cut out to pierce through it just after we started.

Murdoch must not have perceived haze. If he had, there is little doubt he would have notified the captain as required by his night orders. Instead, the first officer may have quite correctly taken the dim, fuzzy line to be a conglomeration of ice. He would have looked for a dark water path through the lighter ice, as he had been doing throughout his watch. There is scant evidence for this speculation, but Murdoch may have aimed the liner directly at the iceberg—thinking he was steering the ship toward a dark opening through the ice. If true, this easily explains why the berg was directly in the ship's path at 11:40 P.M., when the final warning was sounded.

No matter how Murdoch guided the ship's course, however, the ghostly line he saw on the horizon should have been reason enough to call Captain Smith. The fuzzy horizon directly in the ship's path could not have appeared to be the loose mixture of ice through which the ship was then navigating. What Murdoch saw must have looked like what it was: a dense line of field ice. If there ever was a time during his career when the first officer should have called his captain, this was it.

In defense of Murdoch, however, there is no definitive proof he did not notify the captain. Only four men could have observed such an event, three of whom—Captain Smith, Sixth Officer Moody, and Murdoch—died as a result of the sinking. Quartermaster Hitchens alone lived to testify about events on the bridge prior to the accident. Just because Hitchens never mentioned Murdoch's alerting the captain does not mean that it did not happen. Even so, the preponderance of evidence indicates that Captain Smith remained unaware of the conditions surrounding his ship from 11:30 until the impact with the iceberg, and that Murdoch appears to have been derelict in his duties.

John Charles Bigham, Lord Mersey, the wreck commissioner in charge of the British inquiry into the sinking, was skeptical of Fleet's claim of haze on the horizon. "My impression is that the man was trying to make an excuse for not seeing the iceberg," Mersey said. "He thought he could make it out by creating a thick haze. The evidence before and after the accident is that the sky was perfectly clear, and therefore if the evidence of haze is to be accepted, it must have been some extraordinary natural phenomenon—something that sprang up quite suddenly, and then vanished."

Mersey's comments were meant to express doubt that Fleet was telling the truth about what he saw. The wreck commissioner was unaware that an optical phenomenon did "spring up" on that crystal-clear night. In fact, there were two phenomena that likely appeared in front of the speeding liner and its crew. Fleet, Lee, and Murdoch were deluded by ghostlike mirages that night. What their eyes saw in front of the ship was not what their brains perceived.

The primary phenomenon fooling the men was *ice blink,* a "whitish glare on low clouds above an accumulation of distant ice," according to the standard U.S. navigation text, *The American Practical Navigator.* Ice blink occurs when moonlight or starshine reflects off ice and illuminates low-lying moisture in the atmosphere. The ship was approaching the tightly packed ice that had blocked *Californian's* path. Ice blink seen by *Titanic's* lookouts was starshine reflected onto wisps of fog created when the ice chilled the surrounding atmosphere to below its dew point. A thin layer of fog likely formed just above the surface of the ice.

The other phenomenon was *towering,* a pure optical illusion caused by atmospheric conditions in which objects near the horizon appear to be stretched until they are many times their true height. Horizontal size is not affected. Refraction in the atmosphere commonly causes objects beyond the horizon to become visible in this manner. The usual cause of towering is a greater density of the air near the surface of the water compared to the air immediately above. The effect increases in response to a temperature inversion and a rapid decrease in humidity.

These two atmospheric conditions existed simultaneously that night precisely because the air was so still. Dense pack ice chilled the air in contact with it to a temperature lower than the warmer air higher in the atmosphere. Meteorologists call this a *temperature inversion*. Air touching the ice would also have absorbed more moisture than contained by the surrounding atmosphere, producing a rapid decrease in humidity a short distance from the field of ice. Towering resulting from these conditions should have made the front wall of the ice field appear to be much taller. This mirage also may have shimmered in the darkness, heightening an illusion of haze right on the horizon.

The possibility of ice blink was raised by explorer Sir Ernest Shackleton on June 18, 1912, when he appeared before the British inquiry. He was asked to share his expertise on icebergs and other arctic phenomena. "On a night such as you have described," Shackleton told the panel, "if there was a big field of ice, the blink would most certainly be seen very, very clearly. If there was [*sic*] really what we call big fields, miles and miles of ice, then you would see the edge, what we call the water-sky, that is where the ice field ends."

The Antarctic explorer also described how individual icebergs can be of various colors. "There are many bergs I have seen that appear to be black, due to the construction of the berg itself," Shackleton explained. "Again, after a berg has capsized, if it is not of close construction it is more porous and taking up the water does not reflect light in any way." This analysis by a highly experienced ice navigator describes what *Titanic*'s two lookouts observed: a white band of ice blink behind a nonreflecting iceberg that appeared as a black silhouette.

Seven to ten minutes passed between the time Fleet said the lookouts first noticed the "dark mass" and the time the final iceberg alarm was sounded. Some action, or possibly inaction, by the first officer during this period of time angered Fleet and Lee. What happened was serious enough to haunt the two seamen for the rest of their lives. On *Carpathia* after the rescue, both claimed that their iceberg warning just after seven bells went unheeded.

George Behe of the American Titanic Historical Society gives us a hint of what may have angered the lookouts when he says they warned the bridge at least three times of icebergs prior to the accident. Fleet and Lee must have been busy sending down reports all during their watch, but especially during the thirty minutes immediately prior to the accident. The lookouts should have warned the bridge repeatedly about bergs, pack ice, and field ice. Historic accounts of the tragedy speak about "the iceberg" as if it were the only one in the area. It was not. *Titanic* had been steaming for two hours within the ice-filled area that had been reported at 9:40 P.M. by *Mesaba* in the famous message that never got to the bridge. After 11:00 P.M., any warnings from the wireless had become superfluous because the ship was churning through a devil's mixture of ice.

The question may be raised, why did surviving passengers fail to report icebergs sliding past the ship that night? Anyone who has transported large numbers of passengers at sea knows how little they notice. People tend to focus on the ship itself and not on the environment surrounding it. The 10,000 electric light bulbs blazing brightly until the end also hindered the passengers' night vision. An observer must be in total darkness to see unlighted objects on a moonless night. because even the smallest amount of stray light reduces the eye's ability to discern objects in darkness. For this reason, First Officer Murdoch had ordered a forecastle hatch closed at 7:00 P.M. because light from this hatch was partially blinding lookouts in the crow's nest.

Cold weather is another reason passengers did not spot icebergs earlier in the evening. Sauntering in wind from the ship's forward progress would not have been enjoyable in the subfreezing night air. Passengers stayed indoors that Sunday evening for the same reason they would have stayed at home on a cold, windy night. With few people wandering on deck, the chance of a passenger spotting an odd berg was small. Some people did venture outside, of course, and a few even reported seeing bergs prior to the accident. These reports were relegated to the tabloid press and never given much credence.

One thing is certain: there were plenty of icebergs surrounding the lifeboats in the cold light of dawn. Survivors gazing on the restless North Atlantic saw plenty of ice. The image was unforgettable.

We then saw that we were surrounded with icebergs and field ice. Some of the fields of ice were from 16 to 20 miles long.

Seaman Joseph Scarrott

we saw one iceberg in front of us [from lifeboat #8]. After we got aboard the *Carpathia*, we could see 13 icebergs and 45 miles of floating ice, distinctly, right around us in every direction.

Mrs. J. Stuart White

it was broad daylight as we approached the Carpathia. Looking around over the gunwale it seemed to me like the Arctic. Icebergs of huge size ringed the horizon . . .

Marshall Drew

Photographic proof of the ice through which *Titanic* steamed comes from *Carpathia* passenger Mabel Fenwick, who woke up in her cold cabin on the morning of the rescue. Fellow passenger Louis M. Ogden had the same disconcerting experience in his cold stateroom. The cabins were cold because Captain Rostron had ordered all of the rescue ship's steam diverted from the heaters in the passenger cabins and into the racing engines. Both of these passengers decided to investigate, fortunately remembering to take their cameras as they appeared on deck during the rescue. Fenwick snapped *Californian* when it finally arrived at the scene—about six hours too late.

Ogden chose to snap a photograph that does not seem to contain any subject at all. It appears to be just a slightly fuzzy picture of the horizon. Only on second glance does the fuzzy white line reveal itself to be a low-lying line of ice, unbroken across the camera's view. This is the field that had stopped *Californian* the night before. The photograph is technically inferior, but its lack of crispness allows the mind to transform the fuzzy white ice into what might be mistaken for haze on the horizon. All that is missing from Ogden's picture is a "dark mass."

As *Carpathia* began its solemn voyage to New York, Captain Rostron contacted Cunard's New York office by wireless. His message leaves no doubt about ice conditions on the morning of the rescue. The deadly ice that had damaged *Niagara*, trapped *Californian*, and sunk *Titanic* was still very much in evidence.

**Carpathia to Cunard, New York**—LATITUDE 41.45; LONGITUDE 50.20 WEST. AM PROCEEDING NEW YORK . . . LARGE NUMBER ICEBERGS, AND 20 MILES FIELD ICE WITH BERGS AMONGST. ROSTRON.

Both Captain Rostron and *Titanic* survivors reported this field ice that was studded with larger bergs at the accident scene. That grinding mass of deadly ice did not appear mysteriously in the dawn's first light but had been there all night. It had entrapped *Californian* and was the wall of ice that Murdoch saw behind the dark shadow of doom. And, lurking somewhere in all of that ice was The Iceberg.

**11:40 p.m.** Three strokes on alarm bell and lookouts report iceberg dead ahead. Heading 266°; speed 22.25 knots.          —J. MOODY, Sixth Officer

**Range to berg: 912 yards (3 ship lengths)**

At 11:40 P.M. on April 14, First Officer Murdoch was just entering *Titanic's* starboard bridge enclosure for protection from the cold wind. Although seldom seen today, bridge wing enclosures were common on ships of the period. They were slightly larger than a soldier's sentry box outside a land fort and served much the same purpose. Sailors on watch used the enclosures for shelter from wind or rain while still observing the ship and its surroundings. Moving to the outer starboard wing of the bridge gave Murdoch a view forward that was not cluttered by the ship's foremast and rigging. This was a logical location for him to stand if he were becoming uneasy over what he perceived to lie in the path of the ship. Overhead, in the crow's nest, the two lookouts suddenly realized there was a large object directly in the ship's path.

"Iceberg?" Lee asked.

He was questioning the appearance of the dark mass, but his words came out as an emphatic statement. Fleet answered by reaching for the rope of the crow's nest alarm bell. Both men stared into the night for a few heartbeats, transfixed by the sudden change of a seemingly harmless dark spot into a terrifying mountain of ice. Fleet acted.

Clang!

Clang!

Clang!

Three strokes on the alarm bell, the lookout's code for reporting danger directly in the path of the vessel. Fleet was again using the telephone to the wheelhouse. "What have you seen?" came the civilized query from Sixth Officer Moody. "Iceberg right ahead!" Fleet blurted. Moody's calm voice came up the wire. "Thank you, iceberg right ahead."

Moody then shouted the dreaded warning through the starboard wheelhouse door. "Iceberg right ahead!"

# COOL HAND MURDOCH

Sunday, April 14, 1912

**11:40 P.M. to 11:41:13 P.M.**

**P**ARADOXICALLY, the extra ice warnings claimed by author George Behe may have contributed to the misunderstanding of the danger in front of the ship. With large amounts of ice around *Titanic,* neither Murdoch nor the lookouts had enough free time to continuously observe the "black mass" on the horizon. There were too many dangers closer to the ship. The lookouts' attention also would have been diverted by making phone reports to Moody in the wheelhouse. Murdoch's attention was focused on digesting the various warnings and issuing appropriate helm orders. Quite suddenly, the distant "black mass" became a mountain of ice dead ahead of the ship.

No matter how Murdoch perceived the situation prior to the alarm bell, Fleet's final warning of "iceberg right ahead" snapped his perception into line with reality. His was exactly the same shift in perception that the lookouts had experienced a few seconds earlier, when the "black mass" suddenly became an iceberg. What all of these men saw did not change. There was still a ghostly white line on the horizon with a dark spot dead ahead. Their eyes had never deceived them, but their brains, their perceptions, had played tricks on them that night.

First Officer William M. Murdoch began to realize that his perception of the ice had been wrong when the first of the three strokes sounded on the warning bell. He may not have even heard Sixth Officer James Moody repeat the telephone warning because his mind was already sorting out what his eyes were seeing. He had thought he was heading for an opening of dark water in the ice field, but the black area suddenly resolved itself into an iceberg. Now that he perceived the situation correctly, the first officer knew he faced the most difficult decision of his career. He could either steam straight into the looming mountain of ice or attempt to swerve around the berg and take his chances running into the pack ice.

Neither option would allow Murdoch to avoid running into ice. Crashing into the berg would certainly result in massive casualties aboard *Titanic* as the bow first crumpled against the unyielding ice and then the berg caromed down the side of the ship. On the other hand, swerving into the ice field would result in multiple impacts with bergy bits and growlers, each capable of punching a hole in the ship's hull.

Ship officers instinctively avoid allowing their ships to hit anything: not another ship, a quay, a submerged rock, or an iceberg. The desire to avoid a collision is so strong that captains of U.S. Navy landing ships have to be taught to deliberately run their vessels ashore, a highly unnatural act. Because of his experience and training, Murdoch instinctively shied away from hitting the frozen mountain. In an instant he decided to take his chances on *Titanic*'s steel hull being strong enough to brush aside the broken pieces of ice in the field.

**11:40:04 P.M.** First officer orders hard a-starboard. Quartermaster complies.

—J. MOODY, Sixth Officer

**Range to berg: 862 yards (2.9 ship lengths)**

"Hard a-starboard," was Murdoch's irrevocable response to Moody's iceberg warning. Even as he spoke, the first officer was striding toward the center of the liner's bridge. In the wheelhouse, Quartermaster Robert Hitchens began spinning *Titanic*'s primary steering wheel in response to the order. Steering orders in 1912 were given with regard to the tiller and not the bow of the ship. A tiller is simply a lever inside the vessel that moves the rudder. Movement of the tiller is opposite to the swing of the rudder. If the tiller is pushed to port, the vessel turns to starboard.

"Starboarding the helm" in 1912 meant to put the tiller to starboard, causing the rudder to go to port and the bow to turn to its left. This system of giving orders seems backward to anyone raised driving automobiles, but it made perfect sense to generations of sailors trained in wind-powered ships, on which the tiller is pushed to the right to turn the ship to the left.

*Titanic* undoubtedly turned slightly faster to the left (starboard helm in 1912) than to the right because it was driven by three propellers. Every propeller delivers both forward thrust and sideways pressure. A propeller that rotates to the left in forward also pushes the stern to the left. Conversely, a propeller that rotates to the right pushes the stern to the right when the ship is moving forward. Two of *Titanic*'s propellers rotated to the right, giving the ship a slight tendency to swing its stern to the right (turning the bow to the left) when steaming forward. This meant the ship turned a bit faster to the left than to the right. By ordering a left turn, Murdoch took advantage of the ship's handling characteristics.

**11:40:11 P.M.** Helm is hard to starboard (full left rudder).

—J. Moody, Sixth Officer

**Range to berg: 775 yards (2.9 ship lengths)**

11:40:16 P.M.    Moody observed Hitchens inside the wheelhouse. "Hard a-starboard," he repeated the order. When the helmsman complied, Moody sang out "helm's hard over." High above, Lookout Lee watched *Titanic*'s bow begin to curve left.

Within seconds of Fleet's alarm, *Titanic*'s bow began swinging left. The rudder was not yet hard over because the ship's steering engine did not respond to helm orders as quickly as Hitchens turned the steering wheel. This lag time must be considered in reconstructing events of that evening. The quartermaster's wheel did not move the rudder directly. Instead, it controlled two steam-powered steering engines located on C deck at the stern of the ship, more than 600 feet from the wheelhouse. These machines moved the huge steel steering quadrant (a special form of tiller) in response to instructions from the bridge. Movements of the steering engines were ponderous and slow compared to the rapid spinning of the steering wheel, so the steering engine was always several seconds behind the quartermaster's movements.

Once Murdoch ordered the turn, he moved to his best location for judging the iceberg's position relative to *Titanic*'s bow—a small teak grating behind the auxiliary steering wheel on the captain's bridge. From here he could use the frames of the bridge windows, the ship's mast, and the anchor crane at the bow to visualize the swing of the ship's head, much like a marksman uses the sights on a rifle to follow game. Distance to the berg was now approaching 600 yards. Details on the surface of the looming ice monster still were not visible, but Murdoch would not have been concerned with that. He would have been using his "seaman's eye" to judge the motion of the ship relative to the dark spot against the hazy horizon.

The bow was now swinging to the left of the berg, exposing the field of ice in front of it to Murdoch's attention. Perhaps *Titanic's* steel hull could have bulled its way through that floating morass, but it would have been foolhardy to try at full speed. The first officer decided instead to lessen the impact by stopping the rotation of the ship's massive engines, thinking it was better to coast into the tightly packed field ice than to smash into it under full power.

**11:40:24 P.M.** Mr. Murdoch orders ALL STOP to the engines.

—J. MOODY, Sixth Officer

**Range to berg: 600 yards (2 ship lengths)**

Murdoch reached for the brass handles of the engine order telegraphs. According to Fourth Officer Joseph G. Boxhall, the first officer then changed the orders to the two outboard propellers from "ahead full" to "astern full," requesting what sailors call a "crash stop." This is a violent maneuver that can damage the ship's engines, drive shafts, and propellers. For this reason, it is reserved for only the worst of emergencies. Testifying later in London, Boxhall said the engine order telegraphs read "full speed astern" when he stepped into the enclosed section of the bridge.

Unfortunately, Boxhall's recollection seems faulty. *Titanic* never attempted the crash stop that people on land still believe was the obvious way to prevent the ship from slamming into the iceberg. Reverse thrust from the propellers would have eliminated the ability of the single rudder to steer the ship. Murdoch knew this. Under full reverse power, the ship could not have pivoted to the right but would have begun a sideways slide into the iceberg. Trying to turn and stop at the same time had been the ship-handling mistake that caused *Californian* to slew into pack ice earlier that night.

*Titanic* shared certain maneuvering characteristics with all conventional ships of every era, including *Californian*. It steered more rapidly at higher speeds than at lower speeds and responded best with the full wash from its propellers acting on the single rudder. Murdoch rejected a crash stop for these reasons. He had to keep enough speed on the ship to swerve around the iceberg. Because *Titanic's* single rudder required maximum water flow to be effective, a crash stop would have made the ship uncontrollable just when maximum maneuverability was needed.

A second reason for rejecting a crash stop was the short distance between the deadly berg and the wall of packed ice. There could not have been more than two ship lengths (590 yards or a bit more than ¼ nautical mile) of open water between the berg and the field ice. Otherwise, the berg would not have been close enough to the field to have been silhouetted by ice blink from the tightly packed ice. *Titanic* had needed 850 yards (2,550 feet) to make an emergency stop at 20 knots during its abbreviated sea trials. Based on that experience, slamming the engines into reverse still would have put the liner at least 260 yards (780 feet) into the line of ice behind the fatal iceberg. Murdoch was instinctively trying to avoid hitting ice that night, not trying to run into it slowly.

With its rudder hard over to the left, *Titanic* could turn a circle with a 642-yard (1,925-foot) radius. This was one of the few hard facts revealed during its brief sea trials. Although turning required 200 yards less forward travel than did a crash stop, it was only the lesser of two evils. A single turn would have allowed the ship to penetrate the field ice to roughly half the depth (142 yards, or 426 feet) that a crash stop would.

Murdoch knew people would be killed if he allowed the ship to slam head-on into the iceberg. Instead, he seized on the only combination of steering and engine control that offered any possibility of avoiding hundreds of deaths and injuries: stopping the engines while attempting to steer around the berg. Stopping the engines did not slow the liner appreciably during the few seconds before the accident, but it did prevent them from replacing momentum lost to steering around the berg. Murdoch knew that turning a large vessel takes enormous amounts of energy, and he hoped that the loss of speed caused by slewing around the iceberg might help reduce both the inevitable impact with the field ice and any resulting damage.

Nine decks down and 300 feet aft of the bridge, the men who controlled *Titanic*'s mighty engines must have been caught unprepared. The bridge telegraphs were not supposed to clang for another seventy-two hours. Other than speed increases, the engineers on duty to operate the engines that night expected at least three more days of relative inactivity until the ship reached New York. Because it was as unusual for the bridge to send orders in midocean as it was for the boilers to produce green cheese, the engineers knew immediately that the ship faced an emergency demanding quick action on their part.

The three giant machines that powered *Titanic* were not controlled from the bridge like the gasoline engines of a small cruiser are. Men turning valves and pulling levers were needed to slow, stop, or reverse either of the liner's two four-crank triple expansion reciprocating engines as well as to cut steam power to the center turbine engine and redirect it to the condensers. *Titanic*'s turbine—state-of-the-art in steam propulsion for 1912—powered the ship's 16.5-foot-diameter center screw, but only while the ship was moving forward. Lacking reverse, the turbine was secured when the ship was maneuvering on its reciprocating engines.

Engineers qualified to do these jobs must have been scattered throughout the two engine rooms that night. With no telegraph orders expected from the bridge, they would have been tending other responsibilities, such as keeping the bathwater hot, the refrigerated food cold, and the electric lights burning brightly. It is unlikely that anyone remained on the engine maneuvering platform located between the two reciprocating engines during these tasks. Shouts gathered the men to their controls, but valuable seconds were lost during the scramble.

### Range to berg: 512 yards (1.7 ship lengths)          11:40:32 P.M.

Ninety feet above the engine rooms, First Officer Murdoch gauged the swing of the bow to the left, away from the iceberg. At thirty-two seconds after Fleet's warning, a land dweller would have thought *Titanic* had avoided the iceberg. The bow pointed almost 20 degrees to the left of the berg, and the ship appeared well clear of the floating mountain. Murdoch knew better. Ships steer from their sterns, not their bows. Although *Titanic*'s bow was clear of the ice, its stern was actually swinging toward the iceberg.

Virtually every report, book, TV documentary, and motion picture has depicted *Titanic* as sideswiping its starboard bow on the iceberg while turning left, away from danger. Not only did this not happen, but it could not have happened under any circumstances. A starboard bow sideswipe "collision" while turning left would have been impossible for a conventional ship in 1912 as well as today. The manner in which rudder-steered ships pivot in the water does not

67

allow for the actual damage received by *Titanic*'s bow to have occurred during a left turn. Iceberg damage to the starboard bow while turning to the left absolutely would have necessitated bumping and grinding of the ice along the ship's starboard side all the way to its stern.

The impossible "left turn only" scenario would have caused damage to the majority of the ship's sixteen primary watertight compartments. The truth is, *Titanic* did not receive ice damage aft of boiler room #5, which was located approximately below the bridge. This proves that the ship was turning to the right at the time of the accident, *turning toward the iceberg.*

Every conventional power-driven vessel has a "pivot point" located on its centerline roughly one-third of its length aft from the bow. The vessel rotates around this point when its rudder is put over. Because the pivot point is not amidships but is offset toward the bow, the vessel's stern swings a larger arc than its bow does. Turning only to the left (or the right) to avoid a close-aboard object swings the vessel's stern toward that object even though the bow points clear. A side-on impact cannot be avoided. The object then bumps and grinds along the side of the ship, doing damage along the entire length of the hull, from the initial point of impact to the stern.

Sideways impact occurs because a ship in the water acts differently when steered by the rudder at its stern than an automobile does on dry land. The body of a wheeled vehicle is pulled in the direction its front wheels are turned. When the driver attempts to dodge an obstacle, the front wheels take the whole body of the car away from the danger while the back wheels follow within the tracks of the front. On land, only the front fender of an automobile can make grazing contact with the object being avoided. The back end of the land vehicle is not involved.

This highway scenario is what most nonseafaring people envision when they think of *Titanic*'s accident. If the great liner had been a city transit bus, it would have grazed its front right fender on the iceberg without damaging its right side or right rear fender. But ships, of course, are not buses. When Murdoch initiated his left turn, *Titanic* continued moving forward along its original course for some distance while its stern swung outward to the right. (Think of a car sliding sideways when trying to turn on ice.) Movement of a ship in the direction of the original course after the bow starts to pivot is called

*advance.* *Titanic* advanced on the original course while its bow pivoted at an increasing angle to that course and the stern swung outward, toward the iceberg.

Movement of a ship in the direction of the new course it intends to
steer upon completion of the turn is called *transfer.* A vessel the size
of *Titanic* achieves very little transfer during the early portion of a
turn, which explains why the liner continued advancing toward the
iceberg even after its bow appeared to have turned away from the danger. In truth, the bow was clear of the ice until Murdoch executed his
second turn, back toward the berg. This second turn was not a mistake. Even though the bow had been pointed away from the ice, *Titanic's* stern was sliding dangerously toward the berg when Murdoch
shifted the helm. Only when he turned the ship to the right did the
fragile stern swing away from the iceberg and certain disaster.

This "port around" maneuver required the ship to be extremely
close to the berg before Murdoch initiated the second turn. As a result, the iceberg would have appeared to be off the starboard bow
when Murdoch called for "port helm" to turn the ship to the right.
Quartermaster Olliver apparently was fooled by the angle of the
ship to the berg when he said later that Murdoch's "port helm"
order came after the berg passed the bridge. "The iceberg was away
up astern," he told Senator Theodore Elijah Burton at the U.S.
hearings.

If *Titanic* had been turning left (starboard helm in 1912) at the moment of contact, ice and metal should have met roughly in the way
of the bulkhead between boiler rooms #5 and #6. In reality, this is
the approximate location on the hull where damage from the ice
ended. In the mythical left turn, the berg would have bumped and
crashed along the ship's entire starboard side, starting at boiler room
#5 and continuing aft into boiler rooms #4, #3, #2, and #1 and the
two engine rooms. Compartments forward of boiler room #5 would
have remained undamaged and free of water. *Titanic* still would
have foundered, but it would have done so stern first. Of course, the
pattern of damage to be expected during a left-turn collision is exactly the opposite of what actually occurred.

Also, damage during a left turn would have been exacerbated by
suction between the ship and the iceberg, suction that would have
clamped *Titanic's* side against the ice. This did not happen, however, because of the right turn (port helm) that Murdoch initiated to

"port around" the iceberg. The force of the rudder overcame the suction and allowed the hull to rotate clear of the deadly ice.

Two incidents from Captain Smith's career reveal the danger of suction created by large ships. At the start of *Titanic*'s maiden voyage, the ship almost sucked a smaller liner into a collision while departing Southampton. *Titanic* swept past two smaller ships that were rafted to a quay. *New York* was on the outside and the larger *Oceanic* to the land. As Smith's new command passed, suction snapped *New York*'s mooring lines, and the smaller ship began drifting toward *Titanic*. Quick action by the tug *Vulcan* and a burst of reverse on *Titanic*'s port engine avoided a collision by a matter of feet.

In 1911, when he commanded *Olympic*, Captain Smith had a less fortunate experience with suction created between ships. His giant liner sucked a smaller naval vessel, the British HMS *Hawke*, into its starboard quarter. A wedge-shaped hole was punched into *Olympic* by the navy ship's ram bow.

Suction between two moving vessels or between a moving vessel and a stationary object (such as a ship tied to a quay) is created by an action physicists call *Bernoulli's Principle*. Simply stated, when the speed of a fluid or gas is increased, its pressure decreases. This principle explains why airplanes fly and sailboats sail. In the case of large ships operating at close quarters, it also explains why *Hawke* was sucked into the starboard side of *Olympic*.

Bernoulli's Principle also applies when a large vessel is operated at high speed in close proximity to another large object. Low pressure is created between the two, sucking the ship's stern toward the nearby structure (perhaps another ship, a river bank, or an iceberg). Navigators call this effect *bank suction*. Acting strongest on the stern, it causes the ship to turn away from nearby structures in an action that is referred to as *bow cushion*.

If *Titanic* had been under left rudder as the traditional story claims, Bernoulli's suction would have helped pull the midships and stern tightly against the ice. Since only the bow contacted the berg, the ship must have been under enough right rudder (port helm in 1912) to break this suction and allow the stern to swing clear.

Turning a ship's bow away (a left turn for *Titanic*) from a close-aboard iceberg is a maneuver considered so dangerous that it gets special attention in *The American Practical Navigator*. This internationally recognized book specifically describes what happens when a ship collides with ice in the manner described by most *Titanic* historians. The result is more than a "glancing blow" to the bow.

> This maneuver may cause the ship to veer off in a direction which will swing the stern into the ice. . . . the use of full rudder . . . is not recommended because it may swing either the stern or mid-section of the vessel into the ice.

*Bowditch* also cautions mariners to keep clear of projecting points of ice and warns against turning away from a berg in such a manner that might damage the stern of the vessel.

> do so without making sharp turns which may throw the stern against the ice, resulting in a damaged propeller, propeller shaft or rudder.

This highly regarded navigation text states that making a sharp turn away from ice (as the myth claims *Titanic* did) will result in damage along the side of the vessel to the stern. The only way to protect the portion of the ship behind its pivot point is to swing the stern away from the ice. That is exactly what Murdoch accomplished with his "port around" maneuver. The timing of the second turn in his maneuver, the one back toward the danger, is critical. Unfortunately, he started his turn a bit too soon, and the bow came a few yards too close to the berg. Actual damage received by the starboard bow during the accident is irrefutable proof that *Titanic* was under port helm and turning to the right at the moment of impact. Murdoch did, in fact, "port around" the portion of the berg above the water.

One witness at the British proceedings knew the impossibility of explaining *Titanic's* starboard bow damage with only a single left turn. Edward Wilding, an employee of Harland and Wolff and one of the ship's designers, appeared to recognize that the lack of damage to compartments aft of boiler room #5 did not fit the left-turn-only scenario. His testimony gives the impression that Wilding was struggling to accept the conventional version of the accident. He was troubled by the left-turn-only theory, however, because it required damage to parts of the hull that were not involved in the real accident.

> MR. WILDING: After the ship had finished tearing herself at the forward end of No. 5, she would tend to push herself against the iceberg a little, or push herself up the iceberg, and there would be a certain tendency, as the stern came round to aft under the helm, to bang against the iceberg again further aft.

*Titanic*'s inch-thick steel hull was relatively no thicker than the paper of a child's toy model. Ships are strongest in their bows. Every officer knows that if he cannot avoid hitting something, he should hit it head-on. Possibly *Titanic* would have survived such a meeting with an iceberg. Even today *Bowditch* cautions, "If contact with an ice floe is unavoidable, never strike it a glancing blow."

Murdoch rejected a head-on crash because it was almost certain to cause frightful casualties among the passengers and crew. Also, running into things was not Murdoch's way of handling a ship. He was the sort of man who found ways to avoid disaster rather than accept the inevitable. Now, his automatic reaction to steer around the berg had committed him to a swerving, S-shaped maneuver. There was no going back. It would have been harder at this moment to accurately point the ship dead at the berg than it was to swerve around it. Murdoch realized that if he did not hit the berg squarely bow on, the ship would be ripped open along its starboard side. An S curve around the danger—what he later called "porting around"—was his only remaining option to avoid disaster.

11:40:34 P.M.    The berg loomed larger. It was now a bit more than 400 yards from the ship. Murdoch waited, as some 2,200 lives hung on his decision. High in the crow's nest the two lookouts watched the danger grow. "Get out of here," Fleet told his fellow sailor. "The mast will come down if we hit that thing. No sense both of us being killed." From their perch it must have appeared that *Titanic* would slide sideways into the berg with impact coming in line with the crow's nest. Lee began clambering down the ladder inside the hollow steel mast. He had gone only a few steps downward before realizing he could not possibly get to the safety of the deck before impact. So, he scampered up the iron rungs and popped back into the tiny lookout station.

Still Murdoch waited. The mullions of the bridge windows allowed him to gauge the movement of *Titanic* relative to the iceberg. At this point, the ship was actually moving crabwise with the bow clear of the berg but the hull slewing sideways toward it. The first officer knew he would have to swing the stern away from the ice. His problem was judging when to make the turn. If he made it too early, the bow would smash headlong into the berg. Conversely, if he waited too long, the stern would slam sideways into the berg. Murdoch watched and waited. Timing was everything.

There were so many variables to judge as he stared across the top of the auxiliary steering wheel and into the darkness ahead of the ship. How would *Titanic* respond to its rudder? How fast could quartermaster Hitchens spin the wheel hard over to port? How long would it take the steering engine to swing the tiller and rudder in response to the wheel? Murdoch's working life had been spent at sea. His brain called on every minute of that experience to solve these problems.

Now . . . no . . . an instant longer.

Of the officers serving on *Titanic* that night, Murdoch was the one most likely to accomplish this impossible maneuver. While serving as a junior officer in 1905 aboard another White Star ship, *Arabic,* he countermanded a direct order from that ship's captain by physically wresting the steering wheel from the quartermaster. Holding course with his own hands, the younger Murdoch narrowly averted a collision with a sailing vessel. If Murdoch had pulled off *Titanic's* escape from the ice, he surely would have created a legend for himself as the coolest ship driver on the North Atlantic.

Now!

**11:40:36 P.M.** Heading 244°. Mr. Murdoch personally shifts helm to hard a-port. —J. MOODY, Sixth Officer

**Range to berg: 462 yards (1.6 ship lengths)**

"Hard a-port!"

The first officer said it out loud. His words started as an order to quartermaster Hitchens in the wheelhouse but may have ended as if Murdoch were giving an order to himself. This is pure speculation, but as his words blurted out "Hard a-port!" Murdoch may have reached forward instinctively to start the auxiliary steering wheel spinning with his own hands. It was typical of this man to get the job done himself in an emergency. No matter whether he personally steered the ship or Hitchens reversed the helm from the wheelhouse, Murdoch gave a verbal order to turn the ship to the right.

Two quartermasters were assigned to each bridge watch because the task of keeping a huge liner on course was often too demanding on one man for a full four hours. The job was divided, with one man taking a trick at the wheel and the other performing nonsteering duties. Relief quartermaster Alfred Olliver was off the bridge, trim-

ming an oil light in the remote standard compass located on a platform 15 feet above the first-class lounge. He heard Fleet ring the
warning bell just before he started down the ladder from the compass
for the walk back to the bridge. Olliver arrived in time to hear Murdoch say, "Hard a-port!" That meant something was drastically
wrong. Helm orders at sea are small changes of a few degrees. They
are never "hard over," except in response to immediate danger.

In official testimony, the other quartermaster, Hitchens, spoke
only about the first officer's "hard a-starboard" order, turning the
ship to the left. He did not mention Murdoch's turning the ship back
to the right (port helm) at the last second. His omission gave credibility to the physically impossible story of the ship grazing its starboard bow on the berg while making a left turn. Olliver admitted
that he never heard the first "hard a-starboard" order because he was
not inside the bridge when it was given. "I heard 'hard a-port,'" he
told the U.S. investigation. He then confirmed that Hitchens turned
the wheel and that Sixth Officer Moody saw that the order was carried out.

SENATOR BURTON: You do not know whether the helm was put hard
   astarboard first, or not?
MR. OLLIVER: No, sir, I do not know that.
SENATOR BURTON: But you know it was put hard aport after you got
   there?
MR. OLLIVER: After I got there. Yes, sir.
SENATOR BURTON: Where was the iceberg, do you think, when the
   helm was shifted?
MR. OLLIVER: The iceberg was away up stern.
SENATOR BURTON: That is when the "hard aport" was given?
MR. OLLIVER: That is when the order "hard aport" was given. Yes, sir.
SENATOR BURTON: Who gave the [hard a-port] order?
MR. OLLIVER: The first officer.
SENATOR BURTON: And that order was immediately executed?
MR. OLLIVER: Immediately executed, and the sixth officer saw that it
   was carried out.

The left-turn-only myth grew into the accepted version of the
story because most people lack the ship-handling experience to understand why *Titanic* had to turn toward the iceberg, rather than
away, to avoid catastrophe. Only sailors know from daily experience
that a ship's bow sometimes must be turned toward danger to pro-

tect the rest of the hull. The location of the pivot point or fulcrum around which a ship swings requires that somebody must have shifted the helm to port. If Hitchens did not steer the ship, someone else must have. The only other person who could have steered *Titanic* was Murdoch.

### Range to berg: 425 yards (1.4 ship lengths)                     11:40:39 P.M.

Thirty-eight seconds had passed since Fleet's warning. *Titanic* was now beginning to turn back toward its nemesis. Ice and iron were only half a minute—a bit more than 400 yards—apart. The ship did not immediately swing to the right. It took some time for the rudder to overcome the rotational inertia of the original left turn. Murdoch did not wait for this to happen. He was already starting for the wheelhouse.

The berg was slightly more than the length of the ship in front of the bow when the first of several men scrambled to the controls on the reciprocating engine maneuvering platform. This metal grating was located between the two enormous piston engines. The first man must have headed straight for the lever that operated the turbine steam changeover valves. Operating this control shunted steam directly into the condensers instead of through the huge turbine powering the center propeller. The bronze propeller driven by the turbine continued rotating, but now only from the force of being dragged through the ocean.

Next, the man on the platform had to race forward about ten steps to operate the throttle valves on the two reciprocating engines. He was probably joined by another engineer, so this work may have been accomplished in tandem, one man per engine. While the engineers on the platform were operating the control levers, another man was answering the telegraph signals from the bridge by moving the handles on the instruments in the engine room until they matched the pointers indicating what the bridge desired. Up on the bridge, pointers moved and bells rang to show that the engine room had received the message and was obeying.

The engines and associated drive shafts and propeller blades were designed to withstand an instant shift from forward into reverse at harbor speeds. They might have had strength enough to withstand the strain of instant reversal at 22.25 knots, but only if every part from cylinder to tail shaft was totally free of defects. Ships have been

75

known to snap shafts and propeller blades during crash stops. If nothing broke on *Titanic*, a crash stop would have caused a rumbling shudder to convulse through the after third of the hull.

Because none of the seven hundred survivors described such a memorable event, and because the firebox dampers were ordered shut, the engineers could not have performed a crash stop. Instead, they just closed the throttles to the engines to stop them from pushing the liner forward. In sailor terms, *Titanic* was now "shooting," or coasting forward without power.

**11:40:50 P.M.**  **Range to berg: 288 yards (0.9 ship length)**

The toil of sweaty men feeding the fires in the ship's boiler rooms was suddenly interrupted by red warning lights and clanging bells. "Shut the dampers," sang out leading stoker Frederick Barrett. He and Second Engineer James H. Hesketh had been talking in boiler room #6 when the alarms clanged and the lights on the stoking indicators changed from white to red. Chatter among the men stopped in midsentence as they turned to this unexpected work. Closing the dampers on the furnaces was an ordinary precaution for reducing the fires to prevent generating excess steam pressure while the engineers stopped the engines. There were safety valves, of course, but these were not foolproof and had been known to stick on occasion. Nobody wanted to risk building up excessive steam pressure.

The command to close the dampers came just prior to impact, when *Titanic* was perhaps 700 feet from the berg. Closing the furnace dampers is yet another indication that a crash stop was never performed. Full reverse power would have required as much steam as possible from the boilers, making shutting the dampers the worst possible thing to do during a crash stop. Instead, stokers would have been asked to rake the coals in their furnaces, increasing steam output from the boilers in order to get maximum power out of the engines.

*Titanic*'s single rudder was now without wash from the propellers to help it turn the ship. Some writers have speculated that it was not large enough (78 feet tall, 15.5 feet wide, and a weight of 101 tons) to turn the ship from danger. In fact, the opposite is more likely true: *Titanic* turned slightly faster to the right during Murdoch's S-curve maneuver than he anticipated. The rudder was somewhat smaller in area than those fitted to other passenger liners of its time, but well in keeping with rudder sizes today. Current standards dictate that the rudder on a vessel of *Titanic*'s hull form should be equal in area to between 1.5 and 5 percent of the ship's underwater profile. At 1.9 percent, *Titanic*'s rudder falls within this range.

Due to flow characteristics of water, a large, wide rudder is best at slower speeds. A tall, narrow rudder of smaller dimensions is preferred for control at higher speeds, such as the 22.25 knots *Titanic* was making at the time of the accident. At high speeds, the flow of water across a larger rudder easily becomes "detached"—akin to the "stall" of an airplane—if too much steering angle is applied. Detached flow markedly reduces the ability of the rudder to turn the ship in much the same way that lift disappears from a stalled airplane wing. *Titanic*'s relatively smaller rudder (by pre-1912 standards) should have permitted the rapid maneuvers demanded by Murdoch in his attempt to avoid the berg.

The ship's bow, which moments earlier had appeared clear of the berg, was now visibly swinging toward it. Having turned to the left, Murdoch had no choice but to turn back to the right, even though this maneuver rotated the bow perilously close to the floating ice mountain. Up in the crow's nest, Lee and Fleet thought *Titanic* was twisting out of danger. Murdoch did not. "The doors," the first officer shouted. "The watertight doors!"

**11:41 p.m.** Mr. Murdoch closed the watertight doors.

—J. MOODY, Sixth Officer

**Range to berg: 175 yards (0.6 ship length)**

Men in the sweaty hot boiler rooms could not see the looming danger that was about to disrupt their orderly world of coal, dust, and fire. They were just shutting the firebox dampers when Murdoch operated the alarm bells to warn trimmers and stokers who might be in harm's way. The first officer should have paused several seconds after sounding the alarm to let everyone get clear of the doors. Understandably, however, he was flustered. Men in the boiler rooms remembered the alarms coming at almost the same time as the watertight doors began to rumble down like slow-motion guillotine blades. The ship rode onto the ice an instant later.

The releasing mechanisms of the automatic doors were not fine machinery. Each took a slightly different amount of time to react to the electrical current from the bridge. Some doors began closing before impact, while others did not. *Titanic's* watertight doors were huge steel castings that would have caused tremendous damage if they had been allowed to simply fall closed. Instead, the downward movement of each was controlled by a "cataract" escapement. It took almost half a minute for the steel doors to slide down. None had closed completely until after the iceberg accident.

11:41:13 P.M.   **Impact! Heading 255°; range to berg: 0**

According to the traditional story, this is the instant when *Titanic* ran sidelong into its iceberg. Scenes in the movies show the starboard bow of the giant liner slamming against a wall of ice, much like an automobile sideswiping a highway bridge abutment. Nothing could be further from the truth. If the ship had collided with the berg in that manner, the impact would have been devastating. Men sleeping in the bow would have been thrown out of their bunks onto the hard steel decks. Anyone standing in the grand first-class entrance likely would have had their feet knocked from beneath them. Certainly there would have been dozens of injuries: broken arms, legs, and even skulls. More than a few people would have been killed outright as the steel bow collapsed around them.

None of that happened.

# A NARROW SHAVE

Sunday, April 14, 1912
**11:41:13 P.M. to 11:41:30 P.M.**

**11:41:14 P.M.** Per Mr. Murdoch, the ship struck on ice at 11:41:13 P.M. The captain has assumed direct command. Engines stopped.

—J. MOODY, Sixth Officer

FOR most of the 2,200 people on board, the meeting of ship and ice was a nonevent. The majority of passengers slept through the most significant seven seconds of their lives. Aside from deep in the stokeholds, there was no great impact, no deafening roar. Only a slight tremble or a distant noise followed by an unexpected quiet disturbed the night.

> At the time of the collision I was awake and heard the engines stop, but felt no jar. My husband was asleep.
>
> Emily Bosie Ryerson

> I was just sitting on the bed, just ready to turn the lights out. It did not seem to me that there was any very great impact at all. It was just as though we went over a thousand marbles. There was nothing terrifying about it. . . .
>
> Mrs. J. Stuart White

> I was dreaming, and I woke up when I heard a slight crash. I paid no attention to it until I heard the engines stop.
>
> C. E. Henry Stengel

> We felt it under the smoking room. We felt a sort of stopping, a sort of, not exactly a shock, but a sort of slowing down.
>
> Hugh Woolner

Naturally, the force of the impact decreased the farther an observer was from the bow. Crew and steerage passengers unlucky enough to have bunks near the front of the ship knew immediately that something had gone very wrong, but even at the epicenter the event was marked more by noise than by severe jarring.

> The night of the wreck I was sleeping in my room . . . in steerage. I heard some terrible noise and I jumped out on the floor.
>
> Daniel Buckley

Another third-class passenger, Edward Dorking, was enjoying a late-night game of cards with shipboard friends. The impact between iron and ice disrupted their entertainment.

> we were thrown from the bench on which we were sitting. The shock was accompanied by a grinding noise. . . .
>
> Edward Dorking

Time after time, survivors gave one universal description of *Titanic's* contact with the iceberg. The ship quivered or rumbled for a few seconds and then everything seemed normal again. There were no tales of people being flung from their upper bunks by the force of the crash. No first-class passengers were pitched headlong down the famous grand staircase. Tables remained upright and drinks remained unspilled in the smoking rooms. The mast supporting lookouts Reginald Lee and Frederick Fleet did not come plunging down. On D deck, baker Walter Belford suffered more than most when several pans of his fresh rolls slid to the deck.

Looking down on the scene from above, Fleet thought the ship was experiencing "a narrow shave." He and Lee had watched the bow approach the iceberg and curve around it. A distant rumbling began just as the stern seemed to swing away from danger. "There was a rending of metal," Lee recalled in London. "You could hear that from where we were." The berg dumped a small load of ice into the well deck and disappeared astern. The two men wondered what sort of damage had been done.

11:41:15 P.M.　　In the stokeholds there was no mistaking steel crunching ice for a slight quiver or the spilling of a bunch of marbles. The impact produced an earsplitting metallic clatter that drowned out the familiar machinery noises. "It was just like thunder, the roar of thunder," said fireman George W. Beauchamp, who was tending fireboxes at the forward end of boiler room #5. Metal screamed. The deck beneath the feet of the black gang rumbled and shook. The frightened men must have been confused by events around them. Alarm bells were ringing, watertight doors were slamming shut, and steel was being torn by ice. It was a terrifying seven seconds to be in the bowels of the world's largest ship.

Trimmer George Cavell was inside the aft bunker of boiler room #4 when a sudden avalanche of sooty black lumps tumbled down onto him. "I felt a shock," he told the London proceedings, "and with that all the coal round me fell around me. I had a job to get myself out. The coal surrounded me before I knew where I was." Frightened but uninjured, Cavell scrambled out of the bunker just in time for the lights to go out. Only the ruddy glow of the furnaces illuminated the stokeholds.

Events topside were anything but noisy, confusing, or terrifying. With full right rudder (port helm in 1912), *Titanic* was turning to the right as it contacted the ice. Like every other officer on the ship, First Officer William M. Murdoch simply was not familiar enough with *Titanic*'s steering characteristics to conduct a close-quarters maneuver with a high degree of precision. His shift from a left to a right turn (from starboard to port helm in 1912) was made a second or so sooner than it should have been. The ship responded a bit faster than Murdoch anticipated, allowing the bow to pass a few feet closer to the ice than he had intended.

There had been those few quick seconds when it appeared the daring S-curve would succeed. However, as every child learns in school, the bulk of an iceberg lies beneath the water. Murdoch knew it, too. He fully expected what happened next. *Titanic*'s fragile underbelly scraped across an underwater shelf called an *ice ram*. This type of shelf is common enough to warrant special attention in *The American Practical Navigator*. "It is dangerous to approach close to an iceberg of any size because of the possibility of encountering underwater extensions," the navigation text cautions. The great danger of icebergs is "underwater extensions, called *rams*, which are usually formed due to the more intensive melting or erosion of the unsubmerged portion."

Physical evidence and eyewitness accounts prove the accident to be a grounding, not a collision. *Titanic* did not run *into* an iceberg; it ran *over* an iceberg. Both the initial pattern of flooding and the testimony from surviving crew members are consistent on one point: the bottom of the ship—not the side—made solid contact with the ice. Survivors unanimously described the sound and vibration of a ship running aground. There was no sharp jolt of a ship slamming horizontally into an immovable object. Instead, the slight tremble was barely enough to rattle silverware set out for breakfast in the first-class dining saloon.

The difference between a grounding and a collision is far more significant than it appears. Head-on impact with the berg would have sent all of *Titanic*'s 52,310 displacement tons smashing into the ice at a speed of almost 36 feet per second. In the crunch of a head-on impact, the ship's speed would have effectively dropped to zero. Everything inside the bow that was not tied down—people, chairs, bottles of wine, soup tureens—would have continued moving. Sleeping immigrants near the bow would have been sent flying out of their bunks. Farther aft, the impact would have been less forceful, but still substantial. Women could have been hurled down the grand staircase in the first-class section to land in a pile of taffeta. In the second-class smoking room behind the funnel #4, men might have felt their chairs move beneath them.

The field of ice that trapped *Californian* and fatally wounded *Titanic* had claimed its first victim three nights earlier. The French liner *Niagara* ran headlong into the ice on Thursday evening, April 11, 1912. That accident—a head-on impact—occurred while passengers were enjoying dinner. The result was devastating, if press accounts, such as the following from the *New York Herald*, can be believed.

> Passengers were hurled headlong from their chairs and broken dishes and glass were scattered throughout the dining saloons. The next instant there was a panic among the passengers and they raced screaming and shouting to the decks. . . . "I thought we were doomed," said Captain Juham yesterday. "At first I feared we had been in collision with another vessel as I hurried to the bridge. But when I saw it was an iceberg and that we were surrounded by ice as far as we could see through the fog, my fears for the safety of the passengers and the vessel grew. . . . I am sure Captain Smith had a similar experience in practically the same locality when the Titanic went down."

Despite their hair-raising experience, all passengers aboard the French liner survived, and the ship made its way to port. Perhaps because of *Niagara*'s survival, it became fashionable after *Titanic* sank to blame First Officer Murdoch for not hitting the berg squarely on the bow. Edward Wilding, one of the naval architects who designed *Titanic*, testified in London about the effect of a head-on collision. "If she struck a fair blow I think we should have heard a great deal more about the severity of it, and probably the ship would have come into harbor," he said. "I am afraid she would have killed every firemen down in the firemen's quarters, but I feel sure the ship would come in." At the U.S. Senate hearings, Captain John J. Knapp, the U.S. Navy's hydrographer, tried to imagine such an impact for Senator Smith.

> MR. KNAPP: An idea may be formed as to the possible blow by using the accepted formula, the weight multiplied by the square of the velocity divided by twice the gravity. Multiplying . . . will give the blow that would have been struck if she had kept straight on her course against this apparently solid mass of ice, which, at a speed of 21 knots, would have been equal to 1,173,200 foot tons, or energy enough to lift 14 monuments the size of the Washington Monument in one second of time.

Naval architect Wilding raised an interesting point about a head-on accident involving an extremely large ship. The bow of *Titanic* would have crumpled much like the "crumple zone" of a modern automobile. This crumpling would have dissipated much of the force of the blow by spreading it out over several seconds. According to Wilding, telescoping of the ship in this manner would have reduced injuries among passengers and crew who were lucky enough not to have been trapped in crumpled sections of the bow.

While less dramatic, the more often invoked "glancing blow" at 22.25 knots would have created its own kind of havoc. At impact, the deck would have jumped sideways relative to anything not riveted to it. This "rebound effect" would have been as disruptive to people in the forward third of the ship as a major earthquake is in a large hotel ashore: sleeping third-class passengers tossed to the hard steel decks, personal items tumbled off shelves, people thrown down. There would have been fewer injuries and spilled drinks than during a head-on collision, but there would also have been some deaths and broken bones. Either type of horizontal impact—head-on or glancing—would have been an unforgettable experience for a passenger. None of the more than seven hundred survivors recalled such a dramatic event.

What a sailor calls "rebound" is known scientifically as "impulse and momentum," the words naval architect Bill Garzke used to explain the traditional bow sideswipe in an interview with the Discovery Channel. He envisioned the hull striking the ice, then rebounding to strike again . . . and again . . . for nearly 300 feet along the bow. Garzke's description of events may have been inspired by Second Officer Charles H. Lightoller, who described essentially the same type of accident in his autobiography.

The impact flung her bow off, but only by the whip or spring of the ship. Again she struck, this time a little further aft. Each blow stove in a plate, below the water line, as the ship had not the inherent strength to resist.

Lightoller and Garzke undeniably got their Newtonian physics correct. In theory, *Titanic* could have been so unlucky that it pushed its side against an underwater ram with exactly enough force to crack its steel shell plating but not enough to throw people out of bed. A single light bump or two against the berg could have produced this effect, but only if the ship came to a stop against the ice in the same manner that it would make a hard landing against a pier when docking. A few light taps seem highly unlikely, however, given that the ship was making more than 22 knots at impact and continued moving throughout the encounter with the ice.

Alternatively, a single hard sideswipe of the iceberg might have caused enough crumpling of the ship's hull to have cushioned the blow. In this type of impact, the bending, twisting, and shattering of steel would have produced a single huge hole at the point of contact, with no damage anywhere else. Of course, *Titanic* did not receive damage to only one spot on the bow. Damage extended over a distance of nearly 300 feet from the forepeak all the way into boiler room #5. It is the extended nature of this damage that argues most effectively against the "impulse and momentum" type of rebounding impact.

More to the point, the theory of multiple impacts does not fit the experiences described by survivors. Each impulse and rebound would have whipped the deck sideways beneath the feet of passengers and crew—a type of impact no one reported. The universal description of the accident was a rumbling or a vibration, not a side-to-side motion of the deck.

Rapid horizontal motion of a deck knocks people off their feet much quicker than a large roll of a ship does. Friction keeps a person's feet in place on the deck as the deck jerks sideways. At the same time, the person's torso has inertia, which resists sideways movement, with the result that the feet move out from beneath the individual's body. When this happens, the person's center of gravity is suddenly and unexpectedly no longer supported in a straight line by the legs. A fall is almost inevitable.

If the horizontal impact as described by Lightoller and posited by Garzke took place, an indelible memory of a large percentage of surviving third-class passengers who happened to be standing upright in their cabins near the bow would have been an unexpected tumble to the deck. Crew members in their quarters at the very front of the ship would have had the same disquieting experience. Instead, except for one man, passengers and crew universally recalled only a slight trembling as the ship passed over the ice.

Able seaman William Lucas remembered the impact as more intense than did other survivors. He told the British inquiry, "I had just left the mess room," when the impact "very nearly sent me off my feet." Another seaman, John Poingdestre (spelled *Poindestre* in some accounts) was also outside the mess room, on the port side of C deck beneath the forecastle. He was far less impressed by the impact. "I felt the vibration" was his laconic way of describing the same impact.

As has been shown, soft contact with the ice rules against the traditional story of the berg slicing open the side of the ship. All evidence proving exactly how the hull was damaged now lies at the bottom of the North Atlantic, so discussions of ice damage are forced into the realm of speculation. Nobody really knows what happened. Even if we could raise the forward portion of *Titanic* (and assuming that rust has not destroyed the evidence), it would take years of scientific analysis to determine which damage was from the ice and which resulted when the broken hull slammed into the sea bottom after sinking. Since clinical forensic analysis of the ship is impossible, the next best step is to examine the 1912 testimony of experts and eyewitnesses.

When a ship "strikes the ground," the action can be quite stately. Speed often drops so gradually that the first moments of a grounding can go unnoticed even by professional seamen. Sliding onto mud or sand may produce almost no sound or vibration. Striking on a hard surface can sound like marbles pouring over sheet metal. Neither type of grounding produces the smashing impact of iron against an immovable object. Soft or hard, a grounding is exactly what passengers and crew aboard *Titanic* experienced during the seven seconds the ship was in contact with the ice.

Author Lawrence Beesley, a teacher on his way to America for a holiday, was in cabin D-56, just aft of the second-class dining saloon, when the ship slid over the ice. His personal experience is a perfect illustration of a ship going aground, not colliding head-on.

> there came what seemed to me nothing more than an extra heave of the engines and a more than usually obvious dancing motion of the mattress on which I sat. Nothing more than that—no sound of a crash or anything else: no sense of shock, no jar that felt like one heavy body meeting another.

A grounding such as Beesley described is soft because it does not take place in an instant. Only a small portion of the vessel's displacement weight is involved at the beginning. The amount increases as the ship slides onto the ground, but this increase is spread over time. The event is not instantaneous like a head-on collision but takes several seconds from first touch until the ship either stops or breaks free.

11:41:16 P.M. *Titanic*'s steel bottom absorbed just a few ounces of the ship's weight during the first split second of the accident. This weight continuously increased to pounds, and finally to hundreds of tons while the hull was fully on the shelf. However, steel plates in contact with the berg did not carry the total mass of *Titanic* even when the maximum amount of ship was on the ice. The bottom would have supported only that portion of the hull actually riding on the ice shelf. Grounding pressure on the vessel's structure may not have exceeded a minor percentage of the ship's mass. This, too, would have contributed to the soft impact.

Men standing watch on *Titanic*'s bridge knew they had gone across a submerged ice shelf and had not run into the iceberg. "During the time she was crushing the ice, we could hear a grinding noise along the ship's bottom," quartermaster Robert Hitchens confirmed during the U.S. Senate hearings. Note that he stated "along the ship's bottom," and not "along the ship's side." Hitchens believed the damage was located on the underside of *Titanic*'s bottom, and he said so. He also used the phrase "crushing ice," an unlikely way to describe a glancing blow against the side of the bow. "Crushing ice," however, is a perfect description for what happened as the ship slid over the top of the underwater ice shelf.

Sliding across the underwater ice ram would have lifted the starboard side of the ship to a small extent. This lifting would have been virtually unnoticeable inside the hull on the lower passenger decks.

Had their attention not been focused on dodging the berg and closing the watertight doors, the men on the bridge might have noticed it. Two men, lookouts Fleet and Lee, were perfectly positioned to observe the lifting of the starboard bow. The 90-foot height of the crow's nest would have magnified this small roll, which is just what Lee experienced.

"The ship seemed to heel slightly over to port as she struck the berg," Lee recalled in London. "Very slightly to port as she struck along the starboard side."

Eerily, Captain Smith appears to have predicted *Titanic's* accident to a Dr. Williams. His prediction was made around 1910, while he was in command of the White Star Line's *Adriatic* prior to taking command of *Olympic.* "The big icebergs that drift into warmer water melt much more rapidly under water than on the surface, and sometimes a sharp, low reef extending two or three hundred feet beneath the sea is formed," Smith explained. "If a vessel should run on one of these reefs half her bottom might be torn away." The captain predicted that if that happened, "some of us would go to the bottom with the ship."

Captain Smith's hypothesis proved tragically correct in *Titanic's* case. For a hypothesis to be accepted as true by scientists, however, it must produce repeatable results. It must predict accurately the outcomes of experiments done by different people in different situations. Thanks to another British passenger liner, *Queen Elizabeth 2,* we have a second example confirming the softness of a grounding incident involving a high-speed passenger liner. The modern Cunard flagship struck on rocks off the eastern coast of the United States in 1992. Its bottom was ripped open by large boulders in much the same manner that the iceberg damaged *Titanic.* There was no violent impact. Just as in 1912, passengers aboard *QE2* were not thrown about.

Although separated by eighty years, these two events illustrate that a passenger ship can run over a hard object at high speed and still produce a relatively mild impact. The *QE2* incident was not as soft as *Titanic's* because *QE2* ran over rocks that did not move under the weight of the ship the way the iceberg did. Passengers in 1992 received considerably more jostling than those in 1912. "The only thing I can compare it to, being from California," said passenger Linda Robinson of San Diego, "is a major earthquake."

This jarring did not panic *QE2*'s 1,815 passengers or nearly 1,000 crew members. Passenger Nat Welch of Lincoln, Massachusetts, recalled, "The whole ship started to shake quite violently. I went to take a look outside and overheard someone going into a radio room saying it appeared we hit a sand bar." Another passenger told a *New York Times* reporter that the biggest concern after the incident was whether or not the ship's gambling casino would remain open.

Damage done to the outside shell plating of each ship in these individual groundings was remarkably similar. For now, however, the important factor is the similarity of what the passengers experienced. Both ships struck at roughly 20 knots. Passengers felt rumblings and were jostled, but there were no injuries from being thrown to the deck. Panic did not break out on either ship. These similarities serve to confirm Captain Smith's premonition: *Titanic* ran *over* the iceberg, not *into* it.

11:41:19 P.M.  A full-size iceberg has hundreds of times more mass than *Titanic* did. Each cubic yard of berg is roughly a ton of solid ice. In contrast, *Titanic* was a hollow metal structure filled mostly with air. In a head-on collision, there would not have been enough time for the energy of *Titanic* to overcome the inertia of the ice and push the berg sideways. But, as explained above, the ship did not hit the berg. Rather, it spent the seven seconds after impact grinding across the top of an underwater ice shelf. There was plenty of time for the berg to move a bit under the ship's weight. The ice felt the force of the ship as much as the ship felt that of the ice, and the berg rolled ever so slightly toward *Titanic*.

The berg rolled because icebergs are notoriously unstable. Just as Captain Smith told his New York friends, the upper part extending into the atmosphere melts at a different rate than do the underwater portions. This upsets the equilibrium of a berg, which often compensates by suddenly capsizing. "Icebergs that are in the process of disintegrating may suddenly capsize or readjust their masses," warns *Bowditch*. When the ship rode onto the shelf, the berg was forced to support increasing tons of steel, rivets, and passengers well away from its center of gravity. Like any other floating object, the berg tipped toward this extra weight.

As the berg tipped, its upper portions brushed against the ship's topsides at the forward end of the well deck. This contact precipitated the famous mini-avalanche of ice. Brushing against the top of the berg probably did not scratch the liner's fresh paint. During the mid-1990s, scientists studied the impact of icebergs against iron or steel objects. This research was aimed at developing offshore oil rigs for use on the Grand Banks near the spot where *Titanic* now lies. Experiments have shown that ice above a berg's waterline can be relatively soft and often crumbles upon impact. This type of crumbling produced the broken pieces of ice that littered the ship's forward well deck.

"There was quite a lot of ice on the starboard part of the ship," twenty-six-year-old Olaus Abelseth told the U.S. investigation. The young Norwegian was sleeping in the third-class open berthing area on lower deck G, near the bow of the ship. Also near the bow was Frank O. Evans, a twenty-seven-year-old able seaman. "I was sitting at the table reading a book, and all of a sudden I felt a slight jar," he testified in New York. "I did not take any notice of it for a few minutes until one of the other able seamen came down with a big lump of ice in his hands."

Fourth Officer Joseph G. Boxhall also noticed the ice in the well deck but was not impressed by it. "I found just a little ice in the well deck covering a space of about three or four feet from the bulwarks right along the well deck," he said in London. "Small stuff."

Scientific study of icebergs appears to work against the traditional starboard bow "sideswipe." The side of *Titanic* brushed relatively soft, air-filled ice that was not strong enough to pierce steel. The bottom, however, crunched across ice that was capable of tearing the ship's steel plates apart. Severe, if not fatal, damage from running *over* the dense ice of an underwater shelf was almost certain. The same does not appear to be true of running *into* the warmer, less dense ice above the berg's waterline.

Peter Wadhams is one of a group of present-day scientists who determined that solid ice below a berg's waterline is quite different from that extending into the air above. His team found that the crystalline structure of submerged ice is much denser, with smaller trapped gas pockets. Individual ice crystals making up the underwater portion of a berg have also been found to be much larger and stronger than ice crystals exposed to the air. Conversely, the above-water portions of a berg are made of softer ice with larger gas pockets. This modern scientific evidence confirms explorer Ernest

Shackleton's experiences with icebergs that do not reflect light because of porous ice above their waterlines. At the time of the *Titanic* hearings, Shackleton was a respected ice navigator and Antarctic explorer who had become a national hero for his 1908 trek almost to the South Pole.

Icebergs are the subject of continuous study at the Center for Cold Ocean Resource Engineering (C-CORE) in Newfoundland. Stephen Bruneau, a researcher at the center, told the Discovery Channel's Online Service that while cubes in the ice tray of a typical home freezer are only 10 percent as strong as steel, ice deep inside an iceberg can be −25 degrees Celsius. Ice at that temperature is nearly ten times stronger than the average ice cube. This is the type of strong ice *Titanic* would have encountered as it ground across an underwater ice shelf.

11:41:21 P.M.  A paint smear was apparently scraped off the ship's bottom during the accident. According to author Walter Lord, this smear was red, the color of the ship's bottom paint in 1912. The paint smear became visible because *Titanic*'s journey across the submerged ice shelf damaged the berg as well as the ship. Damage to the unstable berg caused it to slightly adjust its position in the water. By the morning, after *Titanic* foundered, the formerly submerged shelf was partially visible above the surface of the Atlantic.

Another photograph—this one taken from the rescue ship *Carpathia* on the morning following the accident—exists of a stained iceberg. Both photos appear to be of the same berg, which has a tall point and two shorter peaks. At night, this silhouette could have been mistaken for a sailing ship, as it was by quartermaster George T. Rowe, who viewed it from the docking bridge on *Titanic*'s stern.

11:41:23 P.M.  Grinding across ice created friction, which helped the vessel pivot more rapidly to its right than would have been possible under the rudder alone. The ship had been steering 266°, or almost due west, when Fleet sounded the alarm. The bow had rotated left to about 240° when Murdoch reversed the rudder and started it swinging back to the right. In all likelihood, the ship's heading had probably come back to approximately 255° when the bottom first touched on the underwater ice shelf.

Note that 255° is 11° left of the ship's original course, prior to Murdoch's "porting around" the iceberg. *Titanic* was probably heading just south of west (south 75 W in 1912) at the moment of impact.

To passengers unfamiliar with ships, it would have appeared that the liner was heading almost straight for the berg at the instant steel crunched ice. In fact, the bow was rotating to the right because of Murdoch's successful attempt to swing the midships and stern away from danger.

In order for *Titanic*'s stern to clear the ice fully, the bow had to reach a heading of at least 270° and possibly as high as 275°. That is, it was heading slightly north of the original course as the hull slid off the underwater ice shelf. Because such a rapid rotation required a fortunate combination of momentum, rudder, and drag on the starboard bottom from the ice, this turn was impossible for *Titanic* under the force of its rudder alone. The bow continued swinging to the north (right) after the ship passed the berg. Eventually, *Titanic* reached a heading of about 010° (a bit east of north) as it coasted to a halt following the accident.

Crunching over the ice ram not only caused the ship to rotate, it also slowed forward progress. In a way, the berg did Murdoch a favor. It eased his second problem: avoiding the field of tightly packed ice behind the deadly berg. The quick turn while still on the shelf, coupled with the loss of momentum, helped the ship stay out of that line of packed ice. The north marker on the steering compass continued to swing closer to the lubber's line (a mark on the compass used to read the vessel's heading) as the ship coasted forward until the bow pointed just east of due north.

Author Leslie Reade spent most of a lifetime attempting to prove the geographic relationship of *Californian* to *Titanic*. His book *The Ship That Stood Still* details the doomed liner's swing to a heading of slightly east of north after the accident. He backs his argument with not only eyewitness accounts but also the positions of the lifeboats when *Carpathia* arrived from the southeast.

Physical evidence remaining at the wreck site also indicates the ship was heading north when it sank. Writing about his discovery in 1987, oceanographer Robert D. Ballard said that the bow points a little east of north as it rests on the bottom. All of the maps and drawings in his book show this orientation with the bow lying about 2,000 feet north of the stern. The bow undoubtedly moved forward as it swept down to the bottom, but its pointed shape would have tended to keep it on nearly the same compass heading as when it left the surface. It would have been virtually impossible

91

for the remains of the bow to be pointed east of north if the ship had been under left rudder (starboard helm in 1912) at the moment of impact. The single left turn of the official myths would have caused the bow to swing first to the southwest and finally to the south.

11:41:24 P.M.     Except when the berg was at the bluff of the bow, the few eyewitnesses who saw the deadly ice did not observe it as close to *Titanic*'s side. They described the ice as passing at an ever-increasing distance from the side of the ship, especially after it came abreast of the bridge wing. Most significantly, they saw the stern swinging *away* from the berg as the ship moved past. The gulf between the hull and the ice was increasing, an occurrence consistent only with a right turn, not with a left.

George Harder and his bride, who were traveling on their honeymoon, were in cabin E-50, an outside room right against the hull on the starboard side.

> I heard this thump, then I could feel the boat quiver and could feel a sort of rumbling, scraping noise along the side of the boat. When I went to the porthole I saw this iceberg go by. The porthole was closed. The iceberg was, I should say, about 50 to 100 feet away.

Seaman Joseph Scarrott was smoking in the forecastle when the ship struck. He scrambled on deck near the bow, where he saw the berg gliding along the ship's starboard side. In London he testified that *Titanic* was under port helm (turning right) and that the stern was swinging away from the ice. Scarrott's description of the ship turning to its right was ignored by the British investigation, possibly because of an article published under his name in the April 1912 issue of a magazine called *The Sphere*. This piece relates the standard story about a crash stop: "The shaking of the ship seemed as though the engines had suddenly been reversed." A few sentences later, he admits, "we did not think then there was anything serious. . . . [We were] cursing the iceberg for disturbing us." The language in this article reads more like the imagination of a deskbound editor than the recollections of an experienced seaman, which is likely how the piece was developed.

Scarrott's factual testimony to the British proceedings about the ship's turning right, toward the berg, was at odds with both the story he told to *The Sphere* and the official myth, making the testimony easy to discount. However, this testimony attests to the maneuver necessary for *Titanic* to absorb damage only to the forward third of its starboard bow. This, of course, is exactly what occurred.

Far to the stern, quartermaster George Rowe paced the ship's dock- 11:41:28 P.M. ing bridge to keep warm. He thought he felt a skip in the beat of the ship's engines. Then he saw what appeared to be a full-rigged ship sailing down *Titanic*'s starboard side, but the illusion lasted only an instant before he recognized the object as an iceberg. Rowe is the one witness who could have confirmed that the engines attempted a crash stop, if this had occurred. Of all the people aboard that night, this trained seaman certainly would have remembered the resulting tumult had the engines shifted into reverse at more than 22 knots. He was standing almost directly above the triple screws on an open platform. Yet, he recalled only a "skip" in the rhythm of the engines. Rowe never mentioned the noise, vibration, and foaming water that accompany a crash stop because none happened.

Seconds after the accident, Rowe checked the spinner of the patent log, which trailed astern from the port side of the docking bridge on the poop deck. He did not say what prompted him to look at the spinner, but it was probably to see whether the iceberg had torn it loose (as happened to *Californian*'s spinner). Rowe found the log was working perfectly. He later remembered that it showed the ship had steamed 260 miles since the odometer had been reset at noon that day. Simple division of 260 miles by the eleven hours and forty-one minutes of steaming gives the average speed of the ship over that distance as 22.25 knots.

Rowe was watching the berg disappear at the same instant that fireman Beauchamp was congratulating himself on being alive in boiler room #5. Beauchamp had been working to shut the dampers in boiler room #6 when the watertight door alarm sounded. An instant later he heard that "roar like thunder," and water shot through a seam in the ship's side just above the tank top deck. Despite the danger of being crushed by the descending steel door, the fireman instinctively dived into boiler room #5 farther aft. The door slammed shut behind him.

Several hundred feet aft, the senior engineer on duty in the reciprocating engine room operated a switch to start alarm bells ringing throughout the engineers' quarters on E deck, awakening the "watch off watch" with a start. These alarms rang only for major emergencies, when all hands were needed. Sleepy engineers began slipping into their coveralls for the last time. None of *Titanic*'s loyal engineering officers would survive the next three hours.

Although passengers initially were largely unaffected by the brush with the iceberg, the black gang in the boiler rooms was not so lucky. After seven seconds of screeching metal, they found themselves in a fiery twilight caused by a temporary electric blackout. A few men were dispatched from each stokehold to make the long climb to E deck in search of portable lights. However, the main electric power came back on after a few dark minutes, and the stokeholds were once again flooded with light.

Stokers and trimmers probably feared for their lives as water poured into boiler room #6. Most likely, however, everyone survived the initial scramble to escape the freezing water. "We heard a crash," stoker Frederick Barrett recalled. "The engineer and I jumped to the next section [boiler room #5]." Barrett became one of the few people to survive after seeing firsthand the damage done to *Titanic* by the iceberg. He told the U.S. Senate that a horizontal opening

> ran past the bulkhead between sections 5 and 6 [boiler rooms #5 and #6], and it was a hole two feet into the coal bunkers. She was torn through Number 6 and also through two feet abaft of the bulkhead at the forward head of Number 5 section.

In London, Barrett told essentially the same tale. "Water came pouring in two feet above the stokehold plate; the ship's side was torn from the third stokehold to the forward end," he testified. The fireman's experience was as frightening as his testimony is illuminating. He did not mention boiler room #6 as suffering any great structural damage, despite the tremendous noise and sudden deluge of freezing sea water. Most important, he did not report that mythical dagger of ice ripping open the side of the ship.

Barrett placed the open seam at "two feet above the floor plates." Those plates were light metal decking designed to give stokers easier access to the furnace openings. The stokers actually worked standing a few feet above the tank top deck, the upper side of *Titanic*'s watertight double bottom, which means the open seam was about 4 feet above the tank top. On the outside of the ship, the seam would have been in the single-thickness vertical side plating just above the turn of the bilge. Barrett's observation confirms that the opening in the side was confined to the very lowest portion of the hull, no more than 10 feet above the keel.

Sprung seams also must have occurred in the four compartments forward of Barrett's position. Recent dives to the wreck have brought back evidence of six or more horizontal openings in the ship's side, in the area from boiler room #6 to the bow. Unfortunately for the hypotheses of modern researchers, however, the surviving crew members did not believe that the open seams in the side of *Titanic* allowed significant amounts of water into the hull. They knew the location of their vessel's mortal wounds: the bottom beneath their feet. Seaman Edward J. Buley described precisely where the fatal water entered the hull. It was coming not through the side but up through the bottom. When the interrogator made a mistake on this, Buley pointedly corrected him.

MR. BULEY: . . . down where we were there was a hatchway, right down below, and there was a tarpaulin across it, with an iron batten. You could hear the water rushing in, and the pressure of air underneath it was such that you could see this bending. In the finish I was told it blew off.

SENATOR FLETCHER: What part of the ship would you call that?

MR. BULEY: The forecastle head.

SENATOR FLETCHER: How far was that from the bow?

MR. BULEY: About 20 yards, I should think.

SENATOR FLETCHER: That condition could not have obtained unless the steel plates had been torn off the side of the ship?

MR. BULEY: From the bottom of the ship. It was well underneath the water line.

The ice was cruel. Rivets must have been stretched and even ripped out of the plating. Seams would have been forced open and butt joints misaligned. Damage on the outside undoubtedly was random. Although the damage would have been horrible to look at, it is unlikely that this exterior ice damage was life-threatening to the ship. The most immediate result of damage to the exterior was flooding of the starboard side tankage located beneath the tank top deck.

One place bears evidence of direct internal damage from the ice: the forward end of hold #2, directly above the spot on the keel where the ship would have first felt full grounding pressure on the ice shelf. According to the British inquiry's report, the impact smashed a metal enclosure around the foot of the double spiral staircase that was used by firemen to go from their quarters on D, E, and F decks to the stokeholds. This damage was followed by substantial flooding of holds #2 and #3 and the passageway. Hold #3 filled rapidly to the vessel's waterline.

Ice damage to the shell plating of the bottom forced the ship to rely on its double bottom to stay afloat. Rending of steel plates on the outside of the outer bottom did not allow significant amounts of water to enter the inside of the hull because the tank top deck was there to stop it. If that deck had remained totally watertight, *Titanic* might have stayed afloat just as *QE2* did eight decades later. However, the tank top deck was no longer watertight after the ship came off the ice. The Atlantic Ocean was boiling up in the forward cargo holds and was also rising in boiler room #6 but at a markedly slower rate.

Rents in the horizontal tank top deck would be expected as a result of upward deflection of longitudinal girders running parallel to the keel within the double bottom. These longitudinals acted much like snow skis carrying the ship over the ice. And, just as skis flex over moguls, *Titanic*'s hull flexed upward as it passed across the ice ram. Upward movement may have created random strained rivets, sprung seams, or cracked plates in the overlying tank top deck. This movement of the ship's structure was greatest at the point where the keel reached its full depth at the base of the spiral staircase, and damage to the metal around this staircase and the rapid flooding of holds #2 and #3 likely resulted from this upward displacement.

Seventy-seven years after *Titanic* sank, the oil tanker *Exxon Valdez* struck Bligh Reef in Alaska's Prince William Sound. The resulting oil spill continues to make headlines. Shipyard workers who repaired the tanker's hull found numerous bent web frames and displaced longitudinals. Similar damage must have occurred to the framework of *Titanic* as a result of crossing the ice shelf.

Although *Titanic* was not cut open by a knife of ice, Barrett's eyewitness account has often been cited as proof of a long slice in the ship's side. The importance of what he saw has been misunderstood, however. When the seam opened, it released the stress created by the ship's squirming off the ice. This release prevented rivets from popping any higher on the ship's side, and the plates in the side above this single horizontal seam remained undamaged and watertight. Barrett's description of a horizontal opening has distorted nearly every discussion of *Titanic*'s demise. Based on what he saw, it has generally been assumed that the berg tore a horizontal gash the length of the first four compartments and into the fifth, but crew members on duty that night did not think that was what happened.

MR. BULEY: . . . according to where the water was, I should say the bottom was really ripped open altogether.
SENATOR SMITH: The steel bottom?
MR. BULEY: Yes, sir.

The pattern of flooding immediately after the accident shows how the upward curve of the keel toward the bow influenced where damage occurred. *Titanic*'s keel ran straight for most of the ship's length but swept upward in a gentle curve beneath hold #1 and the forepeak. This upward curve protected these first two compartments from the full force of the grounding on ice, reserving the brunt of the impact for hold #2, particularly beneath the double spiral staircase, and the forward portion of hold #3, where the keel first reached full depth.

The British inquiry's report found that, following the accident, the forepeak was dry above the orlop for more than an hour. Hold #1 was awash to 7 feet, but holds #2 and #3 were quickly flooded. Water rose 24 feet within the first ten minutes in hold #3, indicating that it had received considerable damage.

Boiler room #6 was protected by holds #2 and #3. While flooding here was immediate, water does not seem to have driven out the majority of stokers and trimmers until they had raked their fires and vented the 215 pounds of steam pressure from their four double-ended boilers. Boiler room #5 remained nearly dry despite a high-pressure fan of water cascading through a sprung seam at its forward end. Significantly, the space beneath this room apparently was dry enough for engineers to open a manhole into the tankage below. There are no reports of ice damage to compartments aft of boiler room #5.

Depending upon the point of measurement, *Titanic*'s tank top was 6 to 8 feet above the keel in the area of the ice damage. The British report noted that damage reported by men in the boiler rooms did not appear more than a few feet above this deck, which means that the observed damage was low on the hull. The wording in the report is somewhat clumsy, as if the writer did not know exactly where the bottom of the ship ended and the side began.

The collision with the iceberg . . . caused damage to the bottom of the starboard side of the vessel at about 10 feet above the level of the keel, but there was no damage above this height.

11:41:30 P.M.     The great liner was doomed from the beginning. Although the decks above the forepeak tank were dry, the next four large compartments (holds #1, #2, and #3, and boiler room #6) began to flood immediately. The rate of flooding in each of these compartments was different, but this is just an incidental detail. That the sea had open access to at least four of the five forward compartments is what proved fatal. The ship could have floated indefinitely if only three of the four were filled, but foundering was inevitable with four large compartments open to the sea. *Titanic* had that and worse: there was also a steady spray of water into a fifth compartment.

> Titanic as constructed could not have remained afloat long with such damage as she received.
> ... The engineers were applying the pumps ... but even if they had succeeded in getting all the pumps in the ship to work they could not have saved the ship or prolonged her life to any appreciable amount.

Exploration of the wreck has focused attention on the steel from which *Titanic*'s plates were rolled. Harland and Wolff purchased the best available "battleship steel" plate for Olympic-class ships. Excellent by 1912 standards, this steel would not be acceptable today because of the impurities it contains. English steel-making technology prior to World War I was not capable of producing rolled plate of higher quality. Tests on actual samples of the hull raised from the Atlantic have confirmed the presence of sulfide occlusions and other impurities. The impure steel in *Titanic* is reportedly most brittle when the water is at freezing temperature—as it was the night of the accident.

Timothy Foecke, a metallurgist at the National Institute of Standards and Technology in Gaithersburg, Maryland, studied the rivets holding *Titanic*'s wreckage together while working in conjunction with a TV documentary presented by the Discovery Channel. The Associated Press quoted him as saying that one-third of the forty rivets he tested from the wreck "have some kind of problem." According to the AP article, the defective rivets contain three to four times more slag than they should. Foecke's research points toward defective rivets as one possible reason such a light impact against an iceberg produced such fatal damage.

Welding the large plates and girders of a ship was impossible when *Titanic* was built. Ship construction in 1911 involved riveting huge plates of steel together. Most of the shell plates in the Olympic-class ships were 30 feet long and 6 feet tall and weighed about 3 tons each. These plates were attached to internal frames in the same pattern as common bond bricking, each meeting the one below in a horizontal seam. A single line of plates running the full fore and aft direction of the hull was called a *strake*. Strakes were made of individual plates connected by vertical joints called *butts*.

As designed, Olympic-class ships had double bottoms and single sides above their tank top decks. The simplest and strongest way to build a steel ship, a double bottom is nothing more than a box girder the width and length of the vessel. *Titanic's* flat plate *keel* was the first piece of steel laid down in Harland and Wolff's yard. This piece was followed by a vertical keel and another flat plate, creating an I beam that became the ship's backbone for the length of the hull.

Horizontal *frames* (called *floors*) were placed at right angles to the keel. These floors were later joined to vertical frames, forming a steel rib cage defining the hull's shape. The horizontal and vertical frames met in a radius known as the *turn of the bilge*, or simply the *bilge*. The ship's outer skin, called the *shell plating*, was installed on the outside of the floors and up the vertical frames. Another layer of slightly thinner steel plating was installed on top of the floors, creating an enclosed space more than 6 feet deep. Much of this space was used for tankage, so the layer of plating over the floors was logically called the *tank top deck*. All of the boilers and engines were mounted on this watertight deck.

The inside of the double bottom was further divided by longitudinals running fore and aft through the tank space to help the keel support the length of the vessel. Some of these longitudinals, such as the vertical keel, were watertight and subdivided the tankage into smaller watertight compartments. Beneath the two engine rooms, the tankage was divided into four watertight cells between each primary bulkhead. Forward and aft of the engine rooms, tank spaces between the bulkheads were divided into two cells along the keel. The forepeak and afterpeak were not divided. Cells near the bow and stern called *void spaces* were kept empty. Some of these cells under the engine rooms served as tanks for nonpotable fresh water destined for the boilers. Others could be filled with seawater for ballast.

Riveted ships can "unzip" along a row of rivets if a seam is put under strain that exceeds the strength of the seam's materials. All of the strength of the seam is concentrated in the rivets and not along the faying surfaces of the plates. In fact, there is nothing holding the plates together between rivets, which explains why the fasteners are spaced so closely together. A riveted seam will hold strain beyond the breaking point of any individual piece in the structure until one rivet fails. Once one rivet goes, the full force is applied to rivets on either side of the broken fastener. If the forces involved are still beyond the strength of these rivets, more fasteners snap and the pressure moves outward to the next set of rivets. "Unzipping" stops when enough strain has been released so that what remains is not forceful enough to break another fastener.

*Titanic*'s entire tank structure—frames, longitudinals, outer plates, and tank top deck—was a tightly riveted unit, a flat, horizontal box roughly ten times as wide as it was tall. This extreme width-to-height ratio allowed the double bottom to flex as one piece while the ship moved across the iceberg. This does not mean *Titanic*'s bottom was excessively limber, however. In fact, the ship was designed to flex as it passed through waves at sea. The difference is that when the ship rode over the iceberg, the flex was concentrated in a small portion of the bow rather than being spread over the entire hull. Strains at the point of maximum grounding pressure likely exceeded the strength of the metal, particularly the rivets holding seams and butt joints together.

Unlike in the double bottom, flexing of the single thickness plating in the side of the hull above the tank top was prevented by its 60-foot vertical dimension. Think of the side of the ship and its double bottom as two sheets of plywood joined at a right angle along their edges. One piece is horizontal; the other is standing vertically on its long edge. The horizontal sheet of wood bends easily across its thickness, allowing it to flex when dragged over an uneven surface (such as an underwater ice shelf). The vertical piece similarly accepts the curved shape of the bow, but it cannot be flexed across its vertical height. If the horizontal sheet is forced to flex, strain in the right angle between the two sheets of plywood causes that joint to fail.

Similarly, the steel side of *Titanic*'s hull resisted upward flexing while the double bottom was able to bend a bit while riding over the iceberg. Caught between the flexing bottom and the inflexible side was the horizontal seam that Barrett saw open. Strain concentrated in that seam would have sheared rivets and forced the plates to move relative to one another. The seam failed, and water began spraying into the hull as Barrett watched. The overlapping plates of the seam remained in contact with each other, which limited the flow of water between them. A ship with randomly sprung seams over one-third of its length is in trouble. However, considerably less water entered *Titanic* through its randomly sprung seams than would have come through the mythical iceberg gash. By themselves, these open seams were not the fatal wounds.

Nor were the brittle steel and riveted construction used in *Titanic's* hull fatal construction flaws. Recent tests on steel and rivets taken from the wreck have falsely been interpreted to show they were too weak for safety. Tests on metal from the ship reportedly show it to be equal in tensile strength to modern steel. Also, *Titanic* was not fatally compromised by brittleness caused by the freezing temperatures that April night. Its sister ship *Olympic* steamed into the 1930s without any reported cold weather fractures. *Olympic's* steel was strong enough to ram and sink a German U-boat during World War I. (It also rammed and sank the *Nantucket* lightship in a nonhostile, but equally fatal, encounter.) The sister ship shared metal identical to its ill-fated sibling. Metallurgy proves only that *Titanic's* hull was at its most vulnerable at the temperature of the sea that April night. Malleable steel presumably would have suffered less damage because it would have deformed rather than fractured.

In his autobiography, Second Officer Lightoller correctly assessed the strength-of-materials problem in large ships. This problem does not come from the materials themselves, but from the immense bulk of huge liners. *Titanic's* plates were no weaker than those of any other ship of its day, nor were they all that much weaker than modern steel. The problem was sheer size. Steel does not get any stronger just because the ship gets bigger.

> Had it been, for instance, the old *Majestic* or even the *Oceanic* the chances are that either of them would have been strong enough to take the blow and be thrown off without serious damage. For instance, coming alongside with the old *Majestic*, it was no uncommon thing for her to hit a knuckle of the wharf a good healthy bump, but beyond perhaps, scraping off the paint, no damage was ever done. . . .
>
> Then ships grew in size, out of all proportion to their strength, till one would see a modern liner brought with all the skill and care possible, fall slowly, and ever so gently on a knuckle, to bend and dent a plate like a piece of tin.

101

The first and, to this day, most knowledgeable attempt to quantify the damage was done by naval architect Edward Wilding of Harland & Wolff, who had been associated with the ship from the first sheet of clean drawing paper to *Titanic*'s final launch. Wilding took over shipbuilder Thomas Andrews's job after the disaster. Using actual dimensions of the ship's first five compartments, Wilding reduced the probable length of the damaged area on *Titanic* from 300 to about 200 feet. His more accurate estimate was part of official testimony but was overlooked in later retellings of the story, including Wreck Commissioner's Report.

Having established the length of the damage, Wilding next assessed its nature. He argued that contact with ice could not have ripped the ship open like a knife because *Titanic* took too long to sink. Based on the length of time the ship floated, he was the first to argue that a continuous "slice" would have allowed too much water to enter too quickly. Instead, Wilding suggested that the berg loosened rivets and distorted plating as the ship bumped along. He envisioned fatal damage consisting of a series of modest openings rather than one continuous gash. Water entered the hull through sporadic sprung seams, popped rivets, loosened butts, and fractured steel plates.

> MR. WILDING: I cannot believe that the wound was absolutely contiguous the whole way. I believe that it was in a series of steps, and that from what we heard Barrett say in his evidence it was the end of one of the series of wounds which flooded the different spaces.

Etymological evidence that the ship ran over the ice and not into it is contained in the consistent use of the word *struck* by Lightoller and other members of *Titanic*'s crew whenever they described the accident. Sailors almost universally claimed the ship "struck" the ice. In 1912, the verb *to strike* was reserved by seamen specifically to describe a ship running into the bottom—that is, going aground (even if the "ground" was ice). Striking was a common enough occurrence to warrant its own nautical word in 1912, prior to the invention of radar and other electronic navigation aids.

Based on the flooding that occurred during the first ten minutes, naval architect Wilding calculated the combined surface area of all of the openings through which the sea entered the main compartments above the tank top deck. He concluded that an aggregate hole with an area of 12 square feet was necessary to allow the correct amount of water into the ship. That is an opening only slightly larger than the front door of the average suburban house. Assuming Wilding was correct, the significance of this aggregate opening is its small area relative to the huge exterior surface of the ship. It is hard to imagine that ramming 52,310 displacement tons (actual weight) of ship into a mountain of ice would do so little damage over up to 300 linear feet of hull.

Bumping and grinding over the underwater shelf must have opened holes in the bottom considerably larger in area than 12 square feet. It is possible that some exterior plates may have been ripped off the ship. Photographs taken of QE2's bottom after its grounding give a hint of the type of punishment done to Titanic's brittle shell plating. After viewing the 1992 photos, it is easy to conclude that Titanic absorbed far more punishment than Wilding's calculations seem to indicate. Openings totalling more than 12 square feet must have been punched through the doomed liner's outer hull. Why the apparent discrepancy between Wilding's calculations and real-world experience?

It turns out there is none. Wilding calculated only the combined size of the holes that penetrated through the tank top deck and resulted in the flooding of the three holds and boiler room #6. These fatal holes should not be confused with the massive destruction that must have occurred to shell plating on the outside of the ship's bottom. Wilding ignored this exterior damage because it did not cause the interior hull to flood. He was interested only in the aggregate size of the openings that did allow the flooding. Holes that did not allow water into the holds and boiler rooms were of no consequence in the ship's ultimate foundering.

Ripping open the bottom from forepeak to the after end of boiler room #6 on the starboard side caused the immediate list noted by Captain Smith following the accident. This list is another indication that the ship ran over the ice and not into it. If the side of the vessel had been sliced open, incoming water would have flooded the full width of the hull, not just one side of the tankage. The bow would have tipped downward almost immediately, with negligible listing. In fact, the opposite happened. Titanic remained on a nearly even keel but quickly developed a 5-degree list to starboard.

This immediate listing was the logical result of extensive damage to the outer double bottom on the starboard side forward. Empty tank spaces (*voids*) inside the double bottom on the right side of the ship flooded instantly. Port side voids, protected by a watertight longitudinal along the keel, stayed dry. This unbalanced condition gave the ship more buoyancy on its port (left) side, resulting in an immediate starboard list.

Loss of buoyancy in the starboard tankage would not have caused the bow to tip downward significantly because the ship was about ten times longer than it was wide. *Titanic* lost buoyancy for half its 92.5-foot breadth beneath the first five compartments, but for less than a third of its 852.5-foot length. This disparity resulted in the ship listing quickly but not tipping down by the bow to the same degree. It took several minutes longer for the weight of water above the tankage to cause the bow to sag deeply into the water. Once the bow did tip, *Titanic* straightened its starboard lean and then listed to port. This change occurred when flooding of the larger main compartments above the tank top became the deciding factor in transverse stability.

The ship took alternate port and starboard cants as the night wore on. Toward the end, listing depended upon random flooding of the larger compartments above the tank top. At one point the ship took a pronounced lean to port. Alternate port and starboard listing of this type is known as *lolling*. It is typical of a damaged vessel that is losing transverse stability, or its ability to float upright.

The growing instability of *Titanic* was partially caused by the remaining buoyancy in the undamaged tankage forward. This buoyancy tried to push its way to the surface but could not do so because of flooded compartments above. Instead, the buoyancy tried to get around by rolling the hull to one side. Loss of stability in this manner is normal for a foundering ship. Second Officer Lightoller managed to get laughs from the gallery during the official British inquiry. His inquisitor was apparently unaware that ships can list either toward or away from damage as they flood and stability is lost.

MR. EDWARDS: Does not she usually list to the side from which the water is pouring in?

MR. LIGHTOLLER: Not necessarily.

MR. EDWARDS: Would you expect there would be a list to that side in which the water comes in, would you not?

MR. LIGHTOLLER: No.

MR. EDWARDS: Why not?

MR. LIGHTOLLER: Why should I? (laughter)

As it left the ice, *Titanic* immediately began floating on its inner bottom, the tank top deck. This was exactly what Wilding and the other naval architects at Harland and Wolff intended should happen in just such an emergency. The tank top deck in *Titanic* can be thought of as a "back-up bottom." Part of its purpose was to prevent the ship from flooding in case its real bottom was ever torn apart by a grounding on rocks or ice. Unfortunately, damage from scraping across the iceberg was not confined to the exterior plating. The vital inner bottom suffered openings as well, probably caused by stretching and cracking resulting from the displacement of longitudinal framing within the double bottom. This upward movement must have stretched or sheared rivets holding the steel plates of the tank top together. The damage at the foot of the spiral staircase inside the ship was minor compared to what occurred to the outer bottom, but it was sufficient to create substantial flooding in the three holds and allow significant water into boiler room #6.

An aggregate opening equal in area to 12 square feet did not likely result from the sprung seam described by stoker Barrett. Water entering through that seam did not cause significant flooding of boiler room #5, so the actual slit must have been quite narrow. If we assume the plates were pushed apart to a uniform width of one inch, it would have taken 114 linear feet of open seam to equal a 12-square-foot hole. Sonic imaging seems to indicate six open seams totaling 31 meters, or 101.7 feet. If these were the fatal damage, they would have had to be 1½ inches wide to have provided fatal ingress of water. In reality Barrett's sprung seam proved to be only a nuisance that did not flood boiler room #5. This indicates that while open seams above the tank top undoubtedly played a role in the flooding, they were not the fatal wounds.

Another problem with the sonic imaging is the location of the damage. Published drawings show the pattern of open seams follows the curve of the keel. That is, the damage is higher on the hull at the bow where the forefoot sweeps upward than it is along holds #2 and #3 and boiler room #6 where the keel is straight. Damage on the side of a ship caused by running into a fixed object follows a straight line parallel to the ship's waterline at the time of the impact. It does not follow the shape of the keel. Downward movement of the damage toward the stern could only have occurred if the ship took a massive list to port during impact with the berg. Nobody reported anything more than a gentle lifting of the starboard side, not the 25 feet or so of rise that would have been necessary to account for the pattern of opened seams. It is more likely that the sprung seams discovered by sonic imaging resulted from stress relief as the ship rode over the ice, or from the bow's 30-knot impact with the bottom, or a combination of both. Openings in the side are not likely the fatal damage. The place to look for that is in the double bottom, the tank top deck.

The mythical "300-foot gash" probably originated as idle chatter on the tilting decks of *Titanic.* Confused passengers huddling in the public rooms would have shared what few details they could learn or imagine about the accident. It quickly became common knowledge that the bow had been damaged by ice. Some passengers would have learned that flooded compartments extended nearly one-third of the ship's 882.5-foot length. One idle comment about "sliced open like a razor" and the idea of a huge gash would have been born. Of course, if there had been one continuous opening 300 feet long, it would have been like Niagara Falls tumbling into each compartment. The ship would have sunk before any lifeboats could have been launched.

The long gash made good headlines and seemed to explain the lack of impact during the accident. No less an authority than the U.S. Navy's hydrographer Captain John J. Knapp lent his authority to this explanation. He envisioned razor-sharp ice opening *Titanic* like a giant halberd.

> A comparison might be made to striking a sharp instrument at a glancing blow with the hand. There would be no apparent resisting shock. That part of the ice which cut into its outer skin was struck by the ship very much like the edge of a knife would be so struck by the hand.

Fatal damage to *Titanic* most likely resulted from a combination of the initial force of the grounding coupled with the inability of the vessel's structure to accept the twisting and flexing caused by running over an underwater ice shelf. The box girder structure of the bottom had been subjected to increasing strain as more of the ship's weight came on the ice. This strain caused the starboard side of the forward third of the hull to lift and flex. The portion grinding over the ice was higher than those sections ahead or behind that were not supported by the berg. An upward flex traveled along the forward third of the ship like a wave. (This was the upward lifting of the starboard side noted by lookout Lee.)

*Titanic*'s right turn caused the hull to slide off the berg as boiler room #6 was passing over the ice shelf. Sideways movement put particular strain at the turn of the bilge forward of the bulkhead between boiler rooms #5 and #6. A 1998 article by Dan Dietz, executive editor of *Mechanical Engineering* magazine, gives a hint as to why the inside damage was so much less than that to the outside shell plating. Dietz claimed the steel in *Titanic*'s decks had a finer grain structure than did the metal in the hull. If true, the decks would have been able to bend a bit more without breaking than the shell plating could. Dietz raised this issue as part of his theory of why the ship broke apart near the surface, but it is also possible that more ductile steel in the tank top deck actually reduced the damage.

Starting with Ballard, all of the adventurers who have made the perilous descent to *Titanic* have looked for "the gash." Such curiosity is human nature. Ballard's *The Discovery of the Titanic* shows the obligatory photograph of a sprung seam on the starboard side of the hull. This damage is indicated on an accompanying drawing as a jagged line through boiler room #6. The line is placed higher than stoker Frederick Barrett described, but the positioning in Ballard's book is likely the result of artistic license.

Later expeditions have used special side-scan echo sounding devices in high-tech attempts to find the elusive "fatal wound" in the shell plating of the ship's side. Not surprisingly, everyone has found what they sought: there are numerous open seams along the starboard bow. Chief among the visitors to the wreck has been RMS Titanic, a company holding the quaint title of "salvor-in-possession" of the ship. As such, it claims ownership of the rapidly disintegrating hulk.

George Tulloch, president of RMS Titanic, told television reporter Bryan Jackson that the greatest accomplishment of his company's expeditions was proving how the ship sank. He said the magnetic imaging and sonar imaging used in 1996 showed six small finger-sized cuts in the side plating of the bow. RMS Titanic has released electronic images of what appear to be damaged seams in the vertical single-thickness plating of starboard bow. Tulloch said company scientists used the presumably undamaged port side of the bow to set up its instrumentations before searching the starboard side. An undamaged port side would suggest that the damage Tulloch's expedition observed on the starboard side was caused by the iceberg as it passed along the side of the vessel.

Tulloch made an understandable leap of faith by saying the starboard side openings were caused directly by the iceberg. Unfortunately for the credibility of his claims, there seems to be equal evidence that the seams split open when the bow section smashed into the bottom after sinking. During visits to the wreckage site in the French submersible *Nautile*, Paul Matthias reportedly found more, not less, damage to the port bow than to the starboard bow. Matthias's observation was available from Discovery Channel Online in a report that claims there seems to be more damage on the port side than on the starboard side. Matthias is quoted as saying that he believes he was seeing not ice damage but crumpling due to impact with the ocean floor.

Whether or not there is more damage to the starboard side or to the port, these finger-size horizontal openings cannot be the fatal wounds. They simply are not big enough in aggregate size to equal the necessary 12 square feet of opening. Despite their sophisticated imaging equipment, none of the visitors to the wreck has yet found *Titanic*'s fatal wounds because they lie underneath the hull, buried in 60 feet of mud.

"Discoveries" made by undersea explorers are not news to anyone who has studied the 1912 evidence. The existence of open seams above the turn of the bilge has been known since the night of the sinking. However, the horizontal openings found by modern expeditions are almost certainly not the result of ice damage. They were more likely caused by *Titanic*'s second, and far more violent, collision that night: smashing into the ocean floor. Every subsea visitor to the bow has noted several obvious folds and distortions in the plating that are mute evidence of this second impact.

Ballard estimated that the bow section of *Titanic* was falling at up to 30 miles per hour when it plowed into the bottom. Water pressure from this forward motion is thought to have bent the ship's foremast back onto the top of the bridge, where it lies today. When the bow finally hit bottom, the force of impact was enough to plow it into the mud to a depth of almost 60 feet. Damage to a ship from such a crash is almost unimaginable because we have never seen it happen on the surface.

Because it requires getting underneath the ship, serious forensic analysis of the wreck remains impossible until the bow can be raised intact to the surface and taken ashore. Photos of the 1992 damage to QE2 show a series of rips and tears along the bottom plating. The ship struck several rocks, leaving multiple damage trails on either side of the keel, the longest extending 74 feet along the bottom. Most damage consisted of small cracks and tears, some only an inch wide and a few feet long. This pattern of damage to QE2's bottom is eerily similar to what naval architect Wilding speculated happened to Titanic in 1912. QE2 survived because it was built in 1967 of more malleable steel than that of Titanic, and the new ship was of all-welded construction.

Fatal damage did not necessarily mean the sudden death for Titanic that the British report implied. There is evidence from the ship's chief engineer that the pumps were successful in slowing the flooding of boiler room #6 during the first ten minutes after the accident. Pumping definitely was able to keep even with the inrush of water into boiler room #5. This is not to suggest that the ship would have floated indefinitely, only that Titanic might have floated as long as there was bunker coal to keep its pumps running. The ship could not founder until boiler room #6 flooded beyond the ability of the pumps, which does not appear to have happened until after 11:50 P.M.

During the first ten minutes after the accident, the ship's passengers and crew needed both outside help and time to survive. They got help, but the time needed was squandered by a fatal error in seamanship that pushed boiler room #6 under 8 feet of water.

# BLIND FAITH

Sunday, April 14, 1912

**11:41:35 P.M. to 11:51 P.M.**

**11:41:35 P.M.** I have assumed command of bridge from First Officer Murdoch. Watertight doors are closed. Engines stopped. —E. J. SMITH, Master

*ITANIC* shot past the iceberg even though the ship's speed was greatly reduced by the accident. Friction created by grinding on the ice shelf and momentum lost by "porting around" the berg had taken their toll on the ship's speed. Up to one-third of the 22.25 knots it had been making prior to the accident may have been lost while it was on the ice. The liner coasted away from the berg in a sweeping curve to the north at perhaps 13 to 15 knots. This 7- to 9-knot deceleration was significant for the huge ship, but it would have been virtually imperceptible to passengers because the loss of speed had been spread over more than a minute.

The berg was still alongside when First Officer William M. Murdoch started for the starboard bridge wing only to meet Captain Edward J. Smith emerging from his quarters. There was no need to call the captain now; he already knew that something unusual had occurred. "What have we struck?" the gray-bearded captain asked. *Titanic* had been dodging ice ever since his visit to the bridge at the end of Second Officer Charles H. Lightoller's watch, so Smith must have suspected the answer even before he left the warmth of his cabin.

"An iceberg" was the first officer's direct reply.

"Close the emergency doors."

"The doors are already closed."

"Did you ring the warning bells?"

"Yes."

Fourth Officer Joseph G. Boxhall had been just leaving the starboard entrance to the officers' quarters on the boat deck when the lookout's alarm bell sounded. He walked forward, toward the bridge, and was abreast of the captain's quarters when *Titanic* struck. Boxhall stepped into the bridge just as the captain was questioning Murdoch. "I put her hard a-starboard and rang the engine room for full astern, but it was too close," Boxhall claimed that Murdoch told the captain.

"She hit it." Boxhall made these comments in testimony to the U.S. probe and repeated his story almost word-for-word to the British proceedings. Based on what Boxhall said, this is what nearly every history of the accident claims happened that night. The standard hypothesis is that slamming the propellers into reverse prevented Murdoch from steering around the iceberg. The hard fact is that Boxhall's account was wrong. Murdoch never attempted a crash stop.

There are only two logical possibilities for why the ship's engines did not slam into reverse. One is that engineers disobeyed the "astern full" order that Boxhall claimed was telegraphed from the bridge. Such a quasi-mutiny is unlikely, however. *Titanic's* engineers followed every other order that evening so loyally they were lost to a man when the ship sank. This performance would tend to suggest that all of Murdoch's engine orders were obeyed. If there were no mutiny, the remaining logical possibility is that a crash stop was never requested. Except for Boxhall's statements, all other evidence shows that Murdoch told the engineers simply to stop their engines, not the ship.

Boxhall may have made an honest mistake in recalling the exact words spoken, but it is more likely that he chose his words deliberately to present events in their most positive light. The general public would understand a crash stop to avoid the iceberg. This was the obvious thing to do in the eyes of nonseafarers, who would be unaware that such a maneuver would have caused the ship to skid sideways into the iceberg. What Boxhall must have heard Murdoch say was "I rang the engine room for *all stop*." This more logical order would have reduced the ship's forward drive with the least amount of steering loss possible under the circumstances. It also matches the engine telegraph orders that members of the crew in the engine spaces remembered coming down from the bridge.

Greaser Frederick Scott was in the engine room at the opposite end of the telegraphs from Murdoch on the bridge. "I noticed STOP first," he told the British proceedings, "on the main engines." Murdoch's orders came down on both the main engine order telegraphs and on what Scott described as an "emergency" set. "All four went together: *Stop*. Two greasers at the bottom rang back. They were feeding the engines and were close handy at the time," Scott said.

Revising Boxhall's version of events from a "crash stop" to a simple "all stop" resolves a handful of issues: it allows for the lack of vibration and noise from a crash stop; it accounts for the ship's coasting forward after the accident; it closely matches the actions to be expected of a seasoned deck officer; it permits the "port around" maneuver Murdoch said he used to prevent damage to the ship's entire starboard side; and it matches what eyewitnesses in the engine and boiler rooms experienced.

Murdoch slightly reduced the force of the impact that he knew was coming by shutting down the engines. Probably he was also thinking ahead, preparing engineers for the crash stop he must have anticipated making after the ship "ported around" the iceberg. As late as the instant of impact, Murdoch must have been expecting *Titanic* to slide into that dense pack of ice after clearing the iceberg. (This was the same field ice that surrounded *Californian* a few miles to the north.) Based on his actions, Murdoch apparently intended to swerve around the berg, then do a crash stop to keep out of the ice field that lay behind the deadly floating ice mountain.

However, the rapid pivoting of *Titanic* on top of the berg combined with the ship's continuing curve to the right as it coasted after the accident eventually brought the hull roughly parallel to the edge of the tightly packed field ice. Murdoch's anticipated crash stop became unnecessary and so was never performed. The two giant "up-and-down" steam engines simply rolled to a halt about the time Murdoch met Captain Smith after the accident. Without thrust from its three propellers, the ship gradually lost speed as it coasted forward.

One comment Murdoch did make comes to us apparently unaltered through Boxhall. "I intended to port around it," Murdoch explained, "but she hit before I could do anything more." These words are traditionally interpreted to mean that he intended to swerve around the berg but never accomplished the maneuver. The standard version of the story holds that the ship struck before the first officer had time to complete the second half of his swerving S-turn. The physics that control the way ships steer demand otherwise. Murdoch must have completed "porting around" the berg because *Titanic* damaged only its starboard bow. If Murdoch had failed to port around, damage would have occurred along the starboard side from about the bridge to the stern.

There were witnesses to Murdoch's cool shiphandling: observers on *Californian*, which had been trapped earlier that evening by the same densely packed ice field, watched the liner swerve around the iceberg. Shortly after 11:00 P.M. (*Californian* time, which was about ten minutes behind *Titanic*'s clocks), *Californian*'s second officer, Charles Groves, saw the lights of a large steamer to his south approaching from the east. "There was absolutely no doubt about her being a passenger steamer, at least in my mind," he testified before the London proceedings.

*Californian*'s captain, Stanley Lord, immediately identified the stranger. "That will be the *Titanic* on her maiden voyage," he told Groves, who responded that the ship had apparently stopped and turned out her lights. Captain Lord remained in his cabin and did not come on deck to observe the lights personally. He based his identification on the aborted attempt to warn the new liner by wireless of ice in its path. At about 11:30 P.M. *Californian* time (11:40 P.M. *Titanic* time), the other ship appeared to stop and turn out most of its deck lights. Groves commented that he did not think this was the sort of behavior expected from a large North Atlantic passenger liner. "Well, the only passenger steamer near us is the *Titanic*," Lord answered.

*Titanic*, of course, had not turned out its lights. It had rotated sharply to starboard. Instead of presenting its brightly lighted broadside to *Californian*, the liner was now showing its relatively narrow, dark bow, which was devoid of lights to avoid blinding its own lookouts. Groves could no longer see a mass of illuminated portholes and deck lights. Groves noted that he could see the white masthead light and red (port) sidelight of this stranger. That pattern of navigation lights meant the other ship must have been heading just east of north—exactly the course *Titanic* took after it swerved around the iceberg.

**11:41:45 P.M.** Engineers venting steam from boiler room #6.

—J. MOODY, Sixth Officer

A shriek from steam vent pipes on funnel #1 suddenly shattered the midocean quiet of *Titanic*'s decks. One or more courageous men in boiler room #6 had had enough presence of mind to realize that the cold water washing over the stokehold deck plates could spell instant doom for the ship. Freezing water striking a hot boiler, it was believed, would cause a massive explosion. Some unknown hero must have taken it on his own initiative to pause during his headlong rush to escape the flooding compartment. With water swirling around his knees, he stopped long enough to open the vent line. Venting started too soon after the accident for instructions from the senior engineer in the reciprocating engine room to have reached the damaged boiler room.

One by one, those passengers who were awake noticed the familiar vibrations of the massive power plant disappear. In stateroom C-70, Jack Thayer had been enjoying a breeze through his room's porthole. It stopped. René Harris, wife of Broadway theatrical producer Henry B. Harris, wondered why clothes in the closet of C-83 were no longer swaying. Lawrence Beesley, in D-56, was concerned when his mattress stopped moving to the pounding of the engines.

The ship coasted forward during the minutes immediately after the accident while Boxhall, Murdoch, and Smith peered astern for a glimpse of the berg. It was during this period that Second Officer Lightoller claimed he poked his head out of the officers' quarters. He could see his two superiors looking aft, but otherwise everything appeared normal.

> I instantly leapt out of my bunk and ran out on deck, in my pajamas; peered over the port side, but could see nothing there; ran across to the starboard side, but neither was there anything there, and as the cold was cutting like a knife, I hopped back into my bunk.

Somehow this explanation for remaining in his cabin does not fit Lightoller. Given his career history, he should have voluntarily appeared on the bridge immediately following the accident, even if he was wearing pajamas. On this particular night, however, he started for the bridge and then deliberately went back to his cabin. He claimed that curiosity was not enough motive for an officer to barge onto the bridge when he was not on duty. It was a strange decision for a man who was always at the center of the action during the rest of his seafaring career. He seems to have deliberately chosen to disassociate himself physically from both the bridge and the decisions made there.

**11:42 P.M.** Ship has taken 5-degree list to starboard. Carpenter told to sound the bow and report damage. Engineers venting more steam.

—E. J. SMITH, Master

Whether Captain Smith ever saw the fatal berg is unknown. He rushed to the bridge from his lighted cabin, so his eyes would not have been adjusted to the darkness, leaving him somewhat night blind. After a few seconds peering into the darkness, he returned to the protection of the captain's bridge, where he caught sight of Quartermaster Alfred Olliver. "Find the carpenter," Smith ordered Olliver. "Tell him to begin sounding the ship for damage."

A *clinometer* is a small instrument that measures the amount of list ("lean") on a ship. *Titanic's* was mounted on the primary binnacle just below the compass, so Captain Smith had to step into the wheelhouse to read this instrument. According to the clinometer, *Titanic* already had a 5-degree list to starboard. Confirmation of the list came from Quartermaster Hitchens in his U.S. Senate testimony. Within five minutes of the accident, the helmsman told Senator William Alden Smith, "the Captain . . . came back to the wheelhouse and looked at the commutator in front of the compass, which is a little instrument like a clock to tell you how the ship is listing. The ship had a list of five degrees to starboard."

**11:43 P.M.** Fourth Officer Boxhall sent forward to check on passengers there.
—E. J. SMITH, Master

An immediate list within moments of the accident confirmed for Captain Smith that his ship had received some damage. His next thought was for the safety of his passengers. Boxhall was quickly dispatched on a check of third-class passengers sleeping near the bow. To accomplish his errand, the young fourth officer had to skip down the starboard stairway to the bridge deck. From there another stairway led down to the forward well deck, where passengers were already skylarking with chunks of ice from the berg. Boxhall pushed into the third-class entrance under the forecastle head.

To the London inquiry, he described his trip "through a staircase under the port side of the forecastle head which takes me down into D deck, and then aft along D deck to just underneath the bridge, and down the staircase there on the port side, and then I went down on E deck near E deck doors, the working alleyway; and then you cross over to the starboard side of E deck and go down another accommodation staircase on to F deck. I am not sure whether I went lower. Anyhow, I went as low as I could possibly get."

Meanwhile, Carpenter John Hutchinson was already at work, apparently accompanying the ship's builder, Thomas Andrews, on a tour of the damage. Hutchinson was looking for flooding when

Quartermaster Olliver found him in a working alleyway (a corridor) forward. The two spoke briefly before officer headed back to the bridge where more errands awaited. The carpenter turned to check on the situation in the ship's post office, where he was told that the mail room on the orlop deck in hold #3 was already wet.

First Officer Murdoch remained as officer of the watch for another half hour, but at this point he fades as the central character in the story. He still has work to do supervising the loading of the starboard side lifeboats, and he will meet his fate in the icy North Atlantic in less than three hours. Before that happens, now is the time to assess what he accomplished by "porting around" the iceberg.

His instantaneous reaction to the final warning from the crow's nest prevented *Titanic* from plowing headlong into the berg. Critics say that swerving around the ice preserved a few hundred lives at the expense of more than 1,500 a few hours later. This criticism ignores that when Captain Smith came on the bridge, there had been no passenger casualties and *Titanic* was still floating on an even keel with only a slight list. If Murdoch's goal was to save lives, he succeeded.

It is unfortunate that a decision made by his superiors some ten minutes after the accident rendered Murdoch's cool shiphandling irrelevant. As will be shown, Murdoch is innocent of blame for the horrible death toll. The more than 1,500 deaths of that night were the result of actions taken by Captain Smith and J. Bruce Ismay after they took direct command of the wounded ship.

According to myth, *Titanic*'s engines never rolled again. At least that is the version of events presented by the surviving officers. A completely contradictory story was told by passengers who were awake and crew members who were on duty. They insisted that the ship steamed away from the scene of its accident. However, everyone agreed the engines were stopped for about ten minutes after the collision while the wounded liner glided in a sweeping curve to the north.

The exact moment when Ismay appeared on the bridge wearing a  11:44 P.M dress coat over his pajamas was not recorded. Based on the events Ismay later described in testimony, it must have been just after Fourth Officer Boxhall was dispatched on his trip forward. As president of International Mercantile Marine and managing director of the White Star Line, Ismay was effectively *Titanic*'s owner. He was taking this trip ostensibly as a passenger, although his de facto role was cocaptain with Edward J. Smith, the titular master.

"I presume the impact awakened me," he later told Senator Smith at the U.S. Senate hearings. "I lay in bed for a moment or two afterwards, not realizing, probably, what had happened."

Ismay wandered into the corridor outside his posh suite (B-52), where he met a steward. "I got up and walked along the passageway and met one of the stewards, and said, 'what happened?' He said, 'I do not know, sir.'" Not satisfied with that answer, Ismay returned to his stateroom, where he slipped an overcoat over his nightclothes and headed straight for the bridge. He met Captain Smith on the bridge just after Murdoch's report. We can only imagine their conversation:

"What happened?" Ismay asked.

"We have struck ice," Smith replied.

"Do you think the ship is seriously damaged?"

"I am afraid she may be."

*Titanic* was not gliding silently as Ismay climbed to the bridge. Fearing an explosion if cold seawater were to hit the hot boilers, engineers began venting steam. Almost immediately steam came from boiler room #6. Within minutes, it started to vent from boiler room #5, which was also open to the sea. Vent pipes ran up the outsides of the funnels. Intended for letting off pressure in port or when the boilers were shut down, this night the pipes served a more urgent purpose. High pressure steam venting from the twenty-four working boilers eventually created such a screech that conversation on the boat deck became nearly impossible. The roar of steam escaping into the cold night air became an indelible memory of survivors who ventured on deck.

11:46:30 P.M.    The iceberg wrongly gets all of the attention of books, movies, and TV documentaries, because the crucial event of the *Titanic* tragedy actually occurred several minutes after the accident. The pivotal event that night was a decision to get the ship moving again. This decision (in which First Officer Murdoch apparently played no part) led to rapid flooding of the bow and ultimately to the horrible loss of life. Considering the personalities of the men involved, it is tempting to speculate that the fatal decision was proposed by an agitated J. Bruce Ismay and accepted by a reluctant Captain Smith. However, which man proposed making way again is not important because both agreed to the plan. Their wounded ship would resume steaming.

Ismay's reasons for wanting to make way again can only be surmised from events of his life prior to that night on *Titanic*. He was, in modern terms, a "pusher." His visionary father started White Star Line and was instrumental in developing the modern ocean liner. The son took over management of the company, then sold it to the American tycoon J. Pierpont Morgan. The junior Ismay finagled a deal that made him president of Morgan's maritime operations, International Mercantile Marine, and managing director of White Star Line.

Ismay was not a sailor, a naval architect, an engineer, or a shipbuilder. He was an aristocrat—an inheritor of position—in an era when amateurism was a British national passion. Robert Falcon Scott was about to march to an icy death in Antarctica for the same reason that Ismay was about to steam his ship into oblivion: the British belief in upper-class amateurs "muddling through" on their social superiority. *Titanic* represented twentieth-century technology bursting through those old ideas. This massive ship required large numbers of educated, skilled people making professional decisions beyond the capacity of well-intentioned amateurs. Ismay may have been an anachronism, but on this night he was still in charge.

The Olympic-class ships had been largely Ismay's project with encouragement from Lord James Pirrie, who was a major partner in the Harland and Wolff shipyard. The concept of the Olympics was to "go one better" Cunard's high-speed competition, *Lusitania* and *Mauritania*. From the beginning the Olympics were to be bigger, more opulent, and more comfortable than the competition. They were not, however, to be faster. (*Mauritania* held the Atlantic speed record for twenty-two years.) Both Cunard ships had received naval subsidies to defray the costs of their high-speed engines and other modifications intended to turn them into armored cruisers during time of war.

We can only suppose Ismay's purpose for planning the high-speed publicity stunt described earlier. His goal may have been to make *Titanic* appear faster than even its owners expected. If the world's largest ship could not win the Atlantic speed record, at least it could appear to be so incredibly fast that even White Star's published schedule could not keep up with it. The increasing speeds desired by Ismay throughout the voyage also indicate he definitely wanted *Titanic* to beat *Olympic*'s best time for the crossing to New York.

Ismay would still have had these thoughts on his mind as the damaged ship slid to a stop.

Far from events on the bridge, the engineers, stokers, and trimmers in the boiler rooms began to recover from the initial shock of the accident. The lights were back on. Junior Second Engineer J. H. Hesketh yelled to the men in boiler room #5, "All hands stand by your stations." Stoker Frederick Barrett and engineer John Shepherd started back for boiler room #6. The usual route through the bulkhead was blocked by the automatic watertight door, so the men had to climb a series of escape ladders. It was a long three-deck climb up the inside of the boiler casing to a doorway, which opened into a wide corridor on the port side of E deck. 11:48 P.M.

To Ismay's chagrin, any speed exhibition by *Titanic* was now obviously impossible. His magnificent ship was sitting in the middle of the Atlantic with what he must have viewed as the nautical equivalent of a bloody nose. This situation was definitely not to the White Star general manager's liking, and he was not the sort of man to sit around waiting for somebody to come to his rescue. Ismay needed a bold stroke to turn a public relations disaster into victory. It must have occurred to him that he could accomplish this quite simply by having the ship rescue itself.

Steaming to safety would have been stunning proof that claims of unsinkability for Olympic-class ships were true. If it had succeeded in reaching Halifax, *Titanic* would have appeared to be invincible. Ismay was shrewd enough to know that reporters would have overlooked the cause of the accident and focused on the amazing self-rescue. The resulting publicity would have made Olympic-class ships appear to be the safest in the world. From his point of view, this "unsinkable" ship had to get moving again as quickly as possible.

Analyzing Ismay's motives from ninety-odd years distant is a risky undertaking. The man cannot speak for himself. Our view of him has been forever colored by the tragic loss of more than 1,500 souls. We know that Ismay was wrong when he decided to move the ship, and we know that he should have been interested only in saving as many lives as possible. In three hours he would know this, too. But at the time of his decision to resume steaming, no one aboard *Titanic* was aware of the horror to come.

The discussion between Ismay and Captain Smith was not recorded. In fact, any hint of this conversation was carefully avoided

119

in testimony before both government probes despite the fact that the two men huddled together on the bridge and Ismay admitted they spoke to each other. Their talk of making way again was probably polite and formal, in keeping with the manner of the age. It may have turned heated if they argued over the condition of the ship. We know the outcome of this conversation even though we do not know the details. A wounded *Titanic* hauled itself slowly northward despite extensive damage to its bottom and flooding of at least four of its sixteen primary watertight compartments.

The ship is usually described as having sixteen watertight compartments created by its fifteen main bulkheads, a description that is only partially true. The interior of the hull did have sixteen primary compartments. However, the number of smaller cells beneath *Titanic's* tank top greatly increased the watertight subdivision of the vessel. In all, there were seventy-three watertight compartments, forty-four contained within the double bottom. Few current passenger ships have more subdivision than Olympic-class vessels did.

The Achilles heel of the Olympic-class vessel, of course, was the height of the fifteen main bulkheads above the tank top. For aesthetic reasons, they did not reach all the way to the weather deck. Passenger comfort demanded free access throughout the ship. A 12-foot-wide corridor on the port side of E deck allowed easy fore and aft passage for third-class passengers. This corridor joined the single men's berths in the bow with similar accommodations for single women in the stern, creating an unbroken passageway nearly the full length of the ship to a watertight door at the reciprocating engine casing. A similar but narrower corridor gave access to first-class staterooms on the starboard side of the ship.

Once water rose to E deck, these two corridors became aqueducts carrying it over top of the compartments below. There was nothing to stop water from rolling over the bulkheads aft of boiler room #4 and filling those compartments from above. Ironically, *Titanic* sank because water poured down from above, not up through the bottom. *Titanic's* bulkheads were only high enough to give adequate freeboard if the hull were damaged by collision with another vessel. The worst scenario envisioned was a "T-bone" collision, in which another ship rammed the hull at a right angle. If the impact took place on a bulkhead, two compartments would be open to the sea.

According to the British inquiry, *Titanic* and her sister ships would have remained safely afloat in such a situation:

> it was arranged that the bulkheads and divisions should be so placed that the ship would remain afloat in the event of any two adjoining compartments being flooded. The minimum freeboard that the vessel would have, in the event of any two compartments being flooded, was between 2 ft. 6 in. and 3 ft. . . .

Naval architects at Harland and Wolff were correct in claiming that extensive subdivision provided Olympic-class vessels with an extraordinary margin of safety for 1912. Still, *Titanic* could not get past its iceberg. The ship was severely if not fatally injured during about seven seconds of bumping and grinding over an underwater ice shelf.

During the first minutes after the accident, pumping gave the appearance of being adequate to keep the ship afloat for an extended period. Chief Engineer Joseph G. Bell made this observation to Ismay at about 11:54 P.M., more than ten minutes after the accident. If Bell's view of the situation was correct, the wounded liner should have been floating well into the next dawn. This would have allowed enough time to transfer passengers to *Carpathia*, or any of the other ships that answered the liner's eventual distress call. If *Titanic* had floated that long, it would have fulfilled the designers' expectations for it to be its own lifeboat.

**11:49 P.M.** Captain Smith allows watertight doors aft of Boiler Room #5 to be opened per request from Chief Engineer Bell. Flooding reported in forward holds and Boiler Room #6. Water reported entering Boiler Room #5. Ship nearly stopped on heading of 010°.          —J. MOODY, Sixth Officer

The British report on the sinking claimed that boiler room #6 flooded to a depth greater than 8 feet, and that boiler room #5 had water shooting into it during the first ten minutes after the accident while Ismay and Smith discussed making way again. Based on what engineers and stokers accomplished in preventing a boiler explosion, the British assessment of the flooding must be wrong with regard to boiler room #6. Circumstantial evidence indicates that this compartment did not flood to a depth of 8 feet until after the ship resumed steaming about twenty minutes after the accident, not the ten minutes that Lord Mersey's report claimed.

The flooding of the watertight compartments forward of the boiler rooms probably took place as described in the British report, although these rooms were unmanned holds and their conditions cannot be determined with certainty. We do know that the watertight pipe tunnel and fireman's passage through these holds flooded immediately after the accident, likely from damage to the tank top deck. The flooding of this passageway may have contributed to high water levels in the three holds forward of boiler room #6.

We can surmise that information coming to the bridge from the engine room must have been reassuring during the first ten minutes after the accident. Chief Engineer Bell requested Captain Smith to shut off the electricity holding the automatic watertight doors locked. The doors were kept closed by the electric current from the bridge to prevent unauthorized opening during an emergency.

It quickly became obvious to Bell and his men that compartments aft of boiler room #5 were not flooding. Closed watertight doors between those spaces prevented engineers from rigging suction lines to stem the flooding forward. Bell's request to unlock the doors was a natural part of damage control efforts. It was not a statement about the condition of the ship, even though that is likely how it was perceived on the bridge. Bell's request to open the doors may have indicated to Captain Smith that the majority of *Titanic*'s hull was uncompromised by the accident.

Moving a damaged ship before it had been thoroughly sounded for damage was definitely not the ordinary practice of seamen. Nor was it the action to be expected of a seasoned veteran such as E. J. Smith. Whether the damage was great or small, *Titanic* was no longer on its way to New York and there was no advantage in risking lives by rushing to Halifax. The only plausible explanation for restarting the engines prior to the report from the carpenter is pressure from the man who stood opposite the captain: his boss, J. Bruce Ismay. Whether or not the captain succumbed to Ismay's pressure and resumed steaming will always remain a mystery, but the IMM president and White Star chairman did have a powerful hold on Smith. Proof of that is Ismay's meddling in the operation of the ship, particularly with regard to speed.

Smith's willingness to honor Ismay's demands may be why he led a charmed life at White Star, where he was said to be the highest-paid captain in the world. The collision a few months earlier with

*Olympic* might have put another caption on the beach. Then there was the prospect of retirement. *Titanic* was not to be Captain Smith's last command. He planned to retire sometime after commanding the third Olympic-class vessel on its maiden voyage. Once he did retire, however, his comfortable retirement income would have come from a White Star pension, also controlled by Ismay.

Pressure from Ismay is likely the reason *Titanic* resumed steaming as early as it did. However, Captain Smith was probably quite willing to resume making way. Based on comments he made during the months prior to *Titanic*, Smith could not imagine that this colossus of steel and steam could be ripped apart. Speaking about *Adriatic*, a smaller ship, the captain stated confidently that he could not conceive of a modern ship being lost at sea:

> I cannot imagine any condition which would cause a ship to founder. I cannot conceive of any vital disaster happening to this vessel. Modern shipbuilding has gone beyond all that.

The captain's inflated belief in the invincibility of modern ships was not immediately challenged by the accident. For ten minutes after the berg passed astern, *Titanic* lived up to Smith's expectations. Everything above the boiler rooms seemed normal. Passengers still slept in warm beds. Late-night card games resumed. Even bad news relayed by telephone from the stokeholds was not all that bad. Only boiler room #6 was flooding fast enough that it might have to be abandoned. The engine rooms were dry and ready, in sailor jargon, to "answer bells."

When Quartermaster Olliver returned to the bridge from his errand to the carpenter, Captain Smith would have been in deep discussion with Ismay. Olliver probably remained at a respectful distance. The captain did not ask Olliver for a report, and the quartermaster did not volunteer information about the flooding. This meant that Captain Smith was not only wrong in his assessment of *Titanic*'s ability to shrug off damage, but that he had access to information proving that he was wrong. If Smith had asked Olliver, the quartermaster's answer would likely have delayed the ship's making way again until carpenter John Hutchinson's full report of the damage had been received. And, not even Bruce Ismay would have considered attempting to make way in light of the flooding already taking place in the first four compartments of the bow.

11:49:30 P.M.

Eight decks below, it had not taken long for Hutchinson to learn the truth. The flooding was obvious. He was returning from checking the mail room when he passed first-class stewardess Annie Robinson, who also had been aroused by the accident. "The man looked absolutely bewildered, distracted. He did not speak," Robinson described Hutchinson to the British inquiry. "He came along when I was looking down at the water. And, he had a lead line in his hands."

Hutchinson passed lamp trimmer Samuel Hemming in the crew's quarters beneath the forecastle on E deck. "She is making water in holds 1, 2, and 3, and the racquet court," the carpenter said. Shortly after that encounter, the visibly upset carpenter saw boatswain A. Nicholls. "Turn out," Hutchinson said. "The ship has half an hour to live, from Mr. Andrews. Don't tell anyone, keep it to ourselves."

Hutchinson's mention of Thomas Andrews is significant. Andrews was aboard as a representative of the company that built the ship, Harland & Wolff. He had supervised construction and knew *Titanic* better than any other man. From what the carpenter said, it appears Andrews felt the initial shock of the accident and went forward to investigate, probably gathering Hutchinson along the way. Andrews would have walked forward on E deck, where he would have met stokers climbing out of boiler room #6 about opposite to the carpenter's cabin. This personal investigation of the damage is the most likely reason why Andrews did not arrive on the bridge until some twenty minutes after the accident.

**11:50 P.M.**  Fourth Officer Boxhall completed his inspection and retraced his route to the bridge. He bounded up the various stairways and was probably puffing a bit while he made his report to the captain. "I found no damage. I found no indications that the ship had damaged herself," the fourth officer later testified to the U.S. Senate about his report to Captain Smith. This would be the last positive news delivered to *Titanic*'s bridge. Boxhall's destination had been to the third-class men's accommodations, which were located above the ship's waterline. Given the contact *Titanic* experienced on the ice, it was unlikely that any damage would have been found here. The energetic young officer seems to have been in the wrong place.

Or was he?

The weak explanation that Boxhall was looking for ice damage is generally accepted as the purpose for his trip. However, at 11:43 P.M., when the fourth officer started on his errand, Captain Smith had been less interested in the condition of his ship than he was in the condition of passengers at the epicenter of the impact. Third-class male passengers sleeping in the bow were those most likely to have been injured or killed. A large number of steerage casualties would have caused unrest or even panic among the other third-class passengers. One thing the captain did not need was panic spreading through steerage, where a considerable percentage of the people did not speak English. Smith was legally and morally correct in being most concerned about his passengers. After determining they were safe, he properly turned his attention back to the condition of his ship.

The captain was uneasy. He immediately asked the fourth officer to get a report from Hutchinson, the carpenter, even though Quartermaster Olliver had barely returned from his errand to request the carpenter to sound the ship. Boxhall's second mission shows that Smith was satisfied with the condition of his passengers but had doubts about the amount of ice damage. Unfortunately, an anxious Ismay was standing at the captain's shoulder. Boxhall's satisfactory report about conditions in third class was the final bit of information that Ismay needed to override any reluctance to begin moving the damaged ship before receiving the carpenter's report on the extent of damage.

Faith in the so-called "unsinkable" ship was still unshaken as late as 11:50 P.M. Only the list to starboard and the barely perceptible downward tip of the bow gave any hint of the massive damage below the waterline. Otherwise, *Titanic* appeared sound. Based on faith, and on Boxhall's first report, both *Titanic*'s commander and owner agreed to begin making way again.

The wounded ship did not resume course for New York, nor did it resume full speed. Instead, Smith appears to have wisely headed for the closest port—Halifax, Nova Scotia—some 450 miles north-northwest. The field of packed ice a few hundred yards west of the ship prevented it from steaming directly to the Canadian port, however. Until dawn, it was safest to head a bit east of north along the edge of the ice field. Witnesses said *Titanic*'s speed was bare steerageway, about 8 knots (9 land miles per hour) as it drew away from both the deadly berg and the line of ice.

Running *over* an underwater ice shelf rather than into the side of the iceberg is a key factor in the two men's decision to head for the closest port. They knew the outer bottom had taken the brunt of the blow. They also knew that *Titanic*'s second bottom, the tank top deck, had been specifically designed to keep the liner afloat if the outer shell became damaged. The ship was designed to float and operate with the tank top deck serving as an inner bottom. On this night, Smith and Ismay simply put too much faith in the inner bottom to keep their ship dry. Their decision was based on a logical, if erroneous, assumption that *Titanic* was relatively sound as it headed northward with steam blasting from its vents.

Halifax was the only possible destination. In addition to being closer than New York, this Nova Scotia port had other attractions for Ismay. It was a major port with facilities that could be stretched to handle the sudden influx of people from the crippled liner. Rail connections would make it possible to get passengers to their final destinations. Also, Halifax was not a major city with a sophisticated network of reporters and wire services. It would be much easier to control the flow of news about the ship in Halifax than it would in the media center of New York.

A basic precept of safe navigation is to never make assumptions, especially assumptions based on scanty information. Ismay and Smith assumed their ship was safe to steam again based on Boxhall's visit to the third-class berths and on scanty information about the extent of damage and the ability of the pumps to cope with the flooding. *Titanic* was more seriously damaged than its two commanders assumed when they started it moving under its own power again. The two men should have waited another quarter hour or so while the engineer and architect who supervised the building of the ship, Thomas Andrews, made a thorough damage inspection. Ismay was not noted for his patience, however.

**11:51 P.M.** Ahead Slow ordered on engines. Course 010. In accordance with Mr. Ismay's desires, we will endeavor to land passengers at Halifax before returning to Belfast for repairs.                                             —E. J. SMITH, Master

According to Quartermaster Olliver, Captain Smith himself stepped to the engine order telegraphs. "Ahead slow" rang down to the engine room. Moments later, *Titanic* was making way for the last time. The course was slightly east of north, shaped to run parallel to the ice field laying to the west. There would be no more close encounters with icebergs. Vibration from the engines confirmed Lightoller's resolve to remain in his cabin.

> to go dashing up to the Bridge in night rig, or even properly clothed, when not on duty, was bound to ensure anything but a hearty welcome. Another thing, to be elsewhere than where you are expected to be found . . . would result in the man who is sent to call you, being utterly unable to find you. So I just waited.

Just as the *QE2* incident in 1992 provided a second experiment regarding the impact of a grounding on passengers, *Titanic*'s younger sister, *Britannic*, provided a second experiment confirming that Olympic-class ships could be driven into their graves. Construction of the third (and last) Olympic had just begun in April 1912. Originally to be called *Gigantic*, the third ship's name was changed after the *Titanic* disaster. Britannic was completed just in time to become a hospital ship during World War I. Steaming through the Mediterranean on November 21, 1916, it struck an antiship mine and received damage remarkably similar to that suffered by *Titanic*. Five forward compartments were opened to the sea. At least one watertight door was reportedly jammed open by the blast.

Captain Charles Bartlett (curiously known as "Iceberg Charlie" to his crew) made the same mistake that Captain Smith did. He decided to drive his wounded ship toward the nearby Greek island of Kea. Bartlett hoped that *Britannic*'s speed would get it into shallow water, where it could be beached before it sank. He was wrong. Pressure from forward motion drove water into the ship until it overwhelmed the bulkheads. *Britannic* plunged bow downward into the Mediterranean in a high-speed replay of *Titanic*. Still-rotating propellers crunched a lifeboat as some of the crew attempted an unauthorized escape. Just like Captain Smith, Bartlett failed to save his Olympic-class ship. Bartlett's mistake serves as a second, forceful reminder proving that when an Olympic-class ship with a damaged bow is driven forward—it sinks.

# STEAMING TO OBLIVION

Sunday, April 14, to Monday, April 15, 1912

**11:51:30 P.M. to 12:09 A.M.**

**11:51:30 P.M.** Wirelessed New York of plan to discharge passengers at Halifax.

—E. J. SMITH, Master

LIFE in stokeholds aft of flooding boiler room #6 was dry but confusing during the first ten minutes after the vessel struck on the iceberg. The natural result of the accident and flooding, this confusion was compounded by orders from the engine room that seemed to conflict with the damaged condition of the ship. Fireman Thomas ("Paddy") Dillon was still struggling to shut the firebox dampers and draw the fires when the lights and bells on the Kilroy electric stoking indicators flashed and rang. The engine room was telling the black gang to "keep up the steam" despite obvious flooding. The men around Dillon shrugged and then began stoking the fires again.

Greaser Frederick Scott recalled the same unexpected orders in his testimony. Unlike Dillon's work, however, Scott's work placed him in contact with the ship's engines, where he could see why it became necessary to keep up steam pressure in the dry boiler rooms. Scott remembered the engines rolling again at "ahead slow" for at least ten minutes. His recollection was supported by Dillon, who later testified that the engines restarted and then ran for several minutes.

Quartermaster Alfred Olliver saw orders to restart the engines sent down by the telegraphs from the bridge. "The *Titanic* went half speed ahead. The Captain telegraphed half speed ahead," Olliver testified to the U.S. Senate hearing. He did not recall whether the engines were stopped at the time of that order or were working slowly astern. He was certain *Titanic* was almost dead in the water when it started moving for the last time.

Olliver's statement about telegraphing "half speed ahead" begs more information than is contained in the available documents. If true, Captain Smith called for a faster speed than bare steerageway. This would have been foolhardy in any damaged ship, even one still believed to be unsinkable. It is possible that urging from J. Bruce Ismay caused Captain Smith to signal "half ahead," but Chief Engineer Joseph G. Bell responded with a much slower speed adapted to the ship's damaged condition and dwindling steam pressure. Another possible answer to the speed mystery is language confusion. *Titanic*'s "bare steerageway" speed was roughly one-third of the speed it had been making prior to the accident. Olliver may have been referring to that fact, not to the printed words on the sides of the drumlike engine order telegraphs. If this was the case, there is no confusion surrounding the speed of the ship. Everyone seems to have agreed that the ship moved slower than half of its cruising speed.

In the wheelhouse, Quartermaster Robert Hitchens must have been told to "steady up" on the ship's heading of just east of north. Otherwise, *Titanic* would have steamed in a giant circle with the full right rudder given by Murdoch as he "ported around" the iceberg. Hitchens was kept at the wheel for more than forty minutes after the accident, a position that would have been unnecessary if the ship had not been moving. No amount of rudder movement has an effect on the heading of a stopped ship. Yet, Hitchens was kept at his usual post instead of being sent to help uncover lifeboats or launch distress rockets. The only logical reason Hitchens remained at the wheel was to steer the ship after it resumed making way following the accident.

It has been suggested that Captain Smith resumed steaming in an attempt to reach the twinkling lights of *Californian*. If this had been true, Ismay would surely have claimed that the ship sank itself during a desperate race to save the passengers' lives. Such a race would have transformed a blatant example of bad seamanship into a failed act of courage. Unfortunately, *Californian* does not appear to have been the destination. The small freighter had not been noticed from the crippled *Titanic* when the liner started moving again. Captain Smith was making for Halifax because it was the closest port for a large ship. The freighter just happened to be along the way.

A curiosity of the evening was the ability of *Californian*'s crew to see *Titanic* for almost half an hour before people on the sinking liner saw the freighter. The answer to this question may lie in the visibility conditions that night. Third Officer Charles V. Groves, Ernest Gill, and other members of the freighter's crew may have been able to peek over the horizon as a result of the same "towering" that combined with ice blink to make the horizon look hazy to *Titanic*'s lookouts. *Californian*'s lights became visible to men on *Titanic*'s bridge only after the damaged ship had steamed about 3 miles northward, almost directly toward the stopped freighter. If this is true, the two ships were a bit more than 20 miles apart when the accident took place and some 17 miles apart when *Titanic* came to its second and final stop.

11:52 P.M.     Quartermaster Olliver caught the captain's eye. Smith had a new job for him, an errand involving a mysterious note to Chief Engineer Bell. The captain wrote his message on a standard White Star Lines form that was used for communications and orders aboard company ships. Smith carefully folded the form in half and then bent the corner before handing it to Olliver, who was instructed to take it to Bell. Olliver found his way to the engine room while carrying the captain's neatly folded paper.

"I delivered the message," the quartermaster later told the U.S. Senate hearings, "and I waited for an answer. I waited two or three minutes. Then he saw me standing, and he asked me what I wanted. I said I was waiting for an answer to the message I took him. He told me to take back—to tell the captain that he would get it done as soon as possible." Olliver did not know the contents of the captain's note, so he could never explain what in particular Bell promised to do.

On E deck, engineer John Shepherd and stoker Frederick Barrett reached the corridor, which stretched nearly the full fore-and-aft length of the ship. They hustled forward to the escape door from boiler room #6, where the pair started down into what must have been a steam-filled hell. Any dry portions of the boiler room deck must have glowed red from the fire raked out of the furnaces. Acrid coal smoke would have mixed with the steam generated by rising water lapping over hot coals.

Fourth Officer Boxhall's second trip below had taken him off the bridge just seconds before the captain ordered the engines to roll again. Boxhall set out to find carpenter Hutchinson, whose shop was forward on C deck, within the forecastle. Boxhall unexpectedly discovered the carpenter on the stairway between the boat deck and A deck. They paused to speak for a few moments. "The ship is making water," Hutchinson blurted out as he explained the extent of the flooding. Boxhall listened; then Hutchinson pushed past in his rush to the bridge with this disturbing news. The fourth officer decided to make a personal inspection of the flooding.

*Titanic*'s fatal decision made, the two men who commanded the ship parted company. The slow speed at which the ship was moving does not seem to have suited Bruce Ismay, who left the bridge for a face-to-face meeting with Chief Engineer Bell. Captain Smith left the bridge for the wireless office, a visit that opens another of the mysteries surrounding the sinking. It is most unusual that any captain would leave the command center of his damaged ship simply to "alert" the radio operators to a "possibility" that some message requesting help would be necessary. This was particularly true in 1912, when wireless was still considered more of a commercial novelty to amuse passengers than a useful tool. Preparing the operators for a possible eventuality was an errand too trivial for the captain's personal attention. It should have been done by Relief Quartermaster Olliver, who would soon return from taking Captain Smith's note to Chief Engineer Bell, or by Sixth Officer James Moody, who was also on the bridge at the time.

Captain Smith must have had a compelling reason for making that trip personally. There is intriguing evidence that the captain's real motivation was to dictate a message to the White Star office in New York. It appears that he wirelessed a message that *Titanic* had struck an iceberg, that everyone was safe, and that they were steaming for Halifax (all of this was true at 11:53 P.M.). A ship from the Allan Line (probably *Virginian*) had reportedly transcribed just such a message and forwarded it to the White Star office in Boston via a Canadian ground station. From Boston it went by land telegraph to the company's New York office.

It is possible that Marconi operator Jack Phillips had difficulty getting this message to a station in North America that could relay it to White Star in New York. Difficult atmospheric conditions commonly affected early radio. Sometimes a ship could reach a distant station, and then the signals would fade (similar to modern AM radio). Distant stations might "boom" in for a few minutes, then disappear. If Phillips temporarily could not raise a coast station, he would naturally have sought another vessel that was in touch with a station like the one on Cape Race.

Was *Virginian* the vessel Phillips used for this relay? If so, it explains why the Cape Race operator contacted this ship twice that night about *Titanic*. If *Virginian* did assist in the transmission of the Halifax message, the ship's captain was never informed. On April 22, 1912, the *Daily Sketch* reported:

> The *Virginian*'s captain states that he can throw no light on the message that the *Virginian* had the *Titanic* in tow, and that other steamers were standing by.

In the same edition, the *Daily Sketch* reported a somewhat complicated hypothesis proposed by Captain Haddock of *Olympic*. He thought it possible that electronic eavesdroppers simply mixed together bits and pieces of two (or more) other messages, creating a nonexistent one about *Virginian*.

Phillips hunched over the telegraph key while he sent Captain Smith's Halifax message. His assistant, Harold Bride, hovered nearby. Bride recalled the captain's visit in a *New York Times* newspaper article. "We've struck an iceberg," Bride claimed the captain told the two Marconi operators. "I'm having an inspection made. You better get ready to send out a call for assistance. But, don't send it until I tell you."

If that is what the captain said, Senior Wireless Operator Phillips was not impressed by the gravity of the situation. Renewed beating of the engines apparently motivated him to send a reassuring message to his parents in England. Although a personal transmission, the content of this message was undoubtedly scrutinized by every electronic eavesdropper who could catch the signal:

> MAKING SLOWLY FOR HALIFAX. PRACTICALLY UNSINKABLE. DON'T WORRY.

In an ironic twist of fate, newspaper accounts said this cheerful message was delivered to Phillips's parents on Monday evening, after they learned that the ship had foundered and that their son was not listed among the survivors.

Reporters and editors apparently obtained erroneous but hopeful early reports from land-based wireless operators who were doing some electronic eavesdropping that night. One of those snoops was David Sarnoff, who kept the *New York Times* on top of the breaking story. Sarnoff gained fame later that night by correctly guessing that the wounded liner had foundered with great loss of life. He based that guess on his interpretation of messages he overheard from *Titanic, Carpathia*, and other ships.

It is questionable that Sarnoff would have been eavesdropping specifically on *Titanic* at 12:15 P.M., when it sent its first distress call except for Captain Smith's 11:52 P.M. message to New York concerning the ship's predicament. Smith's first message was meant only for White Star in New York, but radio in 1912 was a free-for-all. Anyone could (and did) listen to private conversations. Smith's message also gave news organizations on both sides of the Atlantic information about the damaged ship limping to Halifax. Newspapers across Britain carried the good news.

> her fate and that of the thousands on board remained in doubt on both sides of the Atlantic for many hours. It was at length known that every soul was safe, and that the vessel itself was proceeding to Halifax either under her own steam or towed by the Allan liner Virginian.

The time difference between England and America was the *New York Tribune*'s explanation for why British newspapers were wildly optimistic about the ship's safety. Those papers went to press hours before *Titanic*'s fate was known.

> Some of the London newspapers went to press this morning under the belief that all aboard the Titanic were safe and the vessel was proceeding for Halifax. . . . Later dispatches recording the sinking of the Titanic, with loss of life, appear only in the latest editions. All news on the subject still comes exclusively from New York.

During the evening of Monday, April 15, someone in White Star Line's New York office sent a mysterious domestic U.S. telegram to a Mr. Hughes in Huntington, West Virginia. It stated flatly that an injured *Titanic* was steaming for Halifax, Nova Scotia. Of course, the ship was already at the bottom of the North Atlantic when this message was sent. Senator Smith produced a copy of the telegram during the U.S. Senate hearings in New York.

TO: J.A. HUGHES, HUNTINGTON, W. VA.
TITANIC PROCEEDING TO HALIFAX. PASSENGERS WILL PROBABLY LAND THERE WEDNESDAY; ALL SAFE. WHITE STAR LINE

Often branded as a hoax, this telegram was more likely a mistake by a junior White Star employee. This analysis of the incident came during U.S. Senate testimony from Philip A. S. Franklin, the American vice president of International Mercantile Marine, parent company of the White Star Line. He told Senator Smith:

we have had our entire passenger staff in No. 9 Broadway office asked, and we can not find out who sent that message . . . but so far as the White Star Line or its officials were concerned, the officials did not authorize anything of that kind.

While Franklin's explanation is probably the truth, it does not go far enough. This telegram remains troubling on several counts. First, according to myth, *Titanic* never resumed making way after the accident. Second, the myth says it never steamed for Halifax. A third problem is time of day. Franklin carefully pointed out that this telegram was sent at 8:27 P.M. on Monday, April 15. The ship had been down for more than half a day by that time, a fact well-known in White Star's New York offices.

Of course, White Star's office was in an understandable uproar all of Monday, the day of the sinking. It is possible that the telegram was written during those hours when Franklin still believed the ship was afloat. Confusion in the New York office may have delayed its transmission until after *Titanic*'s loss had been confirmed. If this happened, the Hughes telegram would be convincing proof the White Star's New York office believed the ship did steam for Halifax after its iceberg accident.

Although Franklin worked for White Star, he had the same problem on Monday as news reporters: it was almost impossible to separate wild rumors from facts. Maurice I. Farrell, managing editor of the Dow Jones News Agency, explained the confusion in a sworn statement submitted to the U.S. Senate hearings.

As an example of the misunderstandings arising, I am informed that the White Star office in Boston called up the Allan Line in Montreal by telephone to get confirmation of a report that all Titanic passengers were transferred to the Virginian and the Titanic was proceeding to Halifax under her own steam. The Allan Line replied that they had such a statement, meaning that they had heard such a report. The White Star Boston office took this as substantiating the rumor, and accordingly called up the White Star office in New York.

Farrell also related an incident reported by his news service regarding a special train ordered by White Star. According to this report, Franklin requested this train to meet the disabled ship when it docked in Halifax. At 3:01 P.M. on April 15, the Dow Jones News Service published details of the shipping company's plans.

> P. A. S. Franklin, vice president International Mercantile Marine, says arrangements have been made with New Haven Road to send a special train to Halifax to meet passengers of the Titanic. Train will consist of 11 sleepers, 2 diners, and coaches sufficient for 710 people.

Days after the sinking, U.S. Senator William Alden Smith discovered that White Star had dispatched a train to meet the crippled ship in Halifax. He became suspicious not of the Canadian destination but of the number of passengers it could carry—700. That was only one-third the number of people on the ship, but almost exactly the number of survivors plucked from the sea by *Carpathia* (there were 706 survivors according to the U.S. Senate, 711 according to the British Board of Trade). Senator Smith quickly called the vice president of the New York, New Haven and Hartford Railroad Company, Benjamin Campbell, to testify. Campbell confirmed the Dow Jones news report.

> MR. CAMPBELL: Mr. Franklin called me on the telephone between 11 and 11:30 o'clock A.M. Monday, the 15th asking if we would arrange to send sufficient equipment to Halifax to take the Titanic's passengers to New York, which should arrive there sometime Wednesday. He stated there were 325 First Class, 285 Second Class, and 710 Third Class passengers. . . .
> . . . at 1:10 o'clock I called up Mr. Franklin on the telephone. I told him what we had done, that the equipment and trains would be ready to leave Boston at 5 or 6 o'clock that evening. And, it would take about 24 hours to make the trip to Halifax, so that they would arrive there Tuesday evening.

Campbell admitted he was in touch with Franklin at the White Star office in New York all day Monday. At 4:30 P.M., Franklin told the railroad to bill all charges for carrying the passengers and feeding them on the train to the shipping company. Then, at 6:40 P.M., the entire project was canceled when White Star announced that the ship had foundered. The train, which by this time was already rolling north from Boston, was recalled.

Many suggestions have been advanced about the origin of news reports that *Titanic* was steaming for Halifax. It was rumored that the Halifax story was part of a plot to convince insurance companies the ship was still afloat on Monday, well after it sank. This alleged hoax could have allowed White Star to purchase additional insurance on a vessel that had already been lost. Although *Titanic* cost more than $7.5 million to build, White Star had insured the "unsinkable" ship for only $5 million.

Another possible origin for the Halifax story might have been a misunderstanding of transmissions between ships on the Atlantic. Radio was in its infancy in 1912, and range was short while interference ("static") was continuous. Wireless operators in New York, straining to hear anything, might have misunderstood traffic from *Asian* saying it could not help *Titanic* because it had taken the disabled German tankship *Deutschland* in tow. Also, there was obvious confusion that night over the term *standing by*. Land-oriented reporters and editors assumed it meant the ship was alongside. In radio terms, the phrase only meant the ship was listening for more traffic. Eavesdroppers on shore may have thought the ship "standing by" was actually on the scene of the disaster.

Of all the possibilities, *Titanic* itself seems the most plausible origin of the Halifax story. Captain Smith made that unusual first visit to the ship's Marconi office at 11:52 P.M., shortly after the accident. According to operator Harold Bride, the master's purpose was only to alert Bride and Phillips to the possibility that a distress message might be necessary. At the hour of this visit, however, Smith still believed his ship was sound enough to steam slowly for Halifax, the closest port. More important, at 11:52 P.M., all aboard were safe, with most passengers still asleep in their cabins.

There must have been Marconi Company records of messages sent from *Titanic* to New York about steaming for Halifax. If they did exist, however, they are no longer readily available to researchers. Guglielmo Marconi himself wirelessed surviving radio operator Harold Bride to keep quiet until after a secret meeting of all company operators involved in the *Titanic* affair. Bride was promised a great deal of money for his silence. That meeting took place at a hotel after *Carpathia*'s arrival in New York.

In London, two of the key investigators involved in the British *Titanic* inquiry were financially involved in both the European and American Marconi Corporations. Attorney General Sir Rufus Isaacs and his brother, Godfrey, were managing directors of the British Marconi Company. Godfrey also owned considerable interest in the

American Marconi Company. Both were implicated in the "Marconi Scandal" that rocked the British Parliament in 1913.

Based on the situation at the time the ship resumed steaming, the mysterious Halifax message is correct to the last detail. If *Titanic* had been able to keep steaming at bare steerageway (8 knots), the passengers would have arrived in Halifax at midmorning on Wednesday, April 17.

From Captain Smith's point of view during his first visit to the wireless room, notifying New York not only was logical but was also necessary White Star company business. The New York office would have had to deal with the inevitable confusion of getting passengers from Halifax to New York. As much warning as possible would be needed to give time for dispatching the required railroad coaches and reserving other accommodations in time for the ship's arrival. If the captain had sent such a message, its wording would have been strikingly similar to one dispatched eighteen hours later from White Star's New York office. Only the signature would have been different.

TITANIC PROCEEDING TO HALIFAX. PASSENGERS WILL PROBABLY LAND THERE WEDNESDAY; ALL SAFE. SMITH

Carpenter Hutchinson rushed into *Titanic*'s bridge enclosure **11:53 P.M.** only to find that Captain Smith had departed for the Marconi room. His short conversation on the stairway with Fourth Officer Boxhall had delayed him from reaching the captain before the engines were restarted. There is no way to know for sure, but perhaps Hutchinson's report of the flooding mail room would have prevented Captain Smith from bowing to Ismay's demand to resume making way. Unfortunately, the engine room telegraphs were clanging while the Hutchinson and Boxhall spoke on the stairway. By the time Hutchinson reached the bridge, the fatal decision had been made and Captain Smith was on his way to the radio room.

If starting the engines was intended to reassure the passengers, it worked. Lawrence Beesley, the teacher on holiday mentioned earlier, published one of the first survivor accounts of the sinking. His 1912 narrative leaves no doubt that the ship began making way again after striking on the berg. He hammered the point home with incident after incident.

The ship had now resumed her course, moving very slowly through the water with a little white line of foam on each side. I think we were all glad to see this.

Beesley recollected meeting three female acquaintances, who asked, "Why have we stopped?" He replied, "We did stop, but we're now going again." The young teacher countered their doubts that the ship was moving with a demonstration of schoolboy science. He reminded the women that the bathtubs on D deck always vibrated in time with the engines. These tubs were located above and just forward of the ship's two outboard screws, where they concentrated vibrations created by the ship's machinery. Placing the women's hands on a tub, he demonstrated that the metal was again vibrating as usual. This reassured them, and Beesley started for his cabin. Along the way, the vacationing teacher met another acquaintance, who was incongruously fastening his tie in the hallway.

"Anything fresh?" the man asked.

"Not much," Beesley replied. "We are going ahead slowly."

A first-class passenger who reported that the ship begin making way again was leather manufacturer C. E. Henry Stengel. Stengel had considerable experience with machinery in his New York factory, so he was naturally curious about *Titanic*'s engines. At about 10:00 P.M., Stengel had retired to cabin C-116 almost amidships. "I could hear the engines running when I retired and I noticed that the engines were running very fast," he told Senator Smith. "They were running faster than at any time during the trip."

It is true that *Titanic*'s engines had been increased to 75 revolutions that Sunday. However, there is no evidence of a sudden burst of power just prior to the impact with the berg. What Stengel experienced was probably just the illusion of unusual engine speed. He was more aware of the vibration because ships run much quieter in calm water than they do in rough. Ice surrounding the ship dampened wave action, providing calm conditions that made the sound and vibration of the engines more noticeable.

Awakened by Annie May Morris Stengel, his wife, just moments before the ship ground its way across the berg, Stengel experienced the ominous rumbling noted by other witnesses. Then the engines stopped. It was the stopping of the engines, not rumbling over the iceberg, that grabbed Stengel's attention. He told his wife that something serious had happened. At his urging, they dressed and went on deck. After they were on deck for what Stengel estimated as "two or three minutes," he heard the reassuring sound of the ship's engines running again. If those "two or three" minutes are added to the seven or eight it must have taken the Stengels to dress, the result is the nine to ten minutes that *Titanic* coasted after the accident before starting its engines again.

"Then they started again just slightly; just started to move again. I do not know why; whether they were backing off, or not. I do not know. I hardly thought they were backing off because there was not much vibration to the ship," Stengel testified.

Archibald Gracie, a U.S. Civil War historian and retired Army colonel, was in his nightclothes when he felt the shock of the accident. His inside stateroom, C-51, was against the starboard side of the casing for boiler rooms #5 and #6. Gracie carefully removed his pajamas and dressed "in underclothing, shoes and stockings, trousers, and a Norfolk coat" before climbing to the boat deck. All this undressing and dressing must have taken the better part of ten minutes. He walked aft to the first-class entrance and up to the boat deck.

Gracie stepped outside just after the wounded liner picked up headway again. "There was no sign of an officer anywhere," he stated in his book about *Titanic*. Then, he witnessed something that could only have occurred if the ship were moving under its own power: a couple strolling into the wind on a perfectly still night.

> The only other beings I saw were a middle-aged couple of the second cabin promenading unconcernedly, arm in arm, forward on the starboard quarter, against the wind, the man in a gray overcoat and outing cap.

Maritime records for that night agree that for an hour before and an hour after midnight, the weather was marked by what sailors call a "dead calm." The only source for the wind Gracie described was motion of the ship itself, further proof that *Titanic* resumed moving forward after the accident.

**11:55 P.M.** Ship moving at dead slow. Course is nothing west of north 10 east.
—J. MOODY, Sixth Officer

While the captain was visiting the Marconi office, Ismay went "down below" (his words) to confer with Chief Engineer Bell. Ismay knew the route to the engine rooms. He had visited Bell previously and allegedly had his own set of engineer's coveralls. His earlier visit had been to discuss the ship's speed, and this night's visit probably had a similar goal. Ismay appears to have been attempting to circumvent the captain's authority again, if that could be done under the current circumstances, but first he had to know the damage. Was the ship sound enough to increase speed or to resume course for New York?

> MR. ISMAY: I asked if he [Bell] thought the ship was seriously damaged, and he said he thought she was. But [he] was satisfied the pumps would keep her afloat.

Ismay's recollection of this short conversation may be the single most important piece of testimony given during either the British or the American investigation. Without this particular information, the decision to restart the ship's engines is unbelievable. Why would anyone try to steam for Halifax in a sinking ship? Ismay gives us the answer: *Titanic* wasn't sinking when the engines began beating again. According to Ismay, the chief engineer believed as late as 11:54 P.M.—a dozen minutes after the accident—that the pumps were effective against the flooding. If Ismay was correct, Bell did not think the giant liner was foundering for several minutes after the engines began rolling again.

It is hard to imagine that an experienced engineer like Bell could have overlooked the fact that his ship was sinking. Accepting what Bell said at face value is much easier: *Titanic* was seriously wounded but not foundering almost fifteen minutes after the accident, even during the first few moments after it resumed making way. Put another way, it was not the ice that sank *Titanic*, but the actions of its captain and owner.

Bell had good reason for optimism during his conversation with Ismay. Almost immediately after the accident, he had asked Captain Smith to release the watertight doors to allow his engineers to pass between boiler rooms #4 and #5 to rig a 10-inch suction hose. The doors would not have been opened if boiler room #5 had been rapidly filling with water. Watertight doors are opened on a sinking ship only if compartments on either side of the bulkhead are thought to be safe from immediate flooding. Opening the doors is evidence that Barrett's sprung seam was more of an annoyance than a major leak. If the incoming water had been thought dangerous, the door to boiler room #4 would have remained tightly closed.

In any case, the British report stated that the new 10-inch line was enough to handle water spurting through the 2-foot open seam in boiler room #5. More likely, however, this line was part of an apparently successful effort to slow the flooding in boiler room #6. The British report's claim of water 8 feet deep at 11:51 P.M. is undermined by the decision to resume steaming. A flooded stokehold should have sufficiently alarmed even J. Bruce Ismay about the condition of the ship to delay making way again.

No boilers exploded in boiler room #6, another possible indicator that water did not rise above the fireboxes (about waist deep) during the ten minutes the ship drifted after the accident. Those precious minutes gave stokers time enough to rake the coals out of the furnaces and vent off steam pressure. If the British report was correct in saying that water rose 8 feet during the first ten minutes, neither task could have been performed. Eight feet of freezing water might have caused the collapse of one or more hot boilers, possibly resulting in a catastrophic explosion. Since an explosion did not happen, it is likely that boiler room #6 remained inhabitable until after the ship resumed making way.

Fear of exploding boilers also must have been the primary motivation for work taking place in boiler room #5. There had been a short delay caused by a loss of electrical power, but the lights came back and things returned to normal during Ismay's conversation with Chief Engineer Bell. Stokers raked glowing coals out of the fireboxes to reduce the danger of a boiler erupting if cold seawater should flood the compartment. Hot sparks, glowing coals, acrid smoke, and clouds of steam filled the belly of *Titanic*.

A boiler explosion was a life-threatening possibility at all times in steamships. Given his valid concern over explosions, *Titanic*'s chief engineer probably was not overly worried about pumping the damaged cargo holds forward of the boiler room. That flooding would be addressed, but in due time, after the more immediate danger of explosion was removed. Bell's comments about the activity of the pumps prior to 11:54 P.M. likely referred only to their success at keeping boiler room #5 dry and slowing the flooding in boiler room #6. Judging by Ismay's testimony, he took the chief engineer to mean that the pumps could keep the ship afloat indefinitely. And, if the pumps were checking the flooding of Boiler Room #6, that was factually true. The ship would have floated indefinitely in that condition.

**11:56 P.M.** Speed dead slow. Course nothing west of north 10 east. Engineers report they are rigging more suction lines into damaged compartments.

—J. MOODY, Sixth Officer

Confidence in the pumps that night was based on their performance during the moments after the accident. Prior to steaming again at 11:50 P.M., *Titanic*'s pumps and bulkheads were doing a good job of controlling the flooding. Put simply, the ship was floating on its pumps. This was a precarious situation, to be sure, but far from the immediate disaster that ensued after Smith and Ismay resumed making way. Ten minutes after the ship started for Halifax, the pumps were being overwhelmed in boiler room #6. Once this happened, the system of watertight bulkheads was rendered useless. *Titanic* was condemned to a quick end.

What changed?

Certainly not the pumps. If there was a change in the pumps, they would have become more effective as additional suction lines were connected. Surviving stokers and trimmers witnessed engineers rigging more lines to improve the discharge of water. As minutes ticked by, the pumping improved. This means that if the pumps were overwhelmed, there must have been an increase in the rate of flooding. The inescapable conclusion is that *Titanic*'s pumps were swamped by massive amounts of water pushed into the ship by its own forward motion. Water surged to 8 feet deep in boiler room #6 within a few minutes of the engines turning again. *Titanic* appears to have steamed itself into a watery North Atlantic grave.

Coming down the ladder into boiler room #6, Shepherd and Barrett ran into the flooding that would quickly doom the ship. Water was pushing its way into the forwardmost stokeholds. "We could not go in there because there were about eight feet of water when we got there," Barrett reported in London. The stokeholds in boiler room #6 were being abandoned, so the two men made the long climb back up to E deck to get over the watertight bulkhead and go back down into boiler room #5.

Fourth Officer Boxhall was still working his way deeper into the bow when he was stopped by one of the mail clerks, John Richard Jago Smith. "The mail hold is full" was the clerk's unbelievable report. Then, he asked how to get to the captain. Boxhall instructed the man on how to climb to the bridge.

Boxhall decided to see the flooding for himself. He rushed through the roundabout of corridors and stairways leading to the mail room on the lower, or G, deck. This was the same deck he had visited just minutes earlier, except now he was one compartment aft—behind the watertight bulkhead separating the third-class men's open berths from the baggage and mail rooms. The berthing area had no stairways through the deck to the cargo hold below. Behind the bulkhead, an open stairway allowed the fourth officer to look down from the post office to the mail room on the orlop deck.

Boxhall was shocked.

> MR. BOXHALL: . . . I looked through an open door and saw these men working on the racks . . . directly beneath me was the mail hold, and water seemed to be then within two feet of the deck we were standing on and bags of mail floating about. I went right on the bridge again and reported to the Captain.

Five postal workers, three American and two British, struggled vainly to keep the most important sacks of mail dry that night. One of them, Oscar Woody, was celebrating his forty-fourth birthday by slogging in cold seawater. None of these men survived the night. Woody's body was recovered with a pocket watch stopped at the instant the ship plunged beneath the sea.

Boxhall raced back to the bridge from the bow for a second time. He must have been gasping for breath as he burst in upon the captain, who was conferring with Thomas Andrews, of Harland and Wolff, and carpenter John Hutchinson. Andrews was aboard with eight other company employees to handle details overlooked in the rush to commission the new ship. He had been working in cabin A-36, located adjacent to the first-class staircase between the third and fourth funnels, when the ship rumbled across the ice. It appears that Andrews responded by conducting his own inspection of the damage. As a result, his arrival on the bridge was delayed until after Ismay left for the engine room.

**12:00 A.M.** The Captain, Mr. Wilde, and Mr. Andrews leave bridge to inspect damage. Mr. Murdoch has command of bridge. Heading 010°, speed 8 knots. Sea calm. Mr. Moody and Mr. Boxhall are relieved by Mr. Pitman and Mr. Lowe. —H. G. LOWE, Fifth Officer

*Titanic* builder Thomas Andrews already knew the situation was precarious, but he had observed the pumps working well in boiler room #6. Still, he was probably surprised that the ship started moving again so soon after the accident. It was time to share what he had learned about the damage and flooding with Captain Smith. Andrews had just arrived on the bridge when Boxhall suddenly popped up the stairway and gasped that the mail room was filling with water. This confirmed earlier reports from the mail clerk and the carpenter of serious flooding.

Andrews must have pointed out that the fourth compartment aft from the bow was now filled nearly to the ship's normal waterline. That flooding had taken less than twenty minutes. He must have concluded that *Titanic* might sink if they did not save boiler room #6. With that in mind, Andrews appears to have convinced Captain Smith to undertake a personal investigation of the damage. Common sense suggests that Captain Smith should have prudently ordered the ship stopped. However, the evidence from surviving crew members is to the contrary. *Titanic* continued steaming slowly while Captain Smith, Chief Officer Wilde, Andrews, and Hutchinson trooped off the bridge just after the stroke of midnight.

Captain Smith probably restarted the ship simply to placate his irascible employer at a time when *Titanic* did not yet appear to be in serious trouble. The situation had not changed when Andrews appeared on the bridge, although the ship's builder knew that a life-or-death struggle was taking place in boiler room #6 to stem the rising water. If that compartment were lost, the ship would surely sink. Andrews knew about the fire-damaged bulkhead between boiler rooms #5 and #6. This bulkhead was confining the flooding so that pumping could be efficiently concentrated in only one compartment. The builder apparently convinced the captain that it was time for a firsthand inspection of the situation.

At midnight the crow's nest was once again active as two new lookouts, George Hogg and Alfred Evans, climbed the mast to replace Fleet and Lee. This was the normal rotation for the lookouts, who worked two-hour watches with four hours off duty. New lookouts were needed because the ship was slowly making way for Halifax. Undoubtedly, Hogg and Evans were told to keep special watch for growlers. Fleet went to his quarters in the bow but found none of his shipmates there. A few minutes later, he was told to report to the bridge to assist with launching lifeboats.

For the moment, however, *Titanic* was steaming slowly northward at a bit less than half of its cruising speed. Fourth Officer Boxhall, who was officially off duty at midnight, later said he filled his time while the captain was off the bridge by uncovering lifeboats. Lightoller remained stubbornly in his cabin. Most passengers were in bed, still unaware that their ship was mortally wounded.

The Captain's inspection party went down the various stairways to **12:03 A.M.** the forward well deck, where they walked past the crumbled ice. They hurried through the crew's quarters before descending deeper into the bow. Sailors described the incoming water as under more pressure than might be expected during a quiet sinking. Samuel S. Hemming, a forty-three-year-old seaman, was awakened by the accident. About 12:05 A.M., he heard an unusual sound and decided to investigate.

> I went forward under the forecastle head to see where the hissing noise came from. I found it was the air escaping out of the exhaust of the (forepeak) tank. At that time the Chief Officer, Mr. Wilde, put his head around the hawse pipe and says, "What is that, Hemming?" I said, "The air escaping from the forepeak tank. She is making water in the forepeak tank, but the storeroom is quite dry."

Hemming spoke to Wilde while the chief officer was touring the flooding spaces with Captain Smith. What the seaman told Wilde seems to confirm that the ship was pushing water into the bow by steaming northward at several minutes after midnight. Nearby, seaman Frederick Clench had a similar experience. After looking at broken ice on the well deck, Clench went inside to be warm. Another crew member called to him a few minutes later.

> Someone said to me, "did you hear the rush of water?" I said, "No." They said, "Look down under the hatchway." I looked down under the hatchway and I saw the tarpaulin belly out as if there was a lot of wind under it, and I heard the rush of water coming through.

Such eyewitness accounts are not absolute proof that the ship scooped up water as it steamed forward. Incoming water could have forced air to hiss out of the forepeak tank or to balloon a canvas hatch cover even if *Titanic* had been sitting perfectly still. However, what the two men described seems to be more than quiet flooding through relatively small holes in the bottom. Both descriptions give the impression of rapid flooding under pressure, exactly what would have happened if the damaged ship were moving forward under its own power. The captain's inspection of the bow was short. It was obvious that *Titanic* was sinking.

**12:09 A.M.** Captain on bridge. Has ordered Murdoch to stop the ship.

—H. G. LOWE, Fifth Officer

Andrews and the captain hurried back to the bridge. No matter what Ismay demanded, it was time to stop the ship. Fourth Officer Boxhall recalled that First Officer William M. Murdoch operated the engine order telegraph handles to "astern slow." This would have "put the brakes on" to bring the ship to a halt. Someone, probably Andrews, warned him not to stop the ship so quickly because water sloshing inside boiler room #6 might collapse the fire-damaged bulkhead. Murdoch changed the order to "all stop," the last order that greaser Frederick Scott in the engine room remembered coming down from the bridge. Scott testified that the engines ran slow ahead for at least ten minutes before an order came for "astern slow." This was followed by "all stop" a few moments later.

The ship could not have been stopped quickly without excessive strain on the weakened bulkhead. Reversing the engines would have sent water inside the ship sloshing forward, only to have it slam aft with tremendous force, possibly enough to tear the heat-weakened steel between the boiler rooms. The safest way to halt *Titanic* was to let momentum come off naturally so that water inside would stop simultaneously with the hull around it.

Murdoch's final "all stop" order may not have been necessary. Steam had been venting from the ship's boilers during almost the entire twenty minutes since the accident. By 12:08 A.M., there could not have been much pressure left to drive the big reciprocating engines. Perhaps the ship did not coast to a stop because of instructions from the engine order telegraphs but simply because it "ran out of steam." This could be just what Captain Smith requested in his memo to the Chief Engineer. During the remaining minutes of *Titanic*'s life, engineers wisely kept only enough pressure in the system to run the electric dynamos.

Forward motion during the approximately twenty minutes that

the ship was making way must have created enormous hydraulic force on the underside of the tank top deck. This pressure should have caused weakened seams to open wider, increasing the flood of water through missing rivet holes and between the deck plates. As mentioned earlier, there is some evidence of increased flooding while the ship was steaming for Halifax. Crew members in the bow of the ship reported hissing air and other apparent signs of rapid flooding during that time. A slight reduction in flooding seems to have followed the captain's order to stop the engines for the last time. The only possible explanation for even a small reduction of flooding is that less water entered the hull, and the only cause for less water would have been the loss of headway after the ship glided to a halt. Nothing else changed except *Titanic*'s forward momentum.

Stopping the engines did not stop the ship's compounding problems, however. Every additional ton of water inside the hull caused the bow to tip downward. An often-overlooked consequence of this tipping is that it pushed damaged areas deeper underwater, where pressure increases with depth. Increasing pressure forced more water through the existing holes and must have caused other, lightly damaged areas in the bottom to begin leaking.

The effect of steaming is clearly seen in the pattern of flooding. At 11:50 P.M., *Titanic* had lost buoyancy in all three forward holds, but the pumps were keeping down the level in boiler room #6. Water spraying into boiler room #5 was more a nuisance than a threat. According to British Wreck Commissioner Lord Mersey's final report, the ship should have been able to float in this condition.

> Even if the four forward compartments had been flooded the water would not have got into any of the compartments abaft of them though it would have been above the top of some of the forward bulkheads. But the ship, even with these four compartments flooded would have remained afloat.

Things changed quickly as the ship gained forward momentum after restarting. Water was forced into all of the first five compartments. More water made no difference in the three holds that were already flooded beyond pumping. However, forward motion seems to have caused boiler room #6 to flood much faster than the pumps could remove it. The sea rose quickly to a depth of 8 feet and more. This was *Titanic*'s final death blow: the loss of boiler room #6.

But she could not remain afloat with the four forward compartments and the forward boiler room (No. 6) also flooded.

The flooding of these five compartments alone would have sunk the ship sufficiently deeply to have caused the water to rise above the bulkhead at the after end of the forward boiler room (No. 6) and to flow over into the next boiler room (No. 5), and to fill it up until in turn its after bulkhead would be overwhelmed and the water would thereby flow over and fill No. 4 boiler room, and so on in succession to the other boiler rooms til the ship would ultimately fill and sink.

*Titanic* was beginning to tear itself apart even as the engines were turning their last revolutions. This destruction was the result of a condition sailors call *hogging*, in which the hull was being bent by the weight of water in the bow. Although made of steel an inch or more thick, *Titanic* was essentially a hollow metal tube supported by buoyancy along its entire length. Water flooding into the bow put tons of bending force on the ship's structure, force that it was not designed to support. Strain concentrated on the riveted seams caused many to lose watertight integrity, allowing water into areas not damaged by direct contact with the ice.

Additional flooding, also the apparent result of hogging, occurred in the forward end of boiler room #4. This compartment remained dry until about 1:20 A.M., when water in small quantities began coming in from "underneath the floor." This is the slow flooding that would be expected if seams in the tank were being squeezed open under the enormous compression of hogging. It was also the type of flooding that could have been handled by the ship's pumps, as Chief Engineer Bell told Bruce Ismay. Trimmer George Cavell had not quite drawn the fires (pulled the hot coals out of the fireboxes) in boiler room #4 when the sea began creeping upward. "Water started coming up over the stokehold plates. It came gradually," Cavell said later in London, confirming that water came up from the bottom and not through the side of the ship. By the time Cavell left the stokehold, the water in boiler room #4 was knee-deep.

Hogging was the beginning of the process that eventually tore *Titanic* apart like a paper toy. The destruction was slow at first, until hogging contributed to the failure of the fire-damaged bulkhead between boiler rooms #5 and #6. Then, once the bridge sank to the sea, the strain proved more than steel could support. The forward funnel fell. Finally, a vertical crack opened between funnels #3 and #4 and split *Titanic* into two large pieces. Although the end was dramatic, the final breakup of the hull actually began hours earlier, while some passengers were still asleep or were just becoming aware of the accident.

Before the forecastle head went under, the hogging process was more of a nuisance than frightening disintegration of the ship. One famous incident involving tennis star R. Norris Williams indicates that *Titanic*'s hull was bending even before many passengers realized the ship was sinking. Williams and his father had just left their C deck stateroom. They came across a steward trying to open a nearby cabin door that was wedged tight. One explanation for the stuck door is that the jamb had been racked out of square by the hogging of the hull. Williams simply kicked down the door to free the trapped passengers. For his heroism, he was told by the steward that he would be charged for the damage "once the ship reaches New York."

# TIME FOR US TO LEAVE HER

Monday, April 15, 1912

**12:09 A.M. to 12:46 A.M.**

**12:09 A.M.** Mr. Andrews says the ship may float until morning if the bulkheads hold. We are readying the boats and hoping for the best.—E. J. SMITH, Master

FOURTH Officer Joseph G. Boxhall burst in upon a wide-awake Charles H. Lightoller, who had gone back to his cabin after his quick peek on deck. Staying away from the center of the action was out of character for the second officer, yet Lightoller was in bed when Boxhall found him.

"We've struck an iceberg."

"I know we struck something," Lightoller responded.

"Water's up to F deck in the mail room," Boxhall blurted. By now, Lightoller was up and dressing for what would be the coldest night of his life.

The ship's builder, Thomas Andrews, became Captain Smith's focus while Boxhall was rousing the officers. Andrews analyzed what they had seen. Driving the ship forward had increased the rate of flooding, probably beyond the capacity of the pumps in boiler room #6. *Titanic* was still floating and probably could continue floating well into the next day if nothing else went wrong. However, Andrews already knew that the loss of boiler room #6 meant the ship would eventually sink once water in that compartment rose high enough to spill over the top of the bulkhead. The vaunted system of bulkheads and automatic watertight doors had lost all effectiveness. Once boiler room #6 filled to the height of the bulkhead, nothing could prevent the ship from sinking.

Everything now depended upon the pumps and a few plates of distorted steel. If they worked, the ship would probably still be afloat when the *Carpathia* and other rescue ships arrived before dawn. But, if anything failed, *Titanic* would quickly founder, perhaps in as little as one hour.

Inspecting the bow and assessing the damage took an emotional toll on *Titanic*'s builder. Andrews did not openly criticize the decision to resume making way after the accident, but his actions throughout the evening seem to indicate a distrust of the way the ship was evacuated. He continuously exhorted people to put on lifebelts. During the early moments after the ship finally stopped for the last time, he was the only person with enough intimate knowledge of the predicament to urge people to leave the warm public spaces and climb into the cold lifeboats.

"Mr. Andrews told me to put my lifebelt on after I had been on E deck," recalled stewardess Annie Robinson. "Mr. Andrews said to me, 'Put your lifebelt on and walk about and let the passengers see you.' I said to him, 'It looks rather mean,' and he said, 'No, put it on,' and then after he said to me, 'If you value your life put your belt on.'" In the end, Andrews failed to follow his own advice. As the bow dipped beneath the North Atlantic, he appeared too emotionally drained to save himself.

**12:12 A.M.** Marconi operators are instructed to send call for assistance. Position estimated as 41°44′ N, 50°24′ W.                    —E. J. SMITH, Master

Captain Smith now made the longest walk of his career. He stepped from the port side of the wheelhouse into a corridor running the length of the officers' quarters. At the far end was the ship's three-room wireless suite. When he had walked this corridor twenty minutes earlier, the situation had been so much different. During the previous walk, modern shipbuilding still appeared triumphant. Now, the catastrophe he had both predicted and could not envision was unfolding on his ship, and he was powerless to stop it. In his *New York Times* story, Marconi operator Harold Bride also remembered the captain's second visit.

"Send the message," Captain Smith said simply.

"What call should I send?" Phillips asked.

"The regulation international call for help. Just that."

Thirty-five minutes after the accident—time enough to have 12:15:00 A.M. launched ten lifeboats—Jack Phillips started tapping out the 1912 distress signal, "CQD . . . CQD . . . MGY . . . MGY . . . " The letters "MGY" were *Titanic*'s radio call sign. They would be valid for less than two more hours. "CQD . . . MGY . . . LAT 41 44 . . . LON 50 24 . . . CQD . . . MGY."

Back on the bridge, Captain Smith had one more important job for 12:17 A.M. his energetic fourth officer. Boxhall was specially trained in navigation and was considered by Smith to be quite proficient. "Calculate our position," the captain directed. Boxhall stepped into the quiet of the chart room behind the wheelhouse. There was no time to attempt a true fix using the stars. Besides, on such a moonless night it would have been impossible to accurately judge the horizon where sky met sea. Without a distinct horizon, Boxhall did not attempt to use his sextant.

Instead, Boxhall relied on a much older technique of navigation called *dead reckoning*. The last celestial position of *Titanic* had been taken by Lightoller at 7:30 P.M. Boxhall claimed he used this fix as his starting point for calculating the ship's current location. He had to account for *Titanic*'s course and speed during the more than five hours since Lightoller's round of star sights, forcing him to update nearly six hours of steaming. The task took several minutes.

A minor mystery of that night is the inaccuracy of Boxhall's final position. He was noted for his navigational skill, yet he placed the ship about 13 miles west and north of the location of the wreck as it lies today. It was fortunate that Boxhall's position lay beyond the ship's actual location on a direct line from *Carpathia*, allowing the rescue ship to steam straight toward the lifeboats even though they were several miles southeast of where Boxhall said they should be.

Because the rescue ship came right to the boats, *Titanic*'s fourth officer took great pride in his calculation of the ship's final position for the rest of his life. Nevertheless, Captain James H. Moore of *Mount Temple*, another ship that responded to *Titanic*'s distress call, noticed Boxhall's error on the morning after the sinking.

SENATOR SMITH: Does the fact that you found no evidence of the wreck when you got to the Titanic's reported position tend to confirm you in the idea that her position was eight miles to the southward?

MR. MOORE: No; to the eastward.

SENATOR SMITH: To the eastward?

MR. MOORE: Yes . . .

SENATOR SMITH: As I recollect, the captain of the Californian, who was sworn yesterday, and who went to the position given by the Titanic in the C.Q.D., also said that he found nothing there, but cruised around this position.

MR. MOORE: I saw the Californian myself cruising around there, sir.

Many reasons have been suggested for his error, including the unlikely possibility that Boxhall did not use Lightoller's 7:30 star sights for his calculations. Instead, he may have based his dead reckoning on the latitude and longitude of "the Corner" where the ship was to change course at 5:20 P.M. Boxhall likely had committed the latitude and longitude of that spot to memory. If he forgot that the turn was made 25 minutes late, that would account for some of the error.

Then there were the icebergs around the ship. Second Officer Lightoller must have begun dodging icebergs just after 9:00 P.M., while Captain Smith was on the bridge. Circumstantial evidence indicates First Officer William J. Murdoch continued swerving around bergs throughout his watch. Since icebergs float southeastward from Greenland on the Labrador Current, both officers probably dodged south of their intended track when avoiding ice to put their ship farther away from the source of the danger and into presumably less dangerous water. All records of these maneuvers have been lost, so there is no way of knowing how much the swerving influenced Boxhall's calculation of the ship's final position.

*Titanic* steamed northward for about twenty minutes after the accident. Boxhall had to account for this movement in calculating his final position. Even though he never mentioned the liner's restarting to investigators, he had no reason to hide the ship's movements from himself that night. On the contrary, his survival as well as that of every other person aboard the doomed liner depended upon the accuracy of his calculations. An overestimation of the ship's speed (bare steerageway versus "ahead half") might have caused Boxhall's final position of 41°46' N, 50°14' W, to be somewhat north of the actual wreck site.

Dave Gittins, a researcher in South Australia, suggests on his Web site the simplest cause for Boxhall's mistake: a math error. Gittins correctly assumes that *Titanic*'s navigator would have used a set of Traverse Tables to calculate the ship's final position based on its speed and direction since Lightoller's star fix. Prior to the advent of electronic navigation, Traverse Tables enabled the calculation of a ship's position at sea without the need for time-consuming plotting on a chart. Gittins suggests that Boxhall simply read down the wrong column of numbers that night, resulting in the nearly 13-mile error.

**12:18 A.M.** Ordinary operations ended. Crew mustered for launching boats. Murdoch is to launch starboard boats; Lightoller the port. Wilde is told to have passengers put on life vests.          —H. G. LOWE, Fifth Officer

*Titanic's* fifty-nine-year-old master gave out the assignments for abandoning the ship. Lightoller was detailed to launch the port side lifeboats; Murdoch the starboard boats. The memory of the French liner *La Bourgogne* must have flashed through everyone's minds. A horrible panic had broken out on board when that ship went down fourteen years earlier. None of the officers wanted anything similar to happen on *Titanic.* They all knew the truth: there were seats in the lifeboats for only about half the people on board *Titanic.* It would have been extremely dangerous to send people trooping up to the boats. Panic certainly would have resulted when half the passengers found out they could not get into a lifeboat.

Preventing panic was paramount. The maximum number of lives could be saved by loading only those people smart enough or lucky enough to reach the boat deck. No one would be told to go to the boats. In this way, the boat deck would remain free of panic for as long as possible. Those who remained in the warmth and false security of the ship's public rooms would have to fend for themselves after the boats were gone.

In 1911, when *Titanic* was launched, maritime experts openly spoke about large passenger ships serving as their own lifeboats. The belief was that multi-compartment vessels would remain afloat despite any imaginable accident. Today, the public considers this logic specious because of the great ship's maiden voyage tragedy. It is ironic that *Titanic* may have had history's best opportunity to prove that a self-rescuing passenger vessel is possible. Even though mortally wounded from the outset, the huge liner was capable of saving all on board by floating until midmorning, when the rescue ship *Carpathia* arrived on the scene. Unfortunately, this did not happen. *Titanic* failed to be its own lifeboat because of the foolish decision to make way again.

By 12:19 A.M., only the ship's insufficient supply of wooden lifeboats represented any hope of survival. Captain Smith told Murdoch and Lightoller to swing out the boats. "Swinging out" meant moving the fourteen lapstrake boats outboard from their chocks on the boat deck until they hung in their falls over the side. (*Titanic's* two "emergency boats" were kept swung out for immediate use. The four collapsibles could not be readied until the regular boats were launched.) In 1912, swinging out had to be done before passengers could be loaded in the boats. This order was as near as Smith came to giving a classic "abandon ship" command. There was no general alarm, no siren blaring; just a quiet "swing out the boats."

Based on the 65-person capacity of the standard wooden lifeboat, *Titanic* and the other Olympic-class vessels required at least fifty-one boats to accommodate all 3,295 passengers and crew they were authorized to carry. However, *Olympic* and *Titanic* actually sailed with only fourteen full-size and two smaller "emergency" lifeboats. The other thirty-two boats, which theoretically could have saved everyone on board, were never installed. As a last-minute nod to safety, four collapsible Englehardt boats had been added, two on the boat deck and two more on top of the officers' quarters.

Adding the collapsibles brought the total aboard to twenty boats, still well short of the number that could have been carried by the sixteen pairs of davits fitted. Harland and Wolff was in no position to argue with White Star because, in shipbuilding, the buyer's money rules. As a result, the Olympic-class liners went to sea with slightly more lifeboat capacity than required by the Board of Trade's antiquated regulation.

The sixteen noncollapsible lifeboats were slung in davits of the latest design by Axel Welin. The inventor had proudly described the davits he fitted to the Olympic-class ships in a paper presented to the Institute of Naval Architects. Welin's paper indicates that White Star knew the British Board of Trade would shortly increase the number of boats required on larger passenger liners.

> On the boat deck of the White Star Liner Olympic and also of the Titanic this double-acting type of davit has been fitted throughout in view of coming changes in official regulations. It was considered wise by the owners that these changes should be thus anticipated and so make it possible to double, or even treble, the number of boats without any structural alterations should such increase ultimately prove necessary.

White Star correctly claimed that *Titanic* carried more lifeboat seats than required by then-current British Board of Trade regulations. The number of boats required aboard British ships in April 1912 was determined by registered tonnage of the ship, not the number of people on board. Olympic-class liners sailed legally with fewer than half enough lifeboat seats for their maximum capacity of passengers and crew. *Titanic* had emergency accommodations for 1,178 people in its twenty boats. The ship was certified to carry almost triple that—3,300 people—yet the Board of Trade regulations called for only 962 seats. This meant that, under 1912 regulations, *Titanic* had 216 seats in "excess" lifeboat capacity.

Despite that excess capacity, about half the people aboard *Titanic* were condemned to death by the lack of lifeboat seats. It was this somber fact that raised the specter of panic. How could the captain and his officers choose who would live and who would die without raising the ire of those left behind? It became important to divert passenger attention away from the lifeboats to prevent a panic.

Music appears to have been part of someone's plan or impulse to save some passengers' lives by maintaining calm among those who were doomed by the lifeboat shortage. Bandmaster Wallace Hartley and his seven musicians have become legendary for playing ragtime while the ship was sinking beneath their feet. Their story is one of the most poignant to come out of the tragedy, especially because all eight bandsmen were lost. Most research into the last minutes of the ship's orchestra has focused on whether or not they played the hymn "Nearer My God to Thee." There has been little interest in why the band started playing in a first-class lounge at a little past 12:15 A.M. It is reasonable to assume that some members of the band might have gathered on the sloping deck to console themselves with music, but at the hour when they started playing few people except Andrews and the captain knew their "unsinkable" ship was about to founder.

**12:23 A.M.** Quartermaster Hitchens is relieved at the wheel. The ship is still moving forward, but too slowly for the rudder to be effective.

—W. M. Murdoch, First Officer

*Titanic* was coasting to its final stop, its life ebbing like the steam from its boilers. Passenger Lawrence Beesley's "little white line of foam" disappeared from around the cutwater. Without forward motion, the rudder was now useless and there was no longer any need for a quartermaster at the wheel. First Officer Murdoch, who remained as officer of the watch while the ship steamed toward Halifax, had one remaining job to do before attending to his lifeboat duties. It fell to him to issue the last navigation order given on *Titanic*. "That will do at the wheel," he told Quartermaster Hitchens. "It's time to get the boats out." Their ship was almost dead in the water. The world's largest liner was as near to its intended destination as it would ever get.

This is the moment when the story of the sinking began for those passengers who had slept through the actual iceberg accident. Because they were asleep, most passengers had no knowledge of the slight shuddering as the ship ran over the ice shelf or of the engines stopping and restarting. Sleepy passengers naturally assumed that the ship was gliding to a stop for the first time when they were awakened by stewards.

**12:24 A.M.** Final position 41°46′ N × 50°14′ W. Boats ready for lowering. Marconi office contacting nearby vessels. —E. J. SMITH, Master

Fourth Officer Boxhall came out of the chart room with the ship's final position. He passed men on the bridge who were pointing out the lights of a steamer to the north, but he paid little attention. The screech of venting steam was deafening as Boxhall shouted the ship's position at the captain. "Take it to the Marconi room," Smith yelled back. The fourth officer went directly to the wireless office, where he attempted to shout the ship's coordinates to Phillips and Bride. Fearing a misunderstanding due to the roaring steam, Boxhall wrote his famous numbers on a slip of paper: latitude 41°46′ N; longitude 50°14′ W. This corrected position was immediately used to amend the ship's distress call.

The real work of the night was just beginning for Murdoch, Lightoller, Boxhall, Chief Officer Henry Wilde, Third Officer Herbert J. Pitman, and Fifth Officer Harold G. Lowe. They struggled with the lifeboats, lifting them out of their chocks and swinging them over the side. They helped women, children, and some men clamber into the boats before lowering them to the sea. The forward boats had a shorter distance to drop as more of the ship's hull disappeared into the dark water. Considering that *Titanic* was sinking beneath them, the men worked surprisingly slowly at the beginning. More than thirty additional minutes ticked off the ship's life between the captain's "swing out" order and the launching of the first boat.

Procrastination in launching the first boats cannot be attributed either to problems with equipment or to a lack of skilled manpower.

The elite group of skilled seamen who had helped Lightoller perform boat drills for the Board of Trade inspector was still on board. The Welin davits were of the very latest design. Third Officer Pitman actually bragged about the ease of launching boats that night, thanks to Welin's innovative equipment.

> MR. PITMAN: . . . it struck me at the time the easy way the boats went out, the great improvement the modern davits were on the old-fashioned davits. I had about five or six men there, and the boat was out in about two minutes.
>
> SENATOR SMITH: You are referring now to No. 5 Boat?
>
> MR. PITMAN: No. 5 boat.
>
> SENATOR SMITH: The boat at your station?
>
> MR. PITMAN: At my station; yes. The boat went out in two or three minutes. I thought what a jolly fine idea they were, because with the old-fashioned davits it would require about a dozen men to lift her, a dozen men at each end. I got her overboard all right and lowered level with the rail.

There was entertainment during the delay. The ship's orchestra, awake now and properly dressed, struck up a ragtime tune.

> The orchestra was playing a lively tune. They started to lower the lifeboats after a lapse of some minutes. There was little excitement. As the lifeboats were being launched, many of the first-cabin passengers expressed their preference of staying on the ship. The passengers were constantly being assured that there was no danger.

> Nobody ever thought the ship was going down. I do not think there was a person that night, I do not think there was a man on the boat who thought the ship was going down. They speak of the bravery of the men. I do not think there was any particular bravery, because none of the men thought it was going down. . . .

**12:35 A.M.** Lights of a ship visible to north. Distance uncertain. This other vessel seems to be stopped. Mr. Boxhall told to communicate with blinker and rockets. No response. —H. G. LOWE, Fifth Officer

Back on *Titanic*'s bridge, Boxhall had a few moments to study the lights glimmering north of the ship. "It was two masthead lights of a steamer," he recalled in London. "I could see the light with the naked eye, but I could not define what it was. But, by the aid of a pair of glasses I found it was the two masthead lights of a vessel, probably about a half a point on the port bow." That is the expected relative bearing of *Californian* from *Titanic* based on the ships' known positions that night.

**12:40 A.M.** Bulkhead to boiler room #5 has failed. Mr. Andrews says the ship cannot float. We must launch the boats.                —E. J. SMITH, Master

Moving any damaged ship in which the bulkheads have been weakened as *Titanic*'s were is risky enough to warrant special attention in U.S. Navy training manuals. A major danger noted by the Navy is "panting" or a wobbling movement of weakened bulkheads. One possible cause for panting can be the "sloshing" of water inside a compartment resulting from movement of the ship.

> loose rivets, cracked seams and panting of bulkheads are indications of the need for shoring. Panting is a dangerous condition because it causes metal fatigue which in time will result in cracking and splitting.

The situation described by this military training manual sounds much like what happened to the bulkhead between boiler rooms #5 and #6. For almost an hour after the accident, there was no significant water above the tank top in #5. Then, at 12:40 A.M., a sudden rush of water burst out of the coal bunker attached to this bulkhead, forcing the abandonment of boiler room #5.

The British report claimed the coal bunker had been filled by water from the same open seam that was sending a spray into boiler room #5. The report concluded that the relatively thin metal of the bunker was not strong enough to retain the weight of this water, so it broke open under the pressure. Not everyone in London agreed that only the coal bunker had failed and not the bulkhead. Clement Edwards, the counsel for the Dock, Wharf, Riverside, and General Workers Union, voiced his strong belief that it was the bulkhead that let go rather than the bunker.

> MR. EDWARDS: . . . there is grounds for suggesting . . . I am going to suggest that the bulkhead between 5 and 6, on the evidence, did give way.

It is possible that the watertight bulkhead between the two forward boiler rooms (#5 and #6) failed due to a combination of the weight of water and earlier fire damage. This was also the bulkhead that had been heated cherry red by the ten-day bunker fire earlier in the voyage. Heat-weakened metal may have cracked due to panting caused by water sloshing inside flooded boiler room #6. Even minor waves inside this compartment would have meant surge after surge of pressure against the heat-damaged steel. One slosh, even two or three, would not have caused any problem, but several hundred cycles over twenty minutes of steaming may have seriously weakened the metal.

This bulkhead also may have acted as a "stress riser" when the ship slid sideways off the iceberg, resisting thousands of tons of compression during the last split second of contact between ship and ice. How much this pressure affected the heat-weakened steel cannot be known, but it must have increased the likelihood of the bulkhead's eventual failure.

The London proceedings devoted some discussion to an interesting, but probably meaningless, aspect of the bulkhead story. Stoker Frederick Barrett mentioned (apparently off the record) that a hole had been knocked in this bulkhead, possibly as a result of the bunker fire. Investigators were curious about any effect this may have had on the strength of the watertight dividing wall between the two boiler rooms. The existence of the hole was never proven at the hearings, and it may never have existed except as a misunderstanding of Barrett's comments by the British investigators.

The significance of this hole lies in the discussion it caused, not in any impact the opening may have had upon the sinking of the ship. People who were neither sailors nor naval architects mistakenly presumed themselves experts in these highly technical areas by virtue of their participation in the proceedings. All of the speakers were investigators and lawyers, yet they freely came to an engineering conclusion about the importance of a hole that may never have existed. The following discussion is somewhat abridged to remove much legal palaver. The attorney general was Sir Rufus Isaacs, who represented the British Board of Trade.

> THE ATTORNEY-GENERAL: I would like to know where we are upon one point. My friend has raised a point again about the bulkhead between 5 and 6 boiler section . . .
>
> MR. EDWARDS: I think that probably what the learned Attorney-General has in mind is the reference which I made two or three days ago as to the suggestion that a hole had been made.
>
> THE ATTORNEY-GENERAL: Yes.

MR. EDWARDS: What I said then was that, from my information, this had not affected the strength of the bulkhead as affected by the fire; and that, therefore, I deemed it immaterial in any event; but I have not abandoned, and I do not abandon, the suggestion that this bulkhead was seriously damaged by fire on the evidence exactly as it stands before the court.

THE COMMISSIONER: I do not understand that. You seem to be blowing hot and cold.

MR. EDWARDS: That may be due to the fire, my Lord . . . I did say that Barrett, in his evidence, as far as I remember, had spoken about a hole being bored in a watertight compartment between sections 5 and 6. That was not given in evidence. I have caused very careful enquiries to be made, and even supposing the statement to be correct, I am given to understand it would not in the least degree interfere with or detract from the strength of that bulkhead as affected by the fire.

In his book *A Night to Remember*, Walter Lord was not speculating when he related the story of a man trapped in boiler room #5 by the sudden flood of water. Engineer John Shepherd, who had spent much of the time since the accident climbing up and down stairways from boiler room to boiler room, suffered a broken leg when he fell into an open manhole. He simply did not see the opening because of thick steam and smoke filling the stokehold while the fires were being drawn. The injured man was carried into the pump room. He was still resting there when the whole compartment suddenly flooded, killing him.

According to author Lord, the manhole that snared Shepherd was on the starboard side of the tank top deck. Its position lends credence to the theory that iceberg damaged only the starboard bottom of the ship. Engineers would have opened starboard manholes to check for flooding and to rig suction hoses. Those hoses would have prevented the starboard manholes from being closed again. Manholes serving the undamaged void spaces on the port side may have been opened to check for flooding, but they would have been quickly closed for safety.

Significantly, water did not flood upward through this open manhole. From Walter Lord's description, the space beneath the manhole was dry enough for men to work on the bilge pump valves. This indicates that the starboard tank space beneath boiler room #5 either was undamaged or had received such light damage that pumping was

161

keeping it dry. Either way, this reinforces Chief Engineer Joseph G. Bell's statement to J. Bruce Ismay that the pumps kept up with the flooding until after the ship resumed making way.

Lord's description of an injured man unable to escape death from a torrent of water tumbling through a broken bulkhead is unforgettable. However, the men on the bridge knew nothing of Engineer Shepherd's fate. To them, the sudden collapse of the bulkhead meant only one thing: it was time to launch the lifeboats. Murdoch and Lightoller began looking for women and children to load into the fragile wooden craft. Boat #7 was first on the starboard side and #6 first on the port. Both boats were conveniently located outside the entrance to the ship's ornate grand stairway.

Standing on the port side of the boat deck, Lightoller was convinced the lights clearly visible on the northern horizon were a nearby ship. He instructed boats launched from the port side to pull for those lights because they appeared to be so close. *Californian* has always been considered the most likely source of the lights seen from *Titanic* because that freighter's crew also saw lights that night on their ship's southern horizon—in the direction of *Titanic*. The officers who paced *Californian*'s open bridge were certain these lights belonged to a large passenger liner, and *Californian*'s captain, Stanley Lord, even identified them as *Titanic* just prior to the accident. Investigators in 1912 were struck by how closely the actions of the lights seen by *Californian* matched the movements of *Titanic* as it foundered.

Questions regarding the relative positions of *Titanic* and *Californian* eventually focus on their respective latitudes. After 12:15 A.M., the two ships were lying motionless almost north and south of each other on very similar longitudes. This north-south orientation means the difference in their latitudes approximates the distance they were apart in nautical miles using the following formula: 1 minute of latitude equals 1 nautical mile of distance.

*Californian* verified its latitude at 7:30 P.M. by measuring the angle of the Pole Star (Polaris) to the horizon. Captain Lord claimed his ship spent the night surrounded by ice at 42°5′ N, 50°7′ W. Using the actual location of the wreckage, and Captain Lord's Pole Star position at 10:30 P.M., the distance in latitude between the ships after 12:45 P.M. (when *Titanic* finally stopped moving) calculates at 21 miles. The stricken liner had steamed about 3 miles northward following its accident, making the location of the deadly iceberg encounter about 24 miles south of the spot where Captain Lord claimed his ship drifted through the night.

Distances of either 21 or 24 miles raise a significant problem. Due to the curvature of the earth, neither ship could have been seen from the bridge of the other at a range of more than 17 miles. The maximum distance at which officers on the bridges of the two ships could have seen each other can be calculated using Bowditch's table 12, distance of the Horizon. We know that *Titanic*'s bridge was about 60 feet above the water; *Californian*'s about 40 feet. We must add 5 feet to both measurements to approximate the height of the observers' eyes above their respective decks. Referencing table 12 gives the distance to the horizon for an observer on the bridge of either ship. The two resultant horizon distances are added to get the maximum range of visibility at which the officers of the two ships could have seen each other.

### Distance of the Horizon
Based on *Bowditch*, table 12

| Ship | Height of Eye (ft.) | Distance to Horizon (ft.) |
|---|---|---|
| *Titanic* | 65 | 9.4 |
| *Californian* | 45 | 7.8 |
| TOTAL DISTANCE | — | 17.2 |

This table seems to put an end to the *Titanic/Californian* debate. At best, the ships appear to have been too far apart to have observed each other. However, the evidence that the two ships did see each other is compelling. Compare what the watch officers on *Californian* reported seeing with the actual actions of *Titanic:*

### Events of April 14–15, 1912

| *Titanic* Time | *Titanic* | *Californian* |
|---|---|---|
| 10:21 P.M. | Ship is steaming west on course of 266° at 22.25 knots. | Ice prevents steaming; ship stopped at 42°5' N, 57°7' W per Captain Lord. |
| 11:00 P.M. | Steaming westward course 266° crossing longitude 49°45' W. Wireless operator Phillips ignores *Californian*'s ice warning. | Steamer seen approaching from the eastward. Captain Lord believes it to be *Titanic* and has wireless operator warn of packed ice and bergs. The green (starboard) sidelight of steamer is visible as it approaches |
| 11:40 P.M. | Ship makes S turn to "port around" iceberg; strikes on underwater ice shelf and slides to a stop pointing east of north. | Steamer appears to turn out deck lights. After a few minutes, the other ship's red (port) sidelight becomes visible. |

*Titanic*

| Time | *Titanic* | *Californian* |
|---|---|---|
| 11:50 P.M. | Ship resumes steaming at bare steerageway on a course just east of north. | Attempt to contact other ship by Morse lamp fails. Change of watch. |
| 12:10 P.M. | Ship's engines are stopped for last time. Hull shoots forward for some time. | A "bright glow" of lights is noticed on the afterdeck of the other ship. Port sidelight and masthead light continue to be seen. |
| 12:45 A.M. | First lifeboat is launched. Boxhall fires the first socket signal, which throws white pyrotechnic stars into sky above ship. The best estimate by Boxhall and others is that eight socket signals were fired that night. | The other ship is observed to fire white rockets. It is later agreed that the other ship fired a total of eight white rockets. |
| 1:40 A.M. | Launching of lifeboats continues. The last socket signal is fired. The downward tilt of the bow is becoming pronounced, and the foredeck goes underwater. | Second Officer Herbert Stone observes that the other ship is "very queer out of water, her lights looked queer." No more white rockets are observed being fired by other ship. |
| 2:18 A.M. | Lights blink once, then go out forever as the ship begins final breakup. | The other steamer seems to be "disappearing." It is lost to sight at this time. |

Correlations between events on *Titanic* and the actions of "the other ship" observed by *Californian* seem to prove that the freighter's crew watched the giant passenger liner sink. This conclusion was reinforced by members of that crew. *Californian*'s third officer, Charles V. Groves, said in London that he was certain of what he saw, "There was absolutely no doubt of her being a passenger steamer, at least in my mind." Ernest Gill, assistant donkeyman (operator of an auxiliary, or "donkey," steam engine) concurred, "It could not have been anything but a passenger boat, she was too large."

Boxhall continued watching the lights on the northern horizon while he and quartermaster George Rowe prepared distress signals. Although a minor point, *Titanic* did not carry "rockets." Instead, the ship was equipped with "socket signals" manufactured by the Cotton Powder Company. These signals were carried in lieu of both rockets and guns (signaling cannons). They were fired from sockets (hence the name) fixed to either wing of the bridge. When triggered, they shot white balls into the air that exploded with a brilliant flash and a loud report. Although these distress signals were not rockets, everyone including the men who set them off that night called them "rockets," so that is how they are remembered.

"I had sent in the meantime for some rockets," Boxhall recalled in testimony, "and told the Captain . . . I would send them off (fire the rockets) and told him when I saw this light. He said, 'Yes, carry on with it.' I was sending rockets off and watching this steamer." Boxhall and Rowe rigged the first signal in the socket on the starboard side of the bridge. Even though designed for marine use, socket signals were similar to skyrockets and other pyrotechnic devices used at holiday celebrations. They presented some danger to people standing around the launching socket. Boxhall triggered them with a lanyard from the relative safety of the semienclosed captain's bridge.

"Every time I fired a signal I had to clear everybody away from the vicinity of this socket," Boxhall said. "I remember the last one or two distress signals I sent off, the boat [emergency lifeboat #1] had gone, and they were then working on the collapsible boat which was on the deck."

Between rockets, Boxhall attempted to signal the ship to the north with a blinker light. "Come at once, we are sinking" he tapped on the Morse key that controlled the blinker light. Men on the *Californian* attempted to use the same means of communication, but the distance was too great. Due to atmospheric conditions, the natural "twinkle" of distant lights turned the long and short flashes of Morse code into a jumble of light.

**12:45 A.M.** First distress rocket launched. Continuing to Morse ship on northern horizon.                              —J. BOXHALL, Fourth Officer

*Titanic* quartermaster George Rowe recalled firing the first distress rocket at approximately 12:45 P.M. "I assisted the officer to fire them . . . and (continued) firing distress signals until about five and twenty past one," he told the U.S. Senate hearing and later reconfirmed during his London testimony. The rockets produced a brilliant white trail as they ascended into the sky. They detonated aloft with a loud report, throwing numerous white balls in an umbrella of light.

A few miles to the north, Ernest Gill was puffing a cigarette while leaning on *Californian*'s rail. "I could not smoke 'tween decks, so I went on deck again," he told the U.S. Senate in a prepared statement. "I had been on deck when I saw a white rocket about 10 miles away on the starboard side. In 7 or 8 minutes I saw distinctly a second rocket in the same place, and I said to myself, 'that must be a vessel in distress.' " Gill told Senator William Alden Smith that his first rocket sighting took place a little after 12:30 P.M., *Californian* time.

**12:46 A.M.** The first boat is away. Godspeed. —E. J. SMITH, Master

Slightly more than an hour had passed since the ship had run over the ice. Looking down 60 feet to the water alongside the hull, First Officer Murdoch finally felt the situation safe enough to order boat #7 lowered to the sea. *Titanic's* momentum had kept the ship sliding forward through the water for several minutes after the engines were stopped for the last time. Even though the ship was moving too slowly for the rudder to function, it still would have been foolhardy to attempt lowering lifeboats filled with passengers. Even boats skillfully handled by professional sailors might still have been swamped.

The delay until 12:45 A.M. in launching the first boat could only have two causes. Either the officers in charge felt it was too dangerous to launch boats from a moving ship, or they did not believe *Titanic* was foundering until shortly before 12:45. Both reasons are plausible since the ship would have been shooting forward well past 12:15 A.M. Perhaps the officers deliberately procrastinated another few minutes, hoping that taking way off the ship would slow the flooding and allow the pumps to catch up. Then, the bulkhead between boiler rooms #5 and #6 collapsed and the truth was inescapable. As Murdoch sent the first lifeboat down to the sea, Boxhall sent the first distress rocket upward into the heavens. The symbolism of these almost simultaneous acts was not lost on the crew launching the boats.

A few miles to the north, *Californian's* crew watched *Titanic's* final moments. Those who condemn Captain Lord claim that *Californian* failed to respond to obvious distress rockets from a nearby vessel. Defenders of Lord counter with maps and data aimed at proving the *Californian* was too far away to have observed *Titanic* sink. His supporters have claimed he did not refuse to go the aid of the stricken ship because he did not know the tragedy was occurring.

Whether *Californian* was 5 miles or 30 miles from the sinking ship, Lord's inexperience navigating through ice prevented him from going to the rescue of any ship that night. It was a frightened Captain Lord who was trapped by the ice, not his ship. Lord's fear was quite rational, the result of his clash with ice earlier that night. And, his fear was reinforced by what happened when *Titanic* ran into the same ice.

MR. DUNLOP: Can you tell us what the extent of the ice field was?

MR. LORD: The width of it?

MR. DUNLOP: Yes, the width of it from your position to the position of the wreck.

MR. LORD: It was running north and south after the style of a "T," and the "T" was dividing the position where the Titanic was supposed to have sunk and where we were. I suppose for the two or three miles all the way down to where she was, it was studded with bergs and loose ice.

MR. DUNLOP: If any vessel was proceeding in a south-westerly direction towards the place where the Titanic was she would encounter this field ice?

MR. LORD: Yes.

The questioner during these exchanges was Robertson Dunlop, a solicitor who appeared on behalf of the Leland Line, the company that owned *Californian* and employed Captain Lord. As such, he was admittedly a friendly examiner.

MR. DUNLOP: Supposing you had known at 1:15 A.M. that the Titanic was in distress somewhere to the southward and westward of you. Could you, in fact, have reached her before she sank?

MR. LORD: What time did she sink?

MR. DUNLOP: Do you not know?

MR. LORD: I have heard so many different rumors of that out in the States that I really do not know.

MR. DUNLOP: What time do you think she sank?

MR. LORD: Somewhere between 2 and 3 A.M.

MR. DUNLOP: Assuming that she sank somewhere between 2 and 3, could you, in fact, if you had known at 1:15 A.M. in the morning that the Titanic was in distress to the southward and westward of you, have reached her before, say 3 A.M.?

MR. LORD: No, most certainly not.

MR. DUNLOP: Could you have navigated with any degree of safety to your vessel at night through the ice that you, in fact, encountered?

MR. LORD: It would have been most dangerous.

COMMISSIONER MERSEY: Am I to understand that this is what you mean to say, that if he had known the vessel was the Titanic he would have made no attempt whatever to reach it?

MR. DUNLOP: No, my Lord, I do not suggest that. (To witness) What would you have done? No doubt you would have made an attempt?

MR. LORD: Most certainly I would have made every effort to get down to her.

MR. DUNLOP: Would the attempt from what you now know in fact have succeeded?

MR. LORD: I do not think we would have got there before the Carpathia did, if we would have got there as soon.

Captain Lord must have known his actions that night would come into question. At 8:00 A.M. on April 15, however, he probably did not yet realize that he would become the primary scapegoat for such a huge loss of life. It suited both investigations to blame somebody, and this captain who had slept while his crew watched tragedy unfold was a perfect target. Senator Smith summed up the case against Lord in his subcommittee's final report.

> The committee is forced to the inevitable conclusion that the Californian, controlled by the same company, was nearer the Titanic than the 19 miles reported by her captain, and that her officers and crew saw the distress signals of the Titanic and failed to respond to them in accordance with the dictates of humanity, international usage, and the requirements of law. . . . In our opinion such conduct, whether arising from indifference or gross carelessness, is most reprehensible, and places upon the commander of Californian a grave responsibility.

In London, wreck commissioner Lord Mersey's conclusion was the same, even though his criticism of Captain Lord's conduct was worded with typical British reserve. *Californian,* Mersey concluded, had ignored the cry for help from 2,200 people in peril on the sea.

> These circumstances convince me that the ship seen by the Californian was the Titanic and if so, according to Captain Lord, the two vessels were about five miles apart at the time of the disaster. . . . When she first saw the rockets the Californian could have pushed through the ice to the open water without any serious risk and so have come to the assistance of the Titanic. Had she done so she might have saved many if not all of the lives that were lost.

This criticism of Captain Lord assumes that he could have arrived in time to rescue those people trapped aboard the sinking ship. Lord was quite correct in saying that, as of 1:15 A.M., it would have been impossible for him to have arrived on the scene before *Titanic* sank. However, even if Lord had responded to Boxhall's first rocket at 12:45 A.M., it is unlikely that *Californian* could have rescued the 1,500 people without lifeboats still trapped aboard the sinking liner. Such a rescue would have required an extremely risky bit of seamanship. The smaller freighter would have had to go alongside the doomed vessel so people could jump to *Californian* from *Titanic*'s decks. There simply wasn't time to use the lifeboats. Transferring more than 1,500 frightened people from ship to ship would have taken time. Three quarters of an hour would hardly have been long enough, but for sake of argument it will be allowed for that purpose. Considering this requirement, *Californian* would have had to come alongside *Titanic* no later than 1:20 A.M. to have removed the people before the sinking ship became too unstable for safety.

Captain Lord had a scant thirty-five minutes after Boxhall's first rocket during which to have made a hell-for-leather dash through pack ice on a dark night. If the ships had been only 12 miles apart (the maximum distance *Californian* could have been seen from a *Titanic* lifeboat), the freighter would have been forced to achieve 20 knots in order to have performed a successful rescue. Unfortunately, Lord's single-screw ship had an operational speed of only 11 knots and a top speed of about 13 knots. Based on *Californian*'s top speed, the two ships would have had to be no more than 7.6 miles apart for *Californian* to have arrived at *Titanic*'s side in time for a successful rescue.

Even if the two ships had been rafted together, there were no ready-made gangplanks or canvas slides available to help passengers cross from one ship to the other. Escaping from the sloping decks of the liner to those of the freighter would have required negotiating a vertical steel cliff. Most of *Titanic*'s open decks were as much as 20 feet above those of the smaller freighter, and decks at the stern of the liner were actually rising higher as the bow tipped downward. Not many people are capable of dropping from the height of a two-story roof without injury. Only at the forward end of the boat deck would there have been an opportunity for easy movement of people between the two ships. It would have been a dicey rescue in the dark. In order to maintain equal deck heights, *Californian* would have been forced to move backward as *Titanic*'s bow plunged deeper into the ocean.

The other alternative, shuttling passengers in the lifeboats, would have been impossible during the time available. Lifeboats in 1912 were powered by what sailors sarcastically called "Swedish steam": human muscles. It would have taken considerable time to row back and forth ferrying survivors. Reloading boats while they were in the water would have been extremely difficult because of the lack of doors low on *Titanic*'s side. There would have been no time to waste manhandling lifeboats back up to *Titanic*'s boat deck for reloading, but such hoisting would have been necessary. A 1909 rescue made by the White Star liner *Baltic* illustrates the daunting task of transferring people by lifeboats. It took more than ten hours to carry away the passengers and crew from the damaged liner *Florida* after that ship rammed and sank another liner, *Republic*.

In reality, if *Californian* had raced to the site of the disaster, it would only have rescued Captain Lord's reputation and robbed Captain Arthur H. Rostron of *Carpathia* of his moment of fame. At top speed, *Californian* would have arrived just as *Titanic*'s stern pointed into the sky like a black finger of death. A few nearly frozen survivors might have been plucked from the water—but only a few. Survivors bobbing in the lifeboats might have still been waiting in the first light of dawn for rescue, because retrieving lifeboats in darkness would have been dangerous.

Once the liner sank, it would have been almost impossible to rescue individual swimmers from the freezing water on a dark night. Human heads are difficult to spot in full daylight, and night makes the task virtually impossible. Rescue of anyone in the water would have required steaming the freighter into the mass of struggling people left behind by the sunken ship. Freezing survivors would not have been able to swim out of the way of the rescue ship and, undoubtedly, some would have been run over.

Those not killed by the rescue ship would have been rendered helpless by the cold water within minutes of *Titanic*'s disappearance. Few swimmers struggling in below-freezing water would have had enough strength to grab rescue ropes, let alone climb rope ladders. Even those lucky enough to have been hauled to *Californian*'s deck may not have survived. No one in 1912 knew how to treat hypothermia, a potentially fatal condition in which the body temperature has been lowered to the point where the brain and internal organs stop working.

Discussing the difficulties of removing 1,500 people from the decks of the sinking ship is not idle speculation. Once again, proof comes from another ship's misfortune: the *Andrea Doria*, which sank in 1956. Nearby vessels included a tanker, a freighter, and a U.S. Navy transport vessel, none of which was able to assist in the evacuation of the sinking Italian liner. The ships were forced to stand off helplessly and watch the mass of people huddled on the liner's sloping decks. Passengers trapped on the listing *Andrea Doria* could not be rescued until the French passenger liner *Ile de France* arrived with its thirty lifeboats. *Ile* rescued 753 survivors, while 545 were taken aboard *Stockholm*, the other vessel involved in the collision. The three other would-be rescue ships combined carried fewer than 300 people to safety.

The fact that Captain Lord could not have reached the sinking liner in time does not exonerate him in any way from his failure to make the attempt. International law and the customs of the sea do not require that rescue attempts be successful. All they ask is that an honest attempt be made to aid those in peril on the sea.

> THE ATTORNEY-GENERAL: What did you think this vessel was firing rockets for?
>
> MR. LORD: I asked the second officer. I said, "Is that a company's signal?" And, he said he did not know.
>
> THE ATTORNEY-GENERAL: Then that did not satisfy you?
>
> MR. LORD: No, it did not.
>
> THE ATTORNEY-GENERAL: I mean whatever it was it did not satisfy you that it was a company's signal?
>
> MR. LORD: It did not, but I had no reason to think it was anything else.
>
> COMMISSIONER MERSEY: That seems odd. You knew that the vessel was sending up this rocket was in a position of danger.
>
> MR. LORD: No, my Lord, I did not.
>
> COMMISSIONER MERSEY: Well, danger if she moved?
>
> MR. LORD: If she moved, yes.

Captain Lord had one sure way to find out whether the vessel firing rockets was in trouble. He could have awakened his wireless operator and asked him to contact the other ship. As Lord admitted in London, the mystery of the lights would have been solved almost immediately.

> MR. SCANLAN: You had the Marconi?
>
> MR. LORD: Yes, we had.
>
> MR. SCANLAN: Would not it have been quite a simple thing for you at that time when you were in doubt as to what was the name of the ship, and as to what was the reason of her sending up rockets, to have wakened up your Marconi operator and asked him to speak to this ship?
>
> MR. LORD: It would if it had worried me a great deal, but it did not worry me. I was still thinking of the company's signal.

171

MR. SCANLAN: At all events, now in the light of your experience, would it not have been a prudent thing to do?

MR. LORD: Well, we would have got the Titanic's signals if we had done.

Captain Lord could not discount the descriptions of *Titanic*'s white rockets given by members of his crew. Instead, he extended his personal fiction by transforming those pyrotechnics from obvious distress signals to what he called "company signals." It was common practice prior to radio for shipping companies to use various types of flares and rockets to signal among their ships. Lord knew that company signals did not resemble *Titanic*'s rockets, but not to lie to himself in this manner would have forced him to admit his fear of the ice. He was determined to remain stopped until the relative safety of daylight returned. To Lord, remaining motionless was the only prudent thing to do. This ice was dangerous. It had almost claimed his ship, and now the "unsinkable" *Titanic* was in distress because of it. How much more proof of ice danger did a captain need?

# A SHORTAGE OF WOMEN

Monday, April 15, 1912

**12:47 A.M. to 2:20 A.M.**

OFTEN glossed over in the *Titanic* story are claims of ignorance by the ship's officers concerning the improved capabilities of their ship's davits and lifeboats. All said they feared loading the boats to capacity with passengers because, prior to 1911, the davits, tackles, and wooden lifeboats were not strong enough to carry a full load of people. On older ships it had been necessary to lower boats with only a small crew of sailors aboard; the passengers were loaded only after the boats were in the water.

*Titanic's* newer lifeboat/davit combinations were capable of lowering boats fully laden with passengers, but surviving officers claimed they were never told this vital information. These claims are dubious at best. *Titanic's* officers must have seen the Welin Davit Company's advertisements in marine publications touting the new davits, tackle, and boats installed on Olympic-class ships. Some of *Titanic's* officers must have participated in the weight test conducted aboard *Olympic* in 1911. This test involved lowering boats filled with weights equal to a full passenger load. Axel Welin's equipment and the newly designed wooden lifeboats (built by Harland and Wolff specifically for the Olympic-class ships) easily passed the test.

This supposed lack of knowledge on the part of the officers came to light during the U.S. Senate probe when Second Officer Charles H. Lightoller was questioned about launching a half-full lifeboat.

SENATOR SMITH: How did it happen you did not put more people into that boat?

MR. LIGHTOLLER: Because I did not consider it safe.

SENATOR SMITH: In a great emergency like that, where there were limited facilities, could you not have afforded to try to put more people into the boat?

MR. LIGHTOLLER: I did not know it was urgent then. I had no idea it was urgent.

SENATOR SMITH: Did you not know it was urgent?

MR. LIGHTOLLER: Nothing like it.

SENATOR SMITH: Supposing you had known it was urgent, what would you have done?

MR. LIGHTOLLER: I would have acted to the best of my judgement, then.

SENATOR SMITH: Tell me what you would have thought wise—

MR. LIGHTOLLER: (interrupting) I would have taken more risks. I should not have considered it wise to put more in, but I might have taken more risks.

SENATOR SMITH: As a matter of fact, are not these lifeboats so constructed as to accommodate 40 people?

MR. LIGHTOLLER: 65 in the water, sir, in the water.

SENATOR SMITH: 65 in the water and about 40 as they are being put into the water.

MR. LIGHTOLLER: No, sir.

SENATOR SMITH: How?

MR. LIGHTOLLER: No sir, it all depends on your gears. If it were an old ship you would barely dare to put 25 in.

SENATOR SMITH: But, this was a new one.

MR. LIGHTOLLER: And, therefore, I took more chances with her afterwards.

Senator William Alden Smith found it difficult to understand why *Titanic*'s second officer did not consider loading lifeboats on a sinking ship an urgent situation. Lightoller's seemingly inexplicable claim appears to be based on a technicality: he was not present on the bridge when Andrews made his famous pronouncement about water tumbling over the bulkheads. In reality, however, this technicality did not prevent him from noticing the bow sagging into the water, sure proof the ship was sinking beneath his feet.

Fifth Officer Harold G. Lowe said he was afraid that fully loaded boats would break apart while being launched. Calling up fears based on outdated equipment on older ships was the stock alibi for underloading *Titanic*'s lifeboats.

SENATOR SMITH: What is the capacity of a lifeboat like that under the British regulations?

MR. LOWE: Sixty-five point five.

SENATOR SMITH: What do you mean by "point five"? Do you mean a little more?

MR. LOWE: A boy, or something like that.

SENATOR SMITH: A little below 65 or a little above it?

MR. LOWE: More than 65; 65-point-5.

SENATOR SMITH: I want that understood. Do you with the committee to understand that a lifeboat whose capacity is 65 under the British regulations could not be lowered with safety, with new tackle and equipment, containing more than 50 people?

MR. LOWE: The dangers are that if you overcrowd the boat the first thing that you will have will be that the boat will buckle up like that [indicating] at the two ends, because she is suspended from both ends and there is no support in the middle.

SENATOR SMITH: These lifeboats were all on the upper deck?

MR. LOWE: Yes, sir.

SENATOR SMITH: If it is dangerous to lower a boat from the upper deck, filled to capacity prescribed by the British regulations. . . .

MR. LOWE: [interrupting] Yes; that is the floating capacity.

SENATOR SMITH: Sixty-five plus is the floating capacity?

MR. LOWE: That is the floating capacity; that is, in the water, when she is at rest in the water. That is not when she is in the air.

SENATOR SMITH: I am coming to that. Then 50 would be the lowering capacity, in your judgement?

MR. LOWE: Yes; I should not like to put more than 50 in . . .

Even after almost ninety years, Lowe's testimony *sounds* convincing. He seemed to believe that *Titanic*'s lifeboats would buckle if loaded to capacity before being lowered into the water. However, fear of gear failure was not his or anyone else's primary reason for underloading lifeboats that night. Lowe and the other surviving officers seem to have concealed the much darker reason for not cramming each boat with the maximum number of people: it was part of a plan to prevent panic among the doomed passengers.

Although passengers were awakened and told to don lifebelts, they were not systematically herded to the boat deck as would be done today. There was not even a suggestion that they should go to the lifeboats. Instead, confused passengers were left to mill about in the warmth of the public rooms, waiting and wondering what was happening. Relatively few people took the initiative to brave the freezing temperatures on deck until after 1:00 A.M. A Canadian passenger, Major Arthur G. Peuchen, described the situation to the U.S. Senate hearings.

SENATOR SMITH: Do you know . . . whether any alarm was sounded to arouse the passengers from their rooms after the impact?

MAJ. PEUCHEN: There was no alarm sounded whatever. In fact, I talked with two young ladies who claimed to have had a very narrow escape. They said their stateroom was right near the Astors, I think next to it, and they were not awakened.

SENATOR SMITH: They were not awakened?

MAJ. PEUCHEN: They slept through the crash, and they were awakened by Mrs. Astor.

As is typical in oral testimony, the questioning wandered off track for a moment by discussing the location of the two girls' stateroom. After settling that matter, testimony came back to the main topic, the lack of a general alarm.

SENATOR SMITH: I think you said that from your judgement and from your own observation there was no general alarm given?

MAJ. PEUCHEN: No, I did not hear one. I was around the boat all the time . . .

SENATOR FLETCHER: Major, do you mean for us to understand that at the time lifeboat No. 4 and lifeboat No. 6 on the port side of the ship were loaded and lowered every woman in sight was given an opportunity?

MAJ. PEUCHEN: Every woman on the port side was given an opportunity. In fact, we had not enough women to put into the boats. We were looking for them. I can not understand why we did not take some men. The boats would have held more.

At first, only a few lucky *Titanic* passengers found their way to the boat deck and the frigid night air. These hardy explorers found small groups of officers and sailors working on the davits. Women and children who appeared on deck were quickly shuffled into the lifeboats. However, there were so few women and even fewer children that the first lifeboats could only be partially filled. The officers allowed a few men and boys to board when no one else was about, First Office William M. Murdoch being more lenient with the male passengers than Lightoller was. History has asked why so many of the early boats left virtually half empty. The answer is obvious: it was the inevitable result of not calling people to the boats.

SENATOR SMITH: How did it happen that you did not put more people into lifeboat No. 3 than forty-five?

MR. LOWE: There did not seem to be any people there.

SENATOR SMITH: You did not find anybody that wanted to go?

MR. LOWE: These that were there did not seem to want to go. I hollered out, "Who's next for the boat?" and there was no response.

One of the ship's barbers, A. H. Weikman, told a similar story in an affidavit. "I helped to launch the lifeboats," he said in his statement to the U.S. Senate hearings. "There seemed to be a shortage of women." This strange situation was confirmed in London by another member of the crew, seaman William Lucas: "there was not anybody handy. No women. I was singing out for women myself." Lucas helped load boats all along the port side. "They were not all filled," he said, "because there were no women knocking about."

Senator Smith questioned Second Officer Lightoller about the lack of people on the boat deck.

MR. LIGHTOLLER: In the case of the last boat I got out, I had the utmost difficulty in finding women. It was the very last boat of all, after all the other boats were put out and we came forward to put out the collapsible boats. In the meantime the forward emergency boat had been put out by one of the other officers. So we wounded up the tackles and got the collapsible boat to put that over. Then I called for women and could not get hold of any. Somebody said, "There are no women." With this, several men—

SENATOR SMITH: Who said that?

MR. LIGHTOLLER: I do not know, sir.

SENATOR SMITH: On what deck was that?

MR. LIGHTOLLER: On the boat deck.

The accompanying table tells the story. Based on a report by the British Board of Trade, it shows the number of people loaded into the various boats. Early in the loading process, the number of people loaded into each boat was small. Toward the end, when it became increasingly apparent that the ship was sinking, the boats began filling to (or beyond) their rated capacities. The feared rush of people for the boats began. In at least one case, a crush of frightened passengers forced one officer to use his pistol to maintain order. But that was later. During the early minutes, the lifeboats were launched from a boat deck that was largely devoid of passengers.

## Lifeboat Loading

| PORT BOATS | | | STARBOARD BOATS | | |
|---|---|---|---|---|---|
| Boat Number | Time Launched | Total People | Boat Number | Time Launched | Total People |
| 6 | 12:55 | 28 | 7 | 12:45 | 27 |
| 8 | 1:10 | 39 | 5 | 12:55 | 41 |
| 10 | 1:20 | 55 | 3 | 1:00 | 50 |
| 12 | 1:25 | 42 | 1 | 1:10 | 12* |
| 14 | 1:30 | 63 | 9 | 1:20 | 56 |
| 16 | 1:35 | 56 | 11 | 1:25 | 70 |

| | PORT BOATS | | | STARBOARD BOATS | |
|---|---|---|---|---|---|
| Boat Number | Time Launched | Total People | Boat Number | Time Launched | Total People |
| 2 | 1:45 | 26* | 13 | 1:35 | 64 |
| 4 | 1:55 | 40 | 15 | 1:35 | 70 |
| D | 2:05 | 44 | C | 1:40 | 71 |
| B | floated off | | A | floated off | |

* Emergency boats with only a forty-person capacity.

**12:51 A.M.**    The great graybeard of the White Star Line, Captain Edward J. Smith, was in a most awkward situation as he stood on the deserted bridge. He was still master of *Titanic*, but only until the North Atlantic would claim his ship. Inch by inch, his command was disappearing into the sea. All of the necessary orders had been given. The boats were being readied, and passengers were milling about in their lifebelts. Fourth Officer Boxhall was launching rockets, and wireless was calling to ships beyond visual range. Captain Smith had little more to do than let his crew work and watch his ship die.

In fact, Smith found himself in a peculiar circumstance in which he could do the most by doing the least. A dramatic "abandon ship" order would have created the panic he hoped to avoid at all costs. As the ship's captain, he couldn't even walk through the public rooms for fear of letting the bad news slip out. Earlier during the voyage, he had willingly surrendered increasing amounts of his authority to his employer, J. Bruce Ismay. Now, the authority he retained was insufficient to alter the course of events. Captain Smith was a commander with little left to command. He stayed close to his bridge, a control center with nothing left to control. There was no place else for him to go.

Many passengers, especially in third class, did not learn the ship was being abandoned until after the last lifeboats were floating off the top of the officers' quarters. If Captain Smith had made a general "abandon ship" announcement at 12:15 A.M., there is little doubt a panic-stricken rush for the boats would have followed. Even the officers' pistols would not have been able to prevent chaos. It is doubtful that anywhere near seven hundred people would have survived such mayhem. Imagine a mob trying to lower boats full of frightened people the equivalent of six stories without dumping everyone into the icy water.

Instead, eyewitness reports, confirmed by counts of the passengers actually loaded into the lifeboats, show that Captain Smith and his officers wisely filled boats with only those people who were readily available from the boat deck. These people were more likely to have been first- or second-class passengers because the boat deck was a first- and second-class promenade. If the lifeboats had been stored in third-class space, the distribution of deaths among the classes would have been reversed. Either way, however, the captain would still have been faced with the necessity of not issuing a formal "abandon ship" order. Class distinctions may have determined who got to the boat deck, but class was not part of the selection process when it came to boarding the boats.

SENATOR SMITH: [W]as it a part of your duty to select the people who were to get into lifeboat No. 3 and No. 5?

MR. LOWE: Yes, I aided Mr. Murdoch generally, but . . .

SENATOR SMITH: What did you do about it yourself? Did you arbitrarily select from the deck?

MR. LOWE: You say "select." There was no such thing as selecting. It was simply the first woman, whether first class, second class, third class, or sixty-seventh class. It was all the same; women and children were first.

SENATOR SMITH: You mean there was a procession of women . . .

MR. LOWE: A procession at both ends of the boat.

SENATOR SMITH: Coming toward these lifeboats?

MR. LOWE: Yes.

SENATOR SMITH: Did that extend beyond the upper deck?

MR. LOWE: No, no, there were only little knots around the deck, little crowds.

SENATOR SMITH: Now, as they came along, would you pass them, one at a time, into the lifeboat? What orders did you have; to pass women and children?

MR. LOWE: I simply shouted, "Women and children first; men stand back."

SENATOR SMITH: Do you know how many women there were on the boat?

MR. LOWE: I do not, sir.

SENATOR SMITH: You put them aboard as they came along, the first being served first?

MR. LOWE: The first, first; second, second.

SENATOR SMITH: Regardless of class?

MR. LOWE: Regardless of class, or nationality, or pedigree.

With no direct role to play in loading the boats, Captain Smith decided to poke his head inside the wireless office once again. "What are you sending?" operator Harold Bride recalled the captain asking. Senior wireless operator Jack Phillips replied, "CQD." Now it was Bride's turn. Half-jokingly he suggested, "Send SOS. It's the new call, and it may be your last chance to send it." In April of 1912, SOS was the brand-new international distress call. It had been chosen because the combination of letters was simple to recognize: dot-dot-dot . . . dash-dash-dash . . . dot-dot-dot. Land stations in Europe and America caught the signal as did ships on the North Atlantic. One ship, however, did not hear the new signal: *Californian*, whose lights twinkled to the north of the sinking liner.

12:53 A.M. On the port side, Lightoller took a few minutes longer to load his first boat than did Murdoch on the starboard. Just as he was about to give the order to lower away, the Lightoller looked up to see the captain coming on deck. Smith stepped through a doorway in the officers' quarters, nearly opposite to boat #6. This door was adjacent to the wireless office, which Smith had just visited. *Titanic*'s first SOS call crackled through the airwaves as the two men attempted to speak.

Lightoller and Smith did not try to yell over the roar of escaping steam. Instead, the two officers resorted to gestures. Captain Smith's last important order of his long career was a simple nod of his head. Lightoller took this nod to mean "lower away." Suddenly, the roaring steam ended. In its place, the creaking of ropes through the blocks of the lifeboat falls filled the night.

> I will never forget the awful scene of the great steamer as we drew away. From the upper rails heroic husbands and fathers were waving and throwing kisses to their womenfolk in the receding lifeboats.

12:55 A.M. Captain Smith's desire to avoid panic could not prevent both the ship's hotel servants and its passengers from eventually noticing that something was wrong with *Titanic*. In the beginning, the stewards and stewardesses had simply awakened passengers and told them to put on their lifebelts. These hospitality workers increasingly began to push people toward the boat deck as the bow tipped down. No one needed to be told; the truth had become obvious.

Third Officer Herbert J. Pitman was busy loading lifeboat #5 on the starboard side of the boat deck. "I stood on it and said, 'Come along ladies.' There was a big crowd," he told the U.S. inquiry. "I shouted. None [women] were to be seen, so I allowed a few men to get into it. Then I jumped on the ship again."

First Officer Murdoch was supervising the loading of the starboard lifeboats. He saw Pitman jump back onto the ship. "You go away in this boat, old man," Murdoch told Pitman. "Hang around the after gangway." Pitman said he wanted to stay on the ship but did as he was told. According to his testimony, there were about forty people in the boat as it dropped to the sea.

There is evidence of a plan to fill the half-empty boats once they were afloat. Lightoller sent a party to open a sally port for this purpose, but the attempt was unsuccessful. Once the boats were in the water, their occupants feared being overwhelmed by other passengers trying to escape the doomed ship. Lifeboats rowed away and, with a few ineffectual exceptions, did not return.

Several survivors claimed Captain Smith used a megaphone to order boats to return to the sinking liner. His shouted orders may have been those heard by Fourth Officer Boxhall after he took command of lifeboat #2. "I got the crew squared up and the oars out properly and the boat squared when I heard somebody singing out from the ship. I do not know who it was," Boxhall recalled of the man who shouted, "with a megaphone for some of the boats to come back again. And, to the best of my recollection they said, 'Come round the starboard side,' so I pulled round the starboard side to the stern and had a little difficulty in getting round there." 1:45 A.M.

Even when passengers realized the gravity of their situation, they still had difficulty accepting the apparent paradox: this "unsinkable" ship was most certainly foundering. Once the situation was fully grasped, however, everyone realized the importance of the lifeboats. A crowd pushed its way to the boat deck as the launching of the sixteen regular boats neared completion. About 1:30 A.M., Murdoch ordered Steward Joseph T. Wheat to take a group of fellow stewards down to A deck and prepare to load a boat there. "When we got the men down to A deck, I lined them all up two deep round the boats, for fear there was a rush," he recalled. "Then the order was passed to pass the women and children along. After the women and children were all passed in, we filled her up with as many as the boat would possibly hold. And, Mr. Murdoch, looking over the top, said, 'You have got enough there.'"

It is conventional wisdom to say that the crews of the lifeboats feared being swamped by swimmers after the ship sank. A more logical fear was being "bombed" by people jumping six stories from the slanting decks of the sinking ship. This would have motivated the boat crews to row quickly out of range of the jumpers. A 150-pound man falling up to 40 feet into a lifeboat would probably have injured or killed himself as well as people in the boat. Worse, his weight might have splintered the wooden craft. This fear, combined with a rush of people, prompted Fifth Officer Lowe to fire his pistol while being lowered in Boat #14 at 1:30 A.M.

> MR. LOWE: I thought if one additional body was to fall into that boat, that slight jerk of the additional weight might part the hooks or carry away something . . .
>
> . . . I saw a lot of people . . . all along the ship's rails—understand it was open—and they were all glaring, more or less like wild beasts, ready to spring. That is why I yelled out to look out, and let go, bang, right along the ship's side.
>
> SENATOR SMITH: How far from the ship's side was the lifeboat you were in?
>
> MR. LOWE: I really do not know. I should say—oh, 3 or 4 feet.
>
> SENATOR SMITH: And as you went down you fired these shots?
>
> MR. LOWE: As I went down I fired these shots and without intention of hurting anybody and also with the knowledge that I did not hurt anybody.

**2:05 A.M.**   There apparently were gunshots other than those fired by Lowe that night. In his update of the story, *The Night Lives On*, author Walter Lord delved into reports of gunfire around collapsible C, the last boat launched from the starboard side. He also explored the possibility that one person was shot during a scuffle for this last remaining boat. Although there is no proven connection, the reported scuffle took place just as J. Bruce Ismay was crawling into this lifeboat.

Passengers on the port side of the ship remembered vividly seeing what appeared to be the lights of a ship to the north. These were the same lights that Boxhall had tried to signal with blinker lamp and rockets. One passenger, Mrs. J. Stuart White, described the lights and the attempt lifeboat #8 made to reach them. "Oh, it was 10 miles away, but we could see it distinctly. There was no doubt that it was a boat. But we rowed and rowed and rowed, and then we all suggested it was simply impossible for us to get to it," she told the U.S. Senate hearing.

Even though the lifeboats became more crowded with passengers as time passed, the first and second classes were overrepresented. Anyone who studies the *Titanic* tragedy is struck by the unfair distribution of death. Substantially more third-class passengers died than did first- and second-class passengers. This was as true among men as it was among women and children. Modern writers often use this disparity to point out what they view as a clear case of class distinction, but there is no evidence that Captain Smith intended social discrimination that night. His problem was quite simple: there were only 1,178 seats for more than 2,200 people. He had to save as many lives as possible without starting a mad rush for the boats among those passengers sentenced to death by the shortage of equipment.

Despite Lowe's honest efforts to include all classes in the lifeboats, most steerage passengers never found their way to the boat deck. It was more the segregated interior of the huge ship than the locked gates and doors that made it difficult for people in the third-class accommodations to move upward to the boat deck.

Third-class passengers were never intended to have direct access to the boat deck or any of the other upper decks reserved for first- and second-class passengers. Segregating immigrants in steerage was U.S. policy in 1912. American immigration regulations specified that immigrant ships keep third-class passengers physically separated from those in first and second class for "health reasons." *Titanic*'s interior architecture was designed to accomplish this separation with a minimum of doors, gates, and cage-like bars.

Steerage passengers were forced to invent routes to the lifeboats on a night when a minute or two of hesitation separated those who got a seat in a lifeboat from those who saw only empty davits. Some steerage passengers trying to make the climb ran into direct resistance from *Titanic* crew members, who were absurdly still enforcing U.S. immigration regulations.

SENATOR SMITH: Were you permitted to go on up to the top deck without any interference?

MR. BUCKLEY: Yes, sir. They tried to keep us down at first on our steerage deck. They did not want us to go up to the first-class place at all.

SENATOR SMITH: Who tried to do that?

MR. BUCKLEY: I can not say who they were. I think they were sailors.

SENATOR SMITH: What happened then? Did the steerage passengers try to get out?

MR. BUCKLEY: Yes, they did. There was one steerage passenger there, and he was getting up the steps, and just as he was going in a little gate a fellow came along and chucked him down; threw him down into the steerage place. This fellow got excited, and he ran after him, and he could not find him. He got up over the little gate. He did not find him.

SENATOR SMITH: What gate do you mean?

MR. BUCKLEY: There was a gate between the steerage and the first-class deck.

SENATOR SMITH: Was the gate locked?

MR. BUCKLEY: It was not locked at the time we made the attempt to get up there, but the sailor, or whoever it was, locked it. So that this fellow that went up after him broke the lock on it, and he went after the fellow that threw him down. He said if he could get hold of him he would throw him into the ocean.

Just which routes remained closed and which were opened will never be known with certainty. It is indisputably true, however, that the majority of third-class passengers were unable to get to the boat deck until nearly all of the lifeboats had been launched. Few seem to have begun their confusing upward climb until the launching of boats was well under way. This appears to be another consequence of the general lack of knowledge about the ship's condition among all passengers. That ignorance was the result of Captain Smith's deliberate plan to not issue a general "abandon ship" order.

Bureaucrats in Washington and Ellis Island who ordered the segregation of immigrants did not take into account that ships are subject to sinking on occasion. Keeping *Titanic*'s steerage passengers away from first-class territory also kept them away from the boat deck—and survival. Completely forgotten was a plan to provide the immigrants open access to the lifeboats in an emergency. This oversight did not have criminal intent. Rather, it was the logical consequence of thinking that the multicompartment Olympic-class ships were virtually unsinkable.

There was no special evil in the fact that the crew did not have a plan for evacuating third-class passengers. The lack of planning on White Star's part was egalitarian. There were no plans for the orderly evacuation of the millionaires in first class, either. Assistant second steward Joseph T. Wheat hinted at the lack of an organized plan to evacuate the ship during his testimony in London. He was questioned about this by W. D. Harbinson, the solicitor representing third-class passengers.

MR. HARBINSON: Was there any system of organization among the stewards?

MR. WHEAT: No, only among the heads of departments. It was left to them.

MR. HARBINSON: There was no general system which had been established, was there, and positions allotted to the stewards in case of danger?

MR. WHEAT: Yes, all the stewards were allotted to boats. Every man had his boat.

MR. HARBINSON: Then there is no general system or instruction given them as to taking charge of the different classes and the different sections of the passengers?

MR. WHEAT: No, that is understood with regard to then First, Second, and Third. They are each in charge of their own departments.

Preparing an evacuation plan for Olympic-class ships in April of 1912 was simply impossible because they did not carry enough lifeboats. White Star planned to put only enough boats aboard the combined trio of Olympics to save the number people who could be carried aboard just one of the three ships. On the night of the disaster, only if *Olympic* had rushed to the side of its sinking sister would there have been enough lifeboats for everyone aboard *Titanic*. Of course, *Olympic* was well beyond rescue range, and *Britannic* was not yet built.

Some gates or doors blocking steerage passengers eventually were opened, but only when nearly all of the regular lifeboats had been launched. No evidence has been presented to prove that the failure to open the immigrant passageways was more than an oversight caused by unthinking obedience to U.S. regulations. The result, however, was just as deadly for third-class passengers as if there had been a deliberate plan to keep them locked away from the lifeboats.

As time passed, it became increasingly obvious to everyone aboard that the ship was foundering. The forecastle head disappearing into the sea was absolute proof. People in greater numbers sought the boat deck. A few third-class passengers used a novel and dangerous route out of the steerage promenade at the stern of the ship.

MR. ABELSETH: There were a lot of steerage people there that were getting on one of these cranes that they had on deck . . . these steerage passengers were crawling along on this, over the railing, and away up to the boat deck. A lot of them were doing that.

SENATOR SMITH: They could not get up there in any other way?

MR. ABELSETH: This gate was shut.

SENATOR SMITH: Was it locked?

MR. ABELSETH: I do not know whether it was locked, but it was shut so they could not go that way.

For the most part, investigators probing the tragedy overlooked the lack of access from the third-class accommodations to the boat deck. The public became obsessed with only one aspect of the disaster: the number of lifeboats carried by passenger ships. This public focus aided Ismay and White Star in the lifeboat question. The cry "lifeboats for all" drowned any inquiries about why *Titanic* had had only sixteen boats when—save for a White Star request (at Ismay's direction) to reduce the number of lifeboats on an "unsinkable ship"—it could have carried at least thirty-two in its davits.

2:20 A.M.    Even before its ill-fated maiden voyage, *Titanic* had captured the public's imagination. Everything about the ship was spectacular, from the immense size to the sumptuous appointments of its two "millionaire's suites." In death, the ship lived up to the reputation it had created during its short life. The final moments were spectacular—with the stern upended, pointing to the sky like the warning finger of a pagan sea god. The crashing sound of tearing metal preceded this final display but was not the sound most survivors remembered. As the taffrail disappeared, a great keening arose from those poor souls the ship had left behind. This wail continued until the last of more than 1,500 victims succumbed to the freezing water. Now, *Titanic* belonged not to the ages, but to the politicians, lawyers, and tabloid journalists who would create great self-serving myths about the ship's demise.

One of those myths was that *Titanic* sank intact, as perfect as the day it was launched. Thanks to wreckage explorer Robert D. Ballard, we know the ship broke apart either at or near the surface, just as witnesses in the lifeboats claimed. Ballard's photographs show that, after the ship broke apart, the two major sections (the bow and stern) suffered far different fates. The bow planed away to the north, receiving comparatively little damage until it slammed into the bottom.

The stern appears to have been heavily damaged by implosions as air-filled compartments were crushed while the section of hull plunged into the depths.

From the similarities among their accounts, it appears that the surviving officers developed a coordinated story about the final moments of the sinking. They claimed *Titanic* sank intact, and these claims were believed as "facts" for nearly ninety years. At a cost of more than $7.5 million (in pre–World War I dollars) per vessel, White Star would not have wanted any lingering doubts about the soundness of its remaining two Olympic-class ships. Ticket buyers would avoid ships they did not perceive as strong, powerful, and above all seaworthy. A logical goal for Ismay would have been to portray *Titanic* as a sturdy vessel that fought bravely until overwhelmed by conditions beyond human control. If the public accepted this story, the safety of *Olympic* and *Britannic* (still under construction) would not be questioned.

During the British hearings, real concern arose over the issue of scantlings and the size and strength of materials used in the Olympic-class ships. It was reported that these ships were of lighter construction than competitor ships owned by Cunard. The competition, however, received government subsidies for the construction of *Lusitania* and *Mauritania*, with good reason. These Cunard liners were intended to become armed naval vessels during times of war. No such intentions existed for the Olympic sisters, which were intended only for civilian duty.

THE COMMISSIONER: It is not suggested that her scantlings were not right or that her scantlings had anything to do with the disaster.

MR. EDWARDS: Well, my Lord, with very great respect, when I come back to the bulkheads, your Lordship will see that there is a very great deal to do with the question of scantlings . . .

THE COMMISSIONER: I only want to understand it. Are you going to suggest that if the scantlings had been different the iceberg would not have knocked a hole in her side?

MR. EDWARDS: I do not go quite as far as that . . . but I think there is a ground for suggesting . . . either Messrs. Harland and Wolff, the builder, defied the Board of Trade, or that there was an extraordinary laxity on the part of the officials of the Marine Department of the Board of Trade to allow, in the construction of this ship, a departure from those Rules which they have already laid down.

Although the scantlings of Olympic-class ships do not appear to have influenced the fate of *Titanic*, White Star probably did not want to explain the ship's lighter materials to a public that was ignorant of ship construction. Fortunately for the shipping company, arguments over the strength-per-inch of *Titanic*'s hull were too technical to catch the public's fancy. Perhaps the scantlings would have become an issue if it had been widely known that the ship broke apart at the end, but Ismay kept a tight rein on that part of the story.

The breakup of *Titanic* was not common knowledge in 1912, although it had been observed from the lifeboats. Ismay almost certainly witnessed the ship come apart from his lifeboat, despite his protestations to the contrary. Because most people on shore did not know the ship broke apart, the surviving officers were able to perjure themselves with little fear of repercussions.

MR. PITMAN: She gradually disappeared until the forecastle head was submerged to the bridge. Then she turned right on end and went down perpendicularly.

SENATOR SMITH: At about what angle?

MR. PITMAN: She went straight.

SENATOR SMITH: Right straight down?

MR. PITMAN: Absolutely. That was the last I saw of her.

SENATOR SMITH: Did she seem to be broken in two?

MR. PITMAN: Oh, no.

Not only did Third Officer Pitman claim he did not notice the ship break in half, but from this testimony it would appear that he saw *Titanic* swing almost two-thirds of its bulk vertically into the air. Another strong proponent of the intact sinking was Second Officer Lightoller. When the ship broke apart, he was struggling to survive in subfreezing water. Although he was scarcely in a position to be a credible witness, Lightoller's testimony that *Titanic* sank intact is given great weight by both official probes.

Ismay made an unbelievable claim in an extremely confused sworn statement. He said he turned his back on the biggest event of his life. It is hard to imagine that he was so indifferent to the sinking of his multimillion-dollar ship that he did not even sneak a peek. But then, it also appears he did not know a port sidelight from a starboard one, either (that is, red from green).

MR. ISMAY: I did not see her go down.

SENATOR SMITH: You did not see her go down?

MR. ISMAY: No, Sir.

SENATOR SMITH: How far were you from the ship?

MR. ISMAY: I do not know how far we were away. I was sitting with my back to the ship. I was rowing all the time I was in the boat. We were pulling away.

SENATOR SMITH: You were rowing?

MR. ISMAY: I did not wish to see her go down.

SENATOR SMITH: You did not care to see her go down?

MR. ISMAY: No. I am glad I did not.

SENATOR SMITH: When you last saw her, were there indications that she had broken in two?

MR. ISMAY: No, Sir.

SENATOR SMITH: When did you last see her?

MR. ISMAY: I really could not say. It might have been 10 minutes after we left her. It is impossible for me to give any judgement of the time. I could not do it.

SENATOR SMITH: Was there much apparent confusion on board when you last saw her?

MR. ISMAY: I did not look to see, sir. My back was turned to her. I looked around only once, to see her red light—her green light, rather.

Senator Smith was not troubled by Ismay's assertion that he rowed with his back to the sinking ship. Although most rowing is done facing the stern of the boat, so that Ismay would have been looking directly at *Titanic* as his lifeboat pulled away from the foundering liner, it is possible that Ismay was pushing on an oar that was being pulled in normal fashion by another survivor. However, the fact that Senator Smith did not inquire about this apparent inconsistency in Ismay's testimony is graphic evidence of the senator's lack of knowledge about seafaring.

Passenger Lawrence Beesley's book about the sinking—*The Loss of the S.S.* Titanic—became an immediate source of information for *Titanic* historians, a role it continues to fill. It seemed to confirm the intact sinking myth. Beesley heavily criticized a drawing of the sinking made aboard *Carpathia* by L. D. Skidmore of Brooklyn, New York, who followed sixteen-year-old survivor Jack Thayer's description. Beesley took issue with one panel of the sketch that showed the forecastle head resurfacing after the final breakup.

189

No phenomenon like that pictured in some American and English papers occurred—that of the ship breaking in two, and the two ends being raised above the surface. I saw these drawings in preparation aboard the Carpathia, and said at the time that they bore no resemblance to what actually happened.

Beesley was absolutely right. The drawing made aboard *Carpathia* was in error. It shows the bow section floating, prow out of the water, quite separate from the upturned stern section. In fact, the bow did break off, but it sank without ever surfacing again. The stern fell back nearly to horizontal before pitching on end like a giant thumb. Thus, Beesley's valid criticism of the erroneous panel of the drawing was not a denial of the ship's breaking in two. Rather, he just pointed out a mistake in the artwork.

One particularly credible witness did argue in favor of the ship sinking intact: boat designer Edward Wilding. "I have tried to make an approximate calculation, and I feel quite sure it did not happen," he testified in London. "The rough calculation I was able to make as to the probable stress arising when the ship foundered as she got her stern out of the water. I can only do it very roughly, of course. It showed the stress in the ship was probably not greater than she would encounter in a severe Atlantic storm. The ship was made to go through an Atlantic storm, and therefore would be capable of meeting that stress."

It is curious that Wilding, who got the other technical details of the sinking right, was so wrong on this point. There is no evidence linking him to the unified testimony of the ship's surviving officers. Still, the shadow of J. Bruce Ismay lies across Wilding. The White Star Line was not only Harland & Wolff's biggest customer, but it was the shipyard's economic lifeline. Lord William James Pirrie, general manager of Harland & Wolff, had persuaded American financier J. Pierpont Morgan to fund construction of the Olympic-class ships for Ismay and White Star. It was a "cost plus" deal. White Star agreed to pay whatever it actually cost Harland & Wolff to build the ships plus a stated percentage. Obviously, the shipbuilding company could not lose money building the trio of giant liners under these circumstances. Prior to that agreement, the shipyard, Wilding's employer, had suffered financial difficulties.

Because of such testimony, the myth grew that *Titanic* plunged intact to the murky depths of the Atlantic. The sounds of the ship tearing itself apart were ascribed to boilers exploding or falling through the bulkheads. "It sank in one piece," the myth proclaimed, and nobody, not even eyewitnesses to the breakup, successfully challenged that version of the story for nearly ninety years. Survivors who witnessed the breakup and described it in detail to investigators were simply ignored.

> After she got to a certain angle she exploded, broke in halve[sic], and it seemed to me as if all the engines and everything that was in the after part slid out into the forward part, and the after part came up right again, and as soon as it came up right, down it went again.
>
> Frank Osman, Seaman

> She went down as far as the after funnel, and then there was a little roar, as though the engines had rushed forward, and she snapped in two, and the bow part went down and the after part came up and stayed up five minutes before it went down.
>
> She parted at the last, because the afterpart of her settled out of the water horizontally after the other part went down. First of all you could see her propellers and everything. Her rudder was clear out of the water. You could hear the rush of the machinery, and she parted in two, and the afterpart settled down again, and we thought the afterpart would float altogether.
>
> She uprighted herself for about five minutes, and then tipped over and disappeared.
>
> Edward John Buley, Seaman

> She almost stood up perpendicular, and her lights went dim, and presently she broke clean in two, probably two-thirds of the length of the ship.
>
> She broke, and the after part floated back. Then there was an explosion, and the aft part turned on end and sank.
>
> George Frederick Crowe, Steward

The tearing apart of the hull described by these men in 1912, as well as by other members of the crew and passengers, remains visible in the wreckage on the bottom today. There never should have been any doubt: *Titanic* broke apart either at or very near the surface of the sea and sank in pieces.

The amalgam of steel, wood, and paint that had been the world's largest moving object began its descent to the bottom of the Atlantic Ocean at 2:20 A.M. on April 15, 1912. What rests there now is not *Titanic*, but the broken remnants of what was once a magnificent liner. Even as the real ship was disappearing into the dark waters, a new *Titanic* of myth and legend was being launched onto an ocean of public curiosity. It is this mythical ship, not the one of steel launched by Harland and Wolff, that still sails through the public's imagination.

These two *Titanic*s share histories filled with deliberate untruths and human errors. The real ship failed to follow the Rule of Good Seamanship with regard to lookout, speed, and prudence. The mythical ship fails to follow the rules of physics with regard to turning, impact, and even method of flooding. And, while the two ships provide material for an unending stream of sea stories, the harsh reality is that the tragedy underlying them should not have occurred. Posting another lookout, choosing a more southerly course, reducing to a safe speed, or remaining stopped after the accident—any of these actions of ordinary seamen could have prevented the needless loss of life. But, history is not a record of what might have been.

> The loss of the said ship was due to a collision with an iceberg, brought about by the excessive speed at which the ship was being navigated.
>
> *Dated this 30th day of July, 1912*
> MERSEY, *Wreck Commissioner*

# APPENDIX 1

## FATES OF KEY PEOPLE

### THOSE WHO WERE LOST AT SEA

CAPTAIN EDWARD J. SMITH—He was last seen walking toward the bridge just as the bow "took a dive" and the forward funnel collapsed. He was likely killed by the falling funnel. Several people, including wireless operator Harold Bride, claimed to have seen him swimming in the water. Reports that his last words were an exhortation to the crew to "Be British" are apocryphal. His body was never recovered.

In the years following the sinking, Smith was often reported to have been seen in various places, including as a captain of ships on the Great Lakes. One of the most intriguing sightings came in Baltimore on May 20, 1912. A fellow captain, Peter Pryal, claimed he walked up to the man he recognized as his old friend and asked, "Captain Smith, how are you?" The man responded, "Very well, Pryal, but please don't detain me. I am on business. Be a good shipmate until we meet again."

CHIEF ENGINEER JOSEPH G. BELL—He had served aboard *Olympic* before being assigned to *Titanic* while it was still under construction. He had been joined by his adult son on *Titanic*'s short voyage from Belfast to Southampton. The circumstances of Bell's death are unknown, but he was lost along with all thirty-five members of the ship's engineering staff.

CHIEF OFFICER HENRY F. WILDE—Selected at the last minute to transfer from *Olympic* for *Titanic*'s maiden voyage, Wilde was openly reluctant to join the ship and had voiced his apprehensions to his wife in a final letter prior to sailing. He attempted to order Second Officer Lightoller into collapsible lifeboat D, but was rebuffed. "Not damn likely," Lightoller said. After that incident Wilde disappeared with the ship.

FIRST OFFICER WILLIAM M. MURDOCH—While supervising the launching of the starboard side lifeboats, he often shook hands and wished luck to the officers he placed in charge of individual boats. He was last seen working to launch collapsible A just prior to the fall of the forward funnel. Lookouts Reginald Lee and Frederick Fleet claimed he committed suicide by giving a military salute and shooting himself in the head with his pistol. The people who knew and worked with Murdoch doubted he did any such thing. Given the last location he was seen working, Murdoch was also probably killed when the forward funnel collapsed.

SIXTH OFFICER JAMES P. MOODY—After receiving the famous "iceberg right ahead" warning from the lookouts, he helped launch lifeboats. Second Officer Lightoller saw him attempting to launch a collapsible lifeboat minutes before *Titanic* foundered.

THOMAS ANDREWS, BUILDER—After urging passengers and crew to put on lifebelts and board the lifeboats, he went down with the ship he loved. Andrews was last seen standing silently in the first-class smoking room, an unused lifebelt lying on a table next to him. Always a man of vigor, Andrews appeared totally defeated in his last minutes. If he remained in the smoking room until the end, he must have witnessed the ship tear itself apart. Evidence from the wreck shows this room was ripped open and destroyed when *Titanic* broke into two large pieces.

JACK PHILLIPS, SENIOR WIRELESS OPERATOR—He stayed with his equipment right to the last moment, when Captain Smith told him to save himself. He and the ship's other wireless operator, Harold Bride, managed to swim to the overturned collapsible lifeboat eventually commanded by Second Officer Lightoller, but Phillips was overcome by the cold water. He died during the long night before *Carpathia* arrived to rescue the survivors.

## THOSE WHO SURVIVED

J. BRUCE ISMAY—The managing director of White Star never overcame the shame of jumping into a lifeboat at the last minute. He was often called J. "Brute" Ismay in the public press during the investigations. To escape, he retired from White Star in 1913 and became a virtual recluse on his private estate in Northern Ireland. Ismay suffered a stroke and died at his London home in 1937.

SENATOR WILLIAM A. SMITH—Made an eloquent speech about the disaster when he delivered his committee's report on *Titanic* to the full U.S. Senate. He died of a heart attack in 1934 at the age of seventy-three.

MERSEY, LORD JOHN CHARLES BIGHAM—Repeated his role as wreck commissioner during the hearings into the loss of RMS *Lusitania* to a German U-boat torpedo during World War I. As with the *Titanic* investigation, Lord Mersey seemed more concerned with controlling public opinion of the tragic wartime loss of life than with establishing the truth.

SECOND OFFICER CHARLES H. LIGHTOLLER—The company's star witness remained with White Star until taking early retirement in the 1930s. He had been promoted to chief officer of the company's *Celtic*, but it was obvious that his loyalty to Ismay and connection to *Titanic* would forever prevent him from having his own White Star command.

During World War I, Lightoller commanded several British Navy vessels and sank a German U-boat by ramming. His ship was seriously damaged, but he managed to steam backward safely to port—perhaps having learned from *Titanic* about moving a damaged vessel under its own power.

With his wife, Sylvia, Lightoller undertook a covert mission along the coast of Europe in his private yacht just prior to World War II. They spied on potential German ports. After hostilities broke out, he and his son took that same yacht, *Sundowner*, to Dunkirk to help rescue the British Army. Lightoller died December 8, 1952.

THIRD OFFICER HERBERT J. PITMAN—He was sent away in lifeboat #5 by Second Officer Murdoch. Pitman was stopped by passengers in his attempt to row back into the crowd of floating victims left behind by the sinking ship. He continued working for White Star Line, although in the Purser's department because of his diminishing eyesight. He died in 1961 at the age of 84.

FOURTH OFFICER JOSEPH G. BOXHALL—Although his career was stunted by his connection to *Titanic*, Boxhall stuck it out with White Star to retirement. Like Lightoller, Boxhall had an outstanding military career with the Royal Navy. He rose to become first officer of major ships in the Cunard White Star fleet after the two rival companies merged, but was never given a civilian command of his own. He died in 1967 at age eighty-three. His ashes were scattered over the position he calculated as *Titanic*'s final resting place, 41°45′ N 50°16′ W.

FIFTH OFFICER HAROLD G. LOWE—Having reached the rank of commander in the Royal Navy during World War I, he retired from the sea to his native Wales, where he died in 1964 at age sixty-one.

ROBERT HITCHENS, QUARTERMASTER—He disappeared from the sea after the *Titanic* disaster, reportedly having been given the post of harbormaster in Capetown, South Africa.

ALFRED OLLIVER, QUARTERMASTER—He was one of the crew of lifeboat #5. After his *Titanic* adventure he never went to sea again, although he continued to work for White Star Line. Olliver died in June 1934.

FREDERICK FLEET, LOOKOUT—He remained with White Star as a seaman until his retirement, last serving on Titanic's older sister, *Olympic*. Three decades after his retirement, still suffering from flashback memories of the sinking, he committed suicide in 1965.

REGINALD LEE, LOOKOUT—He reportedly drank himself to death in the 1930s in remorse over *Titanic*'s sinking.

CAPTAIN ARTHUR H. ROSTRON—The brave captain of *Carpathia* was knighted, adding the title "Sir" to his name. He rose to the position of commodore of the Cunard White Star Line, the honorary position held by Captain Edward J. Smith when he commanded *Titanic* for the independent White Star Line.

# APPENDIX 2

## A TITAN'S WAKE

HMS *Geary* found itself in trouble during the summer of 1918. The British destroyer had crumpled its bow by ramming a German submarine during a marine dogfight. Water poured into the forward section of the victorious warship despite its crew's best efforts to stay afloat. Fortunately, *Geary*'s captain had survived a similar emergency during his prewar career as second officer of the world's largest passenger liner. Lessons learned by Charles H. Lightoller aboard RMS *Titanic* proved invaluable during combat. His bold seamanship was summed up in a terse radio message:

> Returning under own power . . . stern first . . . 8 knots. . . .

Lightoller's shiphandling was inspired. HMS *Geary* reached port after a harrowing backward ride through submarine-infested waters. This success raises the possibility that Lightoller discovered the secret of how *Titanic* might have been taken to safety six years previously. What if Captain Smith had backed the injured passenger liner to the ship whose lights twinkled so enticingly on the horizon? We will never know, and that element of mystery is a primary attraction of the *Titanic* story.

One reason the truth remains hidden is the liberal coating of "whitewash" that Second Officer Lightoller admitted applying to the truth. However, he wasn't the only one to cover up the truth. Both the American and the British investigations seem to have formed their conclusions before they began hearing testimony. Only those statements that justified their predetermined conclusions were included in the final reports. Not that U.S. Senator William Alden Smith and his British counterpart, John Charles Bigham, Lord Mersey, were involved in any sinister international intrigue. Rather, there seems to have been rivalry between them. Both wanted to be perceived as having done the most thorough investigation. However, like the White Star line, each government appears to have had what today is called a political agenda. The final reports issued on both sides of the Atlantic seem intended to serve purposes other than unbiased forensic investigation.

The London hearings conducted by Lord Mersey, wreck commissioner (a term steeped in English maritime history), gave the pretense of a knowledgeable examination while scrupulously avoiding certain areas of inquiry. Considering the political climate of Europe in 1912, it is easy to surmise Lord Mersey's motives. Britain and Germany were dueling for domination of Europe, and shipping competition on the North Atlantic was just one manifestation of the nationalistic belly bumping that culminated in World War I.

Although fear of lawsuits was not as great in 1912 as it is today, Lord Mersey was certainly aware of the legal implications of his final report. White Star Line might well have been bankrupted by damage claims if Mersey found the company guilty of gross negligence. International Mercantile Marine's owner, J. Pierpont Morgan, likely would not have chosen to use either his personal or coporate funds to pay those judgments. Both remaining Olympic-class ships might have been placed on the auction block to satisfy legal claims.

Among the bidding parties certainly would have been German shipping magnate Albert Ballin, whose Hamburg-America Line was the largest in the world. Ballin was in the process of introducing his own trio of giant liners to compete with Cunard's *Lusitania* and *Mauritania* and with Ismay's Olympic-class ships. (The German ships were to have three funnels, possibly a motivation to add the fourth dummy funnel to the Olympics.) Although he was Jewish, Ballin had a warm relationship with German Kaiser Wilhelm II, through whom he may have obtained funding. If Ballin purchased the two remaining Olympic-class liners, Germany would have instantly become dominant in North Atlantic passenger travel. Germany would have gained hegemony even if the ships were purchased by French or American interests.

Admiralty law is somewhat different from law practiced on land. The total amount of damages for which a shipping company can be held responsible is limited under admiralty law to the value of the ship and its voyage. This limitation is not absolute, however. In 1912 (as today), the limit could be nullified by proof of gross negligence on the part of the shipping company, in this case White Star Line. If that had happened, the company would have been open to damage claims from the families of the more than 1,500 victims.

> Admiralty lawyers in this city believe the courts would be likely to uphold claims against the owners of the Titanic for loss of life and property. . . . If, however, gross negligence, such as running at full speed through dangerous ice fields, could be proven, there is the prospect of obtaining damages. . . .

Senator William Alden Smith's U.S. Senate hearings demonstrated a general lack of knowledge of ships and the sea. The American senator's rush to judgment ultimately focused on *Titanic's* lack of lifeboats. Although he touched on the role of U.S. law in the tragedy, Senator Smith never faulted U.S. immigration regulations, which kept steerage passengers from reaching the lifeboats (see the chapter titled Blind Faith). Also, Senator Smith could not have avoided knowing that International Mercantile Marine, the parent company of White Star, was a U.S. corporation, incorporated within the state of New Jersey.

In the end, both governments tiptoed around how the ship "struck" the berg by developing a carefully slanted (but physically impossible) "left turn only" version of the accident. More important, they turned blind eyes to evidence that Captain Smith and J. Bruce Ismay ordered the damaged ship to steam for Halifax after the accident. They overlooked Chief Engineer Joseph G. Bell's statement to Ismay that the pumps were keeping the liner afloat at 11:50 P.M., which allowed them to avoid discussing the possibility that *Titanic* might have remained afloat long enough for rescue ships to arrive.

A public cry of "lifeboats for all" arose out of the tragedy. On the surface, this demand sounded logical. However, naval architects and sailors have always known that carrying large numbers of lifeboats does not ensure that anyone will be saved in an emergency. This was Lord Charles Beresford's quite valid reasoning in 1887 when he penned his report *Saving Life at Sea* for a select committee of the British House of Commons.

> Many passenger ships could not, without great inconvenience, carry so many of the ordinary wooden boats as would suffice to carry the whole of the passengers and crew with safety in bad weather. Under such circumstances the crew would not be sufficient to man so many boats; nor could they all be got into the water in sufficient time in the event of a very rapid foundering.

The *Titanic* disaster caused Lord Beresford's comments to be trampled by a rush to put lifeboats on ocean liners. To the general public, the logical requirement was obvious: one seat for every man, woman, and child on board. More if possible, but never less than one lifeboat seat per person, including crew and steerage passengers. No one questioned how all those boats would be launched or where the trained boat crews to man them would come from. "More boats" was the cry, not "better seamanship."

Clamor for reform of British Board of Trade lifeboat regulations pushed attention away from White Star Line's deliberate choice to remove the very lifeboats from *Titanic* (and the other two Olympic-class ships) that should have saved everyone. Ismay must have feared public anger over disclosure that all three Olympic-class ships were originally designed to carry sixty-four lifeboats. This admission came during the British hearings from none other than Lord William James Pirrie, the recently retired head of the Harland and Wolff shipyard.

Pirrie revealed a proposal assigning sixty-four lifeboats to each Olympic-class ship, but the proposal never got beyond preliminary drawings. White Star wanted no part of stacks of lifeboats on the open boat deck, which was really a first-class promenade. In the end, White Star (meaning Ismay) deemed sixteen wooden boats sufficient to give Olympic-class ships the appearance of carrying safety equipment without obstructing the vistas of strolling first-class passengers. Ismay never seriously considered that there might be a need to use the boats installed on his trio of superliners.

The most visible change that resulted from the *Titanic* affair was in lifeboat regulations. After 1912, the formerly open promenades on boat decks became jam-packed with lifeboats. For a while, stacks of lifeboats overwhelmed the ships that carried them. Better boat and davit designs solved this problem, but a long line of lifeboats remains the hallmark of passenger vessels. Not since *Titanic* left port for the last time has a major transoceanic passenger vessel departed with less than one lifeboat seat for every person on board.

Less visible than the lifeboats themselves is the training given to crews of passenger vessels. Except for ships sailing under some third-world flags, passenger ships must now carry enough crew members holding "lifeboatman" certificates to man every boat carried. Also quite invisible to the layman are improvements to the lifeboats themselves. *Titanic*'s boats were larger but were otherwise little changed from those used a century earlier. Today, all lifeboats are metal or fiberglass with built-in flotation. Many are motorized. The latest development is the completely enclosed lifeboat that protects its passengers like a cocoon.

Another result of *Titanic*'s sinking was the 1914 establishment of the International Ice Patrol by the U.S. Coast Guard. Information about ice conditions for the North Atlantic is gathered from ships and aircraft and is then sent to vessels in or approaching the area. When icebergs are sighted outside normal limits, special warnings are broadcast from St. Johns, Newfoundland. Iceberg positions in the bulletins are updated at twelve-hour intervals.

Some additional minor safety improvements in passenger vessels also resulted from *Titanic*'s example. Bulkheads generally go higher above the waterline in most passenger ships. Radio communications are considered so vital to safety today that all large ships must station a twenty-four-hour radio watch. No longer can a Cyril Evans turn off his equipment and go to bed as he did that night on *Californian*. Automatic distress alarms sound on the bridges of ships that receive coded messages seeking immediate assistance. Special radio beacons—called EPIRBs (emergency position-indicating radio beacons)—have been developed to send signals to aircraft and orbiting satellites. An EPIRB begins transmitting automatically when it floats off a sinking ship.

Shipping lanes in 1912 were kept as short as possible to prevent burning expensive coal. *Titanic* was not the only vessel to cross with a meager supply of bunker fuel, as shown by *Deutschland*'s embarrassing predicament of being out of coal. The shortest great circle route saved fuel, but it took westbound ships perilously close to waters infested with icebergs from March through July. That route was modified slightly, and today ships run a bit farther south to avoid *Titanic*'s fate.

Through quick wit and careful wording, Second Officer Lightoller was able to deflect much of the blame away from the ship's officers and the White Star Line. Testifying in two governmental probes must have been an ordeal for him. He faced the most extensive questioning of any company employee on either side of the Atlantic, yet for his troubles and loyalty, he was all but shunned by White Star. He was kept on the payroll as a junior officer in smaller ships. Owing (it must be assumed) to his association with *Ti-*

*tanic,* never again would Lightoller stand watch on one of the company's flagships.

> I am never likely to forget that long-drawn-out battle of wits, where it seemed that I must hold that unenviable position of whipping boy. . . . I know when it was all over I felt more like a legal doormat than a Mail Boat Officer.
>
> Perhaps the heads of the White Star Line did not quite realize just what an endless strain it had all been, falling on one man's luckless shoulders, as it needs must, being the sole survivor out of so many departments . . .
>
> Still, just that word of thanks which was lacking, which when the Titanic Enquiry was all over would have been very much appreciated.

The day finally came when Lightoller could no longer remain a White Star officer, and he turned in his resignation after twenty years of loyal service. "Oh, you are leaving us," Lightoller recalled a company official responding. "Well, good-bye." With that, the survivor of *Titanic* walked ashore, where he dabbled in several jobs, including raising chickens for a short while.

The success of Lightoller's efforts on behalf of White Star Lines can be judged by statements printed on page 30 of the British Wreck Commission's final report about the accident. Lord Mersey buried a comment indicating that he anticipated criticism of his findings. He seemed particularly worried by nagging allegations that J. Bruce Ismay pressured Captain Smith into taking unnecessary risks.

> It was suggested at the bar that he [Captain Smith] was yielding to influences which ought not to have affected him: that the presence of Mr. Ismay on board and the knowledge which he perhaps had of a conversation between Mr. Ismay and the Chief Engineer at Queenstown about the speed of the ship and the consumption of coal probably induced him to neglect precautions which he would otherwise have taken. But I do not believe this.

The fitting last words on *Titanic* were not written by an official investigator, nor did they come from one of the survivors. They came from Eleanor Smith, widow of Captain Edward J. Smith, and were posted outside the White Star offices in London on April 17, 1912.

> To my poor fellow-sufferers: My heart overflows with grief for you all and is laden with sorrow that you are weighed down with this terrible burden that has been thrust upon us. May God be with us and comfort us all.
>
> Yours in deep sympathy,
> Eleanor Smith

# Appendix 3

## Nautical Terms

Language plays a pivotal role in many of the misunderstandings that plague histories of *Titanic*. Sailors use a jargon that is both unfamiliar and confusing to those who live ashore. Readers of *Treasure Island* or the *Hornblower* books have been exposed to "sailor talk," but it is one thing to learn the definitions of words and quite another to know how those words are used in everyday conversation.

For example, in 1912 the verb "to strike" was used by sailors almost exclusively to describe a vessel's bottom contacting the seabed. It meant going aground. "Strike" was seldom if ever applied to a vessel colliding with either a floating object or another ship. Those were collisions. When surviving members of the crew talked about the ship "striking" the iceberg, they were not describing either a head-on impact or a sideswipe. Rather, they meant contact with the bottom of the ship, and this traditional nautical meaning of the word "strike" turns out to be factually correct in *Titanic*'s case.

Another problem of language centers around the difference between the engine order "all stop" and the actual conduct of the ship. "All stop" on the engine room telegraph is simply an instruction to cease rotation of the engines. This does not "put the brakes on" the ship. It just stops the propellers from driving forward. The vessel continues moving like a car coasting on a flat, level road in neutral. Frictional resistance of the water against the hull will eventually cause the ship to stop. In a maneuver called a *crash stop*, full reverse thrust is used to bring the ship to a quick halt to avoid danger. The correct telegraph order for this maneuver is "astern full."

The following definitions are presented to help readers understand nautical language as used in this book.

**Admeasurement**—The process of determining a ship's registered tonnage for regulatory purposes. Tonnage for admeasurement is a reckoning of the cubic volume inside the hull, not the weight of the ship.

**Aft**—Toward the stern of a vessel or moving toward the stern of a vessel.

**All stop**—An order to the engine room on the engine order telegraph to stop rotation of the propellers. An "all stop" order does not immediately cause the ship to come to a halt. The ship may continue coasting forward for some distance.

**Amidship**—A location at or near the area halfway from the bow to the stern, or pertaining to a location halfway from the bow to the stern.

**Below**—To go to a lower deck, particularly to a deck within the hull itself, from an outside, or weather, deck. Any space inside the hull below the weather deck.

**Bergy bits**—Pieces of ice broken off larger icebergs, too small to be called *growlers*.

**Bilge**—The lowest portion of the hull, often where water collects. Also, the point where the bottom of the ship curves to meet the vertical hull sides.

**Binnacle**—A tall housing usually made of polished wood and brass that supports the ship's steering compass and may contain other instruments such as a clinometer.

**Black gang**—A nickname for stokers and trimmers, who fed coal to the boiler furnaces. These workers were called *black* because they quickly became covered with coal dust, ashes, and soot. Most of *Titanic*'s *black gang* were from England and Ireland.

**Bow**—The very front of a vessel, but also any part of the hull or deck at or near the front of the vessel.

**Bottom**—That portion of the hull that extends horizontally from the keel outward to where it meets the vertical sides of the ship at what is called the *turn of the bilge.*

**Bridge ("Captain's bridge")**—The main control station of the vessel. It contains the steering wheel, compass, engine room telegraphs, and other equipment necessary for navigation. The term comes from a flimsy platform that bridged the space between sidewheel paddle boxes on early steamboats.

**Bulkhead**—Any "wall" placed across the width of the ship from side to side. Regarding *Titanic*, the word usually refers to the fifteen special watertight divisions that were intended to make the ship virtually unsinkable. A watertight bulkhead prevents water from flowing between the compartments thus formed.

**Bunker**—A storage area or bin specifically for the purpose of stowing fuel for the boilers.

**Captain**—A largely honorary title bestowed upon the person who is the master of the vessel. Also, an appellation used to honor anyone who holds a Master's License, whether that person commands a vessel or not.

**Carpenter**—Originally, a woodworker. In 1912, this was the person responsible for making minor repairs while under way. The carpenter also performed other duties. On *Titanic*, the carpenter was responsible for keeping the drinking water tanks from freezing and for sounding the bilges.

**Chock**—A support that holds a lifeboat upright when it is stored on deck prior to use.

**Companionway**—A small hatch or hatchway with a stairway leading to a cabin or saloon below deck. Or, a small hood with doors over a hatchway on a weather deck to prevent the entry of spray and water.

**Crash stop**—An emergency maneuver in which the ship is halted within the shortest distance possible by applying full reverse thrust on the engines.

**Crow's nest**—A small platform located on a ship's mast for the purpose of sheltering a lookout.

**Davit**—Any type of small crane specifically intended for the launching of boats from a ship, particularly lifeboats. Two davits are needed for each boat, one at the bow and the other at the stern.

**Deck**—Any horizontal surface intended for walking on a ship. On *Titanic*, there were nine decks. Starting from the keel: tank top; lower deck (deck G); middle deck (F); upper deck (E); saloon deck (D); shelter deck (C); bridge deck (B); promenade deck (A); and boat deck.

**Dead reckoning**—The process of determining a ship's most probable position by plotting its movements (speed and direction) since its last known fix. The term is derived from "deduced reckoning."

**Dead water or dead waves**—Waves created by the passage of a ship in the horizontal boundary layer between overlying fresh water and underlying seawater. Dead waves usually occur where large rivers empty into the ocean.

**Displacement**—The actual dead weight of the vessel expressed as the weight of water it displaces when floating. This is real weight, not to be confused with tonnage, which is a measurement of cubic volume.

**Engineer**—Any member of the crew detailed to service or maintain the engines. Also, a rank, such as chief engineer.

**Even keel**—A condition in which the ship draws the same amount of water at the bow as it does at the stern. Normally, ships are trimmed (adjusted with ballast) so the stern is slightly deeper than the bow. As *Titanic* sank, its bow tipped downward, causing its stern to rise like the opposite end of a seesaw.

**Falls**—The ropes of a block and tackle; specifically, the ropes between blocks of a tackle supporting a lifeboat.

**Faying surface**—The area of overlap in a seam where two shell plates are in tight contact with each other.

**Field ice**—Frozen seawater floating in a loose formation.

**Fireman**—Any member of the crew who works at a variety of jobs serving the fireboxes in the boiler rooms.

**Fix**—Navigational term for an exact position of a vessel while under way. Near shore, compass bearings of landmarks may be used to obtain a fix. In 1912, the only way to obtain a fix away from land was to use a sextant and the stars or sun in a process called *celestial navigation*. To obtain an exact position of a vessel while under way.

**Floe (ice floe)**—An area of field ice large enough to pose a danger to navigation.

**Floor**—In naval architecture, the horizontal, transverse framing of the ship giving support to the bottom. The floor frames in *Titanic* were contained within the ship's double bottom. Do not confuse the correct use of this term referring to a structural member of the hull with sailor's slang referring to "decks" as "floors," such as in a house ashore.

**Forecastle**—The raised deck at the very bow of a ship. The crew's berthing space formerly was always located here. *Titanic's* forecastle provided shelter for the third-class promenade space on the forward well deck.

**Foredeck**—The forwardmost upper deck of a ship. On *Titanic* it was a raised area forward of the well deck.

**Forepeak**—A small, triangular compartment at the very bow of a ship, usually kept as a void space.

**Forward**—Toward the bow of a vessel.

**Founder**—To sink completely.

**Funnel**—The nautical term for a smokestack. *Titanic* had four funnels, three of which were functional. The fourth was a "dummy" used to ventilate the engine rooms and galley.

**Greaser**—A member of the engine room crew assigned the duty of lubricating (often with grease) the moving parts of the machinery.

**Growler**—A colloquial term applied to smaller icebergs.

**Hard aport**—In 1912 this was a helm order to the quartermaster to move the ship's tiller to port. This would cause the rudder to swing to starboard and the ship to the right.

**Hard astarboard**—In 1912 this was a helm order to the quartermaster to move the ship's tiller to starboard. This would cause the rudder to swing to port and the ship to the left.

**Hawser**—Originally referring to a type of heavy rope, this word is now applied to any rope or wire cable used when towing astern a barge of large ship.

**Head**—The absolute bow of the ship, especially the uppermost deck area at the bow, which is exposed to weather. Formerly, the "seats of ease" (toilets) were installed at the head because the plunging of the bow into waves would tend to keep them clean. From this practice, the term *head* has come to mean any toilet room at sea.

**Helm**—The steering wheel or, by extension, any of the other equipment used to steer the ship.

**Hogging**—An action in which the keel of a vessel bends upward in the center so that the bow and stern sag lower than amidships. A vessel with such a condition is said to be "hogged."

**Iceberg ("berg")**—A large portion of polar or glacial ice that has become detached and has been carried out to sea. Icebergs are made of freshwater, so they float with only one-eighth of their mass above the surface of the ocean.

**Knot**—A measurement of speed. One knot is equal to 1 nautical mile per hour.

**Ladder**—A nautical term for stairway, usually reserved for stairs intended for crew use only.

**List**—Any lean of a ship to the side, either port or starboard. May be caused by improper loading, water in the hull, or wind. In *Titanic*'s case, listing was caused by water entering the hull as the ship sank.

**Loll**—A list taken by a ship that has lost stability due to damage or improper loading. Lolls may be to port or starboard. Often, the ship takes a loll to one side, then rolls slowly to the other just before capsizing.

**Lookout**—A trained member of the crew specially charged with the duty of observing by sight, hearing, and any other means. Lookouts are to report anything unusual they observe to the bridge. By law, they may have no other duties that interfere with the keeping of an adequate lookout.

**Maiden voyage**—A ship's first paying trip after passing its builder's trials.

**Make water**—Water rising inside the hull.

**Marconi**—Gugliemo Marconi was one of the inventors of wireless telegraphy; *Titanic*'s radio equipment and operator were supplied by his company, Marconi's Wireless Telegraph Company Ltd.

**Marconigram**—A proprietary name for any wireless message sent via the Marconi Company.

**Master**—The person in legal command of the vessel, hence the captain. All ship's masters must hold a Master's License issued by their government. Holding such a license does not guarantee one the position of captain, however. Many of *Titanic*'s officers held Master's Licenses, even though they served in an inferior position to Captain Smith.

**Mercator chart**—The most common type of nautical chart on which all the lines of latitude and longitude cross at right angles. This type of chart is most often used for coastal sailing and in harbors. Because of the natural distortion of Mercator charts over great distances, they are not well suited for great-circle navigation.

**Mile, nautical**—A measurement of distance at sea equal to 1 minute of latitude, or approximately 6,080 feet in 1912.

**Morse code**—A system using dots (short signals) and dashes (long signals) to represent letters of the alphabet in telegraphic transmission. Originated by Samuel F. B. Morse for his land telegraph system, Morse code was adopted by wireless operators after the invention of radio.

**Northing**—Any northerly movement of a ship, regardless of its course.

**Officer**—Any member of the ship's crew operating under an Officer's License. On the *Titanic* there were eight deck officers:

> Master—Captain Edward J. Smith
> Chief Officer—Henry F. Wilde
> First Officer—William M. Murdoch
> Second Officer—Charles H. Lightoller
> Third Officer—Herbert J. Pitman
> Fourth Officer—Joseph G. Boxhall
> Fifth Officer—Harold G. Lowe
> Sixth Officer—James H. Moody

In addition to these well-known deck officers, there were thirty-five men broadly classified as "engineer" aboard *Titanic*. Among these were Chief Engineer Joseph G. Bell, twenty-four engineering officers, two boilermakers, a plumber, and a clerk.

**Orlop (orlop deck)**—On *Titanic*, two short decks extending no farther aft than boiler room #6 and located between the tank top and the lower deck (deck G). Similar orlops were located aft of the turbine engine room. The forward upper orlop deck was used as a mail room. The term is believed to be a contraction of "overlap."

**Pack ice**—Freshwater ice broken from glaciers that covers wide areas of the polar seas, broken into large pieces that are driven (or "packed") together by wind and current.

**Plates (plating)**—The actual flat pieces of metal bent or shaped to become part of the ship's hull. They are attached to the frames and may form either the bottom or the sides of the hull.

**Port**—The left side of the ship when facing forward, or pertaining to the left side of the ship when facing forward.

**Quartermaster**—Job title of the seaman who actually steered the ship.

**RMS**—An abbreviation standing for "Royal Mail Ship." Used to identify British liners that carried mail for the Royal Post Office. Such ships were required to be capable of maintaining a 16-knot speed on the Atlantic.

**Rounds**—A colloquial name given to regular inspection trips of the ship made by senior watch officers when they go off duty.

**Saloon**—On a passenger vessel, any large public room given primarily to passenger use, hence the term *saloon deck*. Does not refer to the sale or consumption of alcoholic beverages as it does ashore in the United States.

**Scantlings**—A collective term for all of the specifications relating to size and strength of materials used in the construction of a ship.

**Seaman**—Any member of the crew, regardless of sex, who works on deck and who handles lines, steers, or stands lookout. Ordinary seamen are of lower rank than able-bodied seamen.

**Secure**—To stop any action, including to shut down equipment (such as the ship's engines) when it is not needed.

**Shoot, Shooting, or Shot**—To move through the water after the propellers have stopped turning, similar to coasting in an automobile without applying any gas.

**Speak**—To share information with another vessel by coming alongside to allow oral communication. The past tense is "spoke," never "spoken." Today, this refers to any communication between ships in visual contact.

**Spring or Sprung**—As a verb, to cause a seam to open, usually through physical damage. As an adjective, it describes a seam that has been damaged and is leaking.

**Starboard**—The right side of the ship when facing forward, or pertaining to the right side of the ship when facing forward.

**Steerage**—The ability of a vessel to be controlled by its own rudder. Usually expressed as a minimum speed for such control. Also, a slang term for third-class passengers, probably because they were formerly housed in the least desirable sections of the ship near the stern, where the tiller and steering equipment are located.

**Stern**—The very back of a vessel, but also any part of the hull or deck at or near the back of the vessel.

**Stokehold**—An obsolete term for "boiler room," derived from the work done there: stoking coal into the fireboxes.

**Stoker**—A member of the crew detailed to shovel coal from the bunkers into the fireboxes of the boiler furnaces.

**Superstructure**—Deck houses or other structures built on top of the ship's hull. On *Titanic,* everything above the shelter deck was considered superstructure.

**Tank top**—The horizontal metal plating that covers the longitudinal and transverse framing in the bottom of a ship and creates spaces called *tanks* between it and the other shell plating, hence the name. The tank top is normally the lowest deck of a ship.

**Telegraph, Engine Order**—The device used on a ship to issue or repeat orders from or to the bridge.

**Tiller**—A lever attached to the rudder post by which the movements of the rudder may be controlled from inside the ship. The tiller is moved to the right (starboard) to turn the ship to the left (port).

**Tip**—Any upward or downward movement of the bow not caused by wave action. The *Titanic's* bow tipped down as it sank. Tipping should not be confused with *listing,* which is a transverse lean of the ship.

**Tonnage**—In commercial vessels, this refers to the ship's ability to carry cargo or passengers. It is not a measurement of weight, but rather of cubic volume within the hull. A ship's registered tonnage may be expressed as gross or net. Gross tonnage is the maximum cubic volume; net tonnage is reduced by space for engines, tankage, and so forth.

**Topsides**—The vertical portion of the hull from the waterline upward. Does not include the portion of the ship that comprises its superstructure.

**Traverse Tables**—A set of mathematical tables arranged to allow computation of a ship's new position by knowing the direction and distance traveled from some previous known location. This allows dead reckoning to be done by reference to tables rather than by plotting on a chart.

**Trimmer**—A member of the crew detailed to rake, or "trim," the burning coal in the boiler furnaces for maximum heat production and complete combustion.

**Triple-Expansion**—Any steam engine having at least three cylinders arranged so that the exhaust steam of one cylinder is used to power the next. The triple-expansion engines of *Titanic* actually had four cylinders: one high pressure, one medium pressure, and two low pressure. These engines were among the largest ever built.

**Watch**—A period of time, usually four hours, during which a member of the crew is actively on duty.

**Westing**—Any westward movement of a ship, regardless of its course.

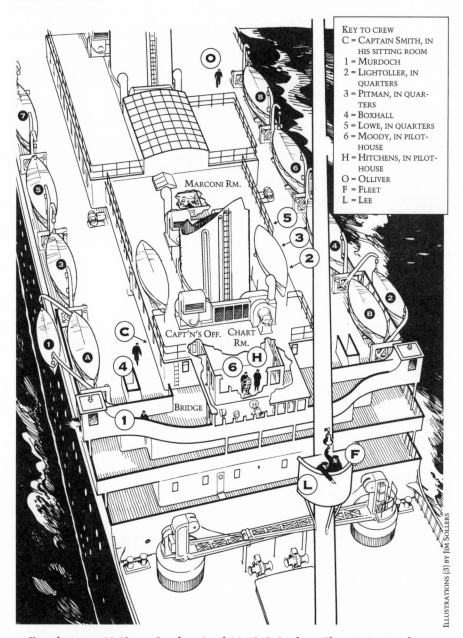

KEY TO CREW
C = CAPTAIN SMITH, IN
    HIS SITTING ROOM
1 = MURDOCH
2 = LIGHTOLLER, IN
    QUARTERS
3 = PITMAN, IN QUAR-
    TERS
4 = BOXHALL
5 = LOWE, IN QUARTERS
6 = MOODY, IN PILOT-
    HOUSE
H = HITCHENS, IN PILOT-
    HOUSE
O = OLLIVER
F = FLEET
L = LEE

MARCONI RM.

CAPT'N'S OFF.   CHART RM.

BRIDGE

ILLUSTRATIONS (3) BY JIM SOLLERS

*Key players at 11:40 P.M. Sunday, April 14, 1912. Lookout Fleet is ringing alarm bell to report "iceberg right ahead" to Sixth Officer Moody in the wheelhouse. First Officer Murdoch is about to enter the starboard bridge wing enclosure, while Fourth Officer Boxhall is walking forward outside Captain Smith's suite.*

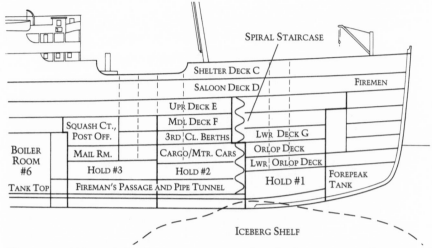

The curve of Titanic's keel as it swept upward in the bow to meet the stem caused the hardest impact on the ice shelf to occur approximately on the bulkhead between holds #1 and #2, directly below the firemen's spiral staircase.

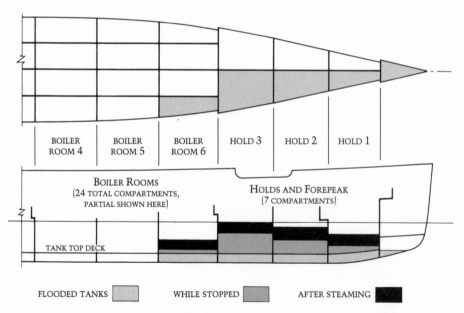

The space inside Titanic's double bottom was subdivided into 44 watertight compartments. Grinding across the ice shelf flooded these on the starboard side, causing the ship's immediate list. Some water entered the holds and boiler room #6 prior to when the ship began making way again, but the fatal loss of boiler room #6 occurred while the ship was steaming for Halifax.

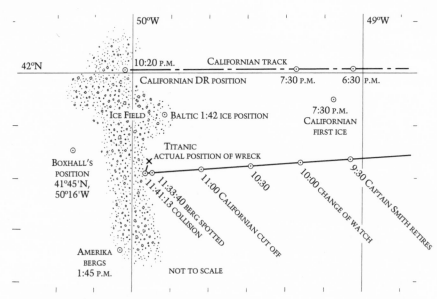

*Plotting the dead-reckoning tracks of* Californian *and* Titanic *shows them to have been about 20 miles apart when the accident took pace. The wounded liner steamed about 3 miles northward, toward* Californian, *before coming to a final stop to launch lifeboats.*

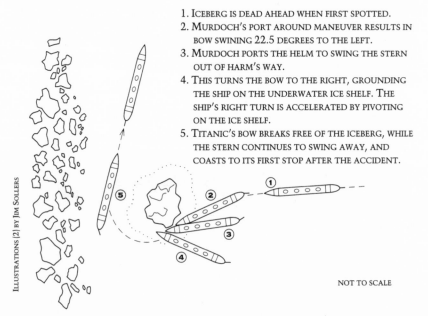

1. ICEBERG IS DEAD AHEAD WHEN FIRST SPOTTED.
2. MURDOCH'S PORT AROUND MANEUVER RESULTS IN BOW SWINING 22.5 DEGREES TO THE LEFT.
3. MURDOCH PORTS THE HELM TO SWING THE STERN OUT OF HARM'S WAY.
4. THIS TURNS THE BOW TO THE RIGHT, GROUNDING THE SHIP ON THE UNDERWATER ICE SHELF. THE SHIP'S RIGHT TURN IS ACCELERATED BY PIVOTING ON THE ICE SHELF.
5. TITANIC'S BOW BREAKS FREE OF THE ICEBERG, WHILE THE STERN CONTINUES TO SWING AWAY, AND COASTS TO ITS FIRST STOP AFTER THE ACCIDENT.

NOT TO SCALE

Titanic's *maneuvers immediately before and after the accident.*

# NOTES

INTRODUCTION

1 **The result was she sank.** U.S. Senate Hearings, April 24, 1912.

1 **a romantic fiction.** Lord, *Night Lives On*, 153–43.

2 **approaching pack ice.** Defense Mapping Agency Hydrographic/Typographic Center, *The American Practical Navigator: An Epitome of Navigation* (Bethesda, Md.: Defense Mapping Agency Hydrographic/Typographic Center, 1995). Multiple editions of Nathaniel Bowditch's classic work exist, but references here are to the 1995 DMA edition, hereafter cited as Bowditch.

2 **everything was against us.** C. H. Lightoller, quoted in John Charles Bigham, Lord Mersey, *Loss of the Steamship "Titanic."* Report of a Formal Investigation into the cirumstances attending the foundering on 15th April, 1912, of the British Steamship "Titanic," of Liverpool, after striking ice in or near Latitude 41° 46′ N., Longitude 50° 14′ W., North Atlantic Ocean, whereby loss of life ensued (London: His Majesty's Stationery Office, July 30, 1912); hereafter cited as Mersey.

3 **hence the whitewash brush.** Lightoller, in Winocour, *Story of the* Titanic, 304–5.

6 **natural under the circumstances.** Mersey, 33.

10 **the chain of tragedy.** Merideth, "Fitting Out," in *1912 Facts about* Titanic.

## COAL AND ICE

15 **about 22.25 knots.** Mersey. This report estimated the speed of the ship at 22.25 knots at the time of the accident. Physical evidence of the wreck indicates *Titanic* was making 20.5 knots from 5:50 P.M. on the evening of the accident. The ship's taffrail log indicated a speed of 22.25 knots.

15 **British Board of Trade records** "The coal on board is certified to amount to 5,892 tons, which is sufficient to take the ship to her next coaling port." British Board of Trade, Report of Survey of an Immigrant Ship (April 10, 1912).

15 **10 percent margin for safety.** A 10 percent fuel reserve is not specified in any regulation but is generally considered to be the minimum required for safety by modern captains. Simple division shows that *Titanic* had about a 10 percent reserve when it departed Southampton, indicating that this was the amount set aside by Captain Smith and the White Star Line for such contingencies as foul weather.

17 **New York the next day.** Ismay categorically denied any involvement in the operation of *Titanic* at any time during the voyage. His most forceful denial came in his famous statement quoted in the *Times* (London) on April 21, 1912. "During the voyage I was a passenger and exercised no greater rights or privileges than any other passenger," he wrote. "I was not consulted by the commander about the ship, her course, speed, navigation or her conduct at sea."

17 **overnight buildup of steam power.** Leading stoker Frederick Barrett told the British proceedings that the last of the double-ended boilers was fired at about 8:00 A.M. He said it took about twelve hours to heat up a boiler and bring it up to the 200 pounds of steam pressure at which Titanic's engines operated.

19 **never eventuated.** J. Bruce Ismay, U.S. Senate Hearings, April 19, 1912.

19 **the more fuel it would burn.** According to H. H. Shufeldt, Capt. USNR, in *Slide Rule for the Mariner* (Annapolis, Md.: Naval Institute Press, 1972), "For large ships steaming at economical speeds, that is, well below hull speed, *fuel consumption varies as the cube of the speed for a given time, and as the square of the speed for a given distance*" (emphasis in the original).

20 **demands of the Musicians Union.** Lord, *Night Lives On*, 145.

21 **"not under control"** This expression arises in the International Rules of the Road, which are designed to prevent collisions at sea. In the modern rules, it has been changed to "not under command."

22 **exclusive control of the Captain.** J. Bruce Ismay, "Statement Issued by J. Bruce Ismay to The Times," *Times* (London), April 21, 1912.

23 **great circle** In navigation, a *great circle* is any circle whose diameter is equal to that of the earth and whose center is concentric with the center of the earth. Great circle routes are the shortest distance between any two points on the globe. On a conventional map, a great circle route appears as a curved line.

23 **rhumb line** A *rhumb line* is a course that crosses all meridians at the same angle. It plots on a mercator chart as a straight line. On the globe, however, it is a curve called a *loxidrome*. Because it is actually a curve on the surface of the globe, a rhumb line is longer than a great circle between any two points. Rhumb lines are easier to follow than are great circles and thus are used for shorter distances.

24 **"North 71 West" (289°).** Rowe gave the "South 85 West" and "North 71 West" courses as he saw them on the ship's steering compass located inside the binnacle in front of the steering wheel. A compass error of 23° West caused by variation and deviation meant the steering compass did not show the ship's true course, which was 266°. True courses are used elsewhere in this book.

27 **six stars that evening.** A single star sight yields only a single line of position. Two lines must cross to obtain a fix, which indicates the location of the ship. It was possible to obtain both latitude and longitude by using several star sights at one time.

27 **to make his sights.** The time of twilight is given in actual Greenwich mean time, which was slightly different than the time shown on *Titanic*'s clocks.

28 **precautions for the winches."** *Titanic* was equipped with steam-powered deck winches for handling cargo and anchors. Cold temperatures could cause water to condense and possibly freeze inside these winches, raising the possibility of cracked castings and other damage caused by ice as it expanded inside the mechanisms.

## PARALLEL TRACKS

30 **bits of their conversation.** Daisy Minahan, affidavit to U.S. Senate Hearings, May 11, 1912.

32 **when conditions warranted.** Bowditch warns, "The best locations for lookouts are generally in a crow's next . . . or housed in a shelter specifically built for a bow lookout in the eyes of the vessel," 474.

33 **I did not hear of any.** Mersey, May 22, 1912.

34 **both months inclusive.** Hydrographic Office of the British Admiralty, *United States (East Coast)* (pilot book), part 1, 34.

34 **seven-eighths being submerged.** Ibid.

36 **embodies careful navigation.** Mersey, May 1912.

37 **becomes thick or hazy.** Mersey, June 21, 1912.

39 **friends and shipmates.** The officer in charge of the watch is responsible for the operational safety of the ship while on duty. However, the ultimate responsibility for the vessel, its crew, and its passengers always resides with the master.

40 **that is all.** Mersey, May 14, 1912.

42 **colder than freezing.** It was standard procedure aboard *Titanic* and other White Star ships to measure the sea temperature every two hours. Second Officer Lightoller explained the procedure, which involved dipping seawater with a bucket, to the U.S. Senate hearings. The salinity of water reduces its freezing point. Seawater can be colder than 32 degrees Fahrenheit (the freezing temperature of pure water) because of its salt content.

43 **aid to navigation.** *Titanic*'s two radio operators were technically not part of the crew. They were employees of the Marconi Company. The two men earned money for their employer by sending private messages for passengers, not by handling traffic about icebergs. There was no requirement in 1912 for passenger liners or other ships to carry radio equipment or to stand radio watches.

## A DARK MASS

47 **to spot dangers.** "Contrary to widespread opinion, it is not always better to search with binoculars instead of using the naked eye." Bill Bearden

and Bill Wedertz, eds., *The Bluejacket's Manual*, 20th ed. (Annapolis: U.S. Naval Institute, 1978), 480.

47 **after they are spotted.** "The first duty of the lookout is to sight the object and report it. His second duty is to identify it." *The Bluejacket's Manual*, 14th ed. (Annapolis: U.S. Naval Institute, 1950), 490. This half-century-old edition of the handbook, issued to every person enlisted in the U.S. Navy, contains language that succinctly describes the dual nature of the lookout's job. Later versions of the book are less precise.

47 **their unprotected eyes.** Experienced lookouts say that the lack of binoculars also would have made it almost painful to stare into a 22.25-knot wind at an air temperature of 31 degrees. They say binoculars are often used in this situation to shield the eyes from a bitter wind. This can result in overuse of the binoculars, which has its own detrimental effect on keeping an effective lookout.

48 **Just after seven bells.** U.S. Senate Hearings, April 23, 1912.

48 **three points on each side."** A point is equal to 11¼° on the compass. Haze 3 points on either side of the bow would have occupied an arc of nearly 70°.

49 **recognizing it as an iceberg.** Reade, *Ship That Stood Still.*

49 **ten minutes after seven bells.** Mersey, May 20, 1912.

50 **No, sir.** U.S. Senate Hearings, April 23, 1912.

51 **ship's standard compass,** *Titanic*'s standard compass was located on a wooden platform some 15 feet above the first-class lounge. This position removed it as much as possible from deviation caused by the magnetic influences of the ship. In the days before gyrocompasses, the standard compass was carefully adjusted to remove all deviation possible. The two steering compasses on the bridge were compared against the standard compass each day to ensure their accuracy.

51 **officers' quarters.** Boxhall never said why he visited the officers' sleeping quarters while on duty. He might have been in his room, which was adjacent to the outside door to the boat deck. However, it was a cold evening, and that door also led to the officers' lavatory.

51 **center with both wings.** Photos show the top of the forward bulwark to be roughly eye level for Captain Smith. A footboard was provided to allow easier viewing. While walking between the center bridge and either wing, a man of average stature would not have been able to observe the horizon ahead of the ship.

52 **other electrical equipment.** "Telephones—Loud speaking telephones of navy pattern were fitted for communication between the following:

"Wheel house on the navigating bridge and the forecastle.

"Wheel house on the navigating bridge and the look-out station on the crow's nest.

"Wheel house on the navigating bridge and the engine room.

"Wheel house on the navigating bridge and the poop.

"Chief engineer's cabin and the engine room.

"Engine room and Nos. 1, 2, 3, 4, 5 and 6 stokeholds." Mersey, 11.

52 **rods and gears.** O'Donnell, *Last Days of the Titanic*, 86. Photographs

from the Father Browne S.J. (Society of Jesuits) Collection. This was deduced from a photograph of *Olympic*'s captain's bridge, showing an auxiliary steering wheel with a rod to an overhead gearbox and a second rod aft to the wheelhouse.

52  **effective service as a lookout.** The telephone instruments were not modern handsets. They were large units affixed to the bulkhead. The person speaking into the mouthpiece faced the instrument in such a way as to preclude maintaining watch on events around the ship.

53  **and this witness [Fleet].** Mersey, May 24, 1912.

54  **I was getting near him,** Captain Rostron's use of the pronoun *him* in this context refers to the captain of *Titanic,* Edward J. Smith. Rostron would have used the pronoun *her* to refer to the ship.

54  **that is right forward.** U.S. Senate Hearings, April 19, 1912.

54  **bridge by an officer.** Mersey, May 1912.

55  **much more than a mile.** John V. Noel Jr., *Knight's Modern Seamanship,* 17th ed. (New York: Van Nostrand Reinhold, 1984), 357–358.

56  **just after we started.** Mersey, May 8, 1912.

56  **his night orders.** Night orders are more than their name implies. These are written orders from the ship's captain concerning standard procedures to be followed by the junior officers when the captain is not present on the bridge, day or night.

57  **accumulation of distant ice,"** Bowditch, 469–70.

57  **surface of the ice.** "The diffusion of light in a fog will produce a blink, or area of whiteness, above and at the sides of an iceberg which will appear to increase the apparent size of its mass." Bowditch, 470.

58  **higher in the atmosphere.** *Warm* and *cold* are relative terms in this discussion. The air temperature was just freezing, but the core temperature of the floating ice was far colder. Thus, air above the ice was "warmer" than the ice.

58  **seven bells went unheeded.** Gardiner and van der Vat, *Titanic Conspiracy,* 83.

59  **discern objects in darkness.** "Exposure to a white light at night greatly reduces vision." K. C. Jacobsen, *Watch Officer's Guide,* 11th ed. (Annapolis: U.S. Naval Institute, 1985), 62.

60  **across the camera's view.** Reade, *Ship That Stood Still,* 175. Mr. Ogden's photograph is in the National Archives, New York City, but is reproduced in Reade.

61  **in the path of the vessel.** Although archaic on modern ships, lookouts still learn these bell signals: one bell for danger to starboard, two bells for danger to port, and three bells for danger dead ahead.

## COOL HAND MURDOCH

63  **to the left.** The origins of cross steering can be seen on the whaleship *Charles W. Morgan* docked at Mystic Seaport Museum in Mystic, Connecticut. The steering wheel is actually mounted on the ship's tiller and

moves in an arc across the deck as the ship is steered. The helmsman must walk with the steering wheel.

64 **events of that evening.** Lord Mersey ordered maneuvering tests conducted with *Olympic* to gain insight into how *Titanic* would have responded to Murdoch's helm orders. Mersey's final report stated, "it was found that travelling at the same rate as the 'Titanic,' about 37 seconds would be required for the ship to change her course to this extent after the helm had been put hard-a-starboard" (Mersey, 30–31).

64 **quartermaster's movements.** *Titanic* had two steering engines to provide for the possibility of breakdown of one machine. Each had three steam cylinders. Mersey, 13.

65 **slide into the iceberg.** "The steering effect of the rudder is the only force turning the ship. . . . The effect of the rudder is reduced as the headway is lost until there is no steering control when the ship is stationary." John V. Noel Jr., *Knight's Modern Seamanship,* 17th ed. (New York: Van Nostrand Reinhold, 1984), 238.

65 **earlier that night.** Some writers have suggested that Murdoch stopped the center turbine engine and called for full reverse on the port propeller. This suggestion is based on modern ship-handling practice, which uses the thrust of propellers more than rudders when maneuvering in harbors. Even today, such a maneuver would be highly unusual. *Titanic,* however, was not designed to be maneuvered on its propellers, which were much closer together than on present-day ships. Today's ships have multiple rudders, one behind each propeller.

65 **than at lower speeds** "A decrease in speed results in a larger turning circle. . . . In making a turn at low speeds, therefore, more rudder is needed." Jacobsen, *Watch Officer's Guide,* 88.

66 **maneuverability was needed.** "Out in the open sea, a crash stop from full-ahead speed is usually less wise than throwing the rudder hard over and going into a tight turn." Harry Benford, *Naval Architecture for Non-Naval Architects* (Jersey City, N.J.: Society of Naval Architects and Marine Engineers, 1991), 185.

66 **abbreviated sea trials.** Merideth, *1912 Facts about* Titanic, 40–41; results of sea trials of *Titanic,* April 2, 1912.

66 **a crash stop would.** These maneuvering characteristics were found either during *Titanic*'s sea trials or by a series of trials conducted by the British inquiry using *Olympic.*

67 **reciprocating engines** Each of *Titanic*'s reciprocating engines had four inverted, direct-acting cylinders. The high-pressure cylinder had a diameter of 54 inches, the intermediate a diameter of 84 inches, and each of the two low-pressure cylinders a diameter of 97 inches. All four cylinders had a stroke of 6 feet, 3 inches. Each engine was reversed by a Brown's type of direct-acting steam and hydraulic engine. The low-pressure turbine was of the Parson's reaction type, direct coupled to the center propeller shaft. Mersey, 21.

67 **lost during the scramble.** The need for engineers to operate control

valves and levers is still a requirement of maneuvering large ships. In fog or other restricted visibility, the International Rules of the Road require ships to have their engines ready for immediate maneuvers to avoid collision. Therefore, the crew who turn the valves or pull the levers must be on duty and at their stations to avoid the loss of valuable time spent running to their stations only when needed.

67 **not their bows.** "The action of the water on the rudder forces the stern of the vessel to the side, and the vessel changes course. . . . For example: With *right* rudder, the stern of the ship will be forced to the *left*, resulting in the bow moving to the *right*." William B. Hayler, *American Merchant Seaman's Manual*, 6th ed. (Centreville, Md.: Cornell Maritime Press, 1980), 9-8.

68 **than its bow does.** Noel Jr., *Knight's Modern Seamanship*, 214.

71 **vessel into the ice.** Bowditch, 474.

71 **propeller shaft or rudder.** Ibid.

71 **further aft.** Mersey, June 1912.

72 **a glancing blow."** Bowditch, 474.

73 **collision with a sailing vessel.** This story is part of a charming biography of William Murdoch, available from the Web site of his hometown, Dalbeattie, Scotland (*www.dalbeattie.com/titanic/wmmlifea.htm*), where he is regarded as a hero. Lee W. Merideth collaborates the story about Murdoch in his *1912 Facts about* Titanic.

74 **remote standard compass** The standard compass was the most accurate instrument on the ship. It was located on a wooden platform some 15 feet above the superstructure to reduce the influence of the ship's magnetic influence. Other compasses, such as the steering compass in the wheelhouse, were checked against the standard compass on a regular basis. Mersey, 11.

74 **it was carried out.** U.S. Senate Hearings, April 1912.

75 **enormous piston engines.** "At the main reciprocating engine manoeuvering platform were grouped all engine controls and from the one position the engineers could operate the engine steam supply valve, reversing mechanism and bridge telegraph." Dr. Dennis Griffiths, "The Titanic's Engineers," Institute of Marine Engineers, online document, March 27, 1997, *http://newwww.livjm.ac.uk/~etmdgril/html_files/titanic1.htm*.

76 **performed a crash stop.** Strictly speaking, one person did report a crash stop—seaman Joseph Scarrott in his magazine article for *The Sphere* (London: April 1912).

77 **falls within this range.** Benford, *Naval Architecture for Non-Naval Architects*, 182.

77 **the time of the accident.** Francis S. Kinney, "Rudders," in *Skene's Elements of Yacht Design*, rev. and updated (New York: Dodd, Mead, 1973).

77 **in harm's way.** Two witnesses (Boxhall and Olliver) said that Murdoch operated the switch closing the watertight doors. The layout of *Titanic's* bridge makes this unlikely. Sixth Officer Moody was in a much better position to have operated the switch.

77 **an instant later.** "The doorplate was of cast iron . . . closed by gravity, and was held in the open position by a clutch which could be released by means of a powerful electro-magnet controlled from the captain's bridge. . . . The time required for the doors to close was between 25 and 30 seconds." Mersey, 17.

## A NARROW SHAVE

79 **a sort of slowing down.** Emily Bosie Ryerson, Affidavit to U.S. Senate Hearings, May 10, 1912; Mrs. J. Stuart White, U.S. Senate Hearings, May 2, 1912; C. E. Henry Stengel, U.S. Senate Hearings, April 30, 1912; Hugh Woolner, U.S. Senate Hearings, April 29, 1912.

79 **jumped out on the floor.** Daniel Buckley, U.S. Senate Hearings, May 3, 1912.

80 **a grinding noise. . . .** "Edward Dorking, Ship Wreck Survivor Appears at Star Theater," *Bureau County Republican* (Princeton, N.J.), May 12, 1912.

81 **the unsubmerged portion"** Bowditch, 456.

82 **52,310 displacement tons** *Titanic's* displacement weight is given variously at between 48,000 and 64,000 tons. This estimate of 52,310 tons at a draft of 34 feet 7 inches comes from testimony by naval architect Edward Wilding to the London proceedings. It should be remembered that *displacement tonnage* is actual weight, whereas *registered tonnage* measures cubic volume.

82 **36 feet per second.** One nautical mile is equal to 6,076.1 feet. At 22.25 knots, *Titanic* was traveling 135,000 feet per hour, which is the equivalent of 37.9 feet per second.

82 **when the Titanic went down."** *New York Herald*, April 17, 1912.

83 **one second of time.** U.S. Senate Hearings, May 18, 1912.

83 **300 feet along the bow.** Jim Boyer, "Day 16," field report cited on the Discovery Channel Online, *www.discovery.com/area/science/titanic/dispatch16.htm*, Aug. 16, 1996.

84 **inherent strength to resist.** Lightoller, in Winocour, *Story of the* Titanic, 286.

85 **by professional seamen.** Based on the author's personal experience operating a passenger vessel in a shallow river.

85 **in contact with the ice.** This time can be calculated by dividing the maximum distance over which the ship was damaged (300 feet) by its maximum speed in feet per second (37.8). The result is 7.9 seconds. The actual time is unknown and may have been longer as a result of friction slowing *Titanic* to some extent.

86 **heavy body meeting another.** Beesley, *Loss of the S.S.* Titanic, 36.

87 **to the bottom with the ship."** "Captain Spoke of Ice Peril," *New York Times*, April 18, 1912. This article is posted on George Behe's Titanic Tidbits Web site at *http://ourworld.compuserve.com/homepages/Carpathia/page2.htm*. A similar story was carried by the *Denver Post* on Thursday, April 18, 1912, in conjunction with articles about *Carpathia's* arrival in New York.

88 **casino would remain open.** McFadden, Robert D., "Passengers Evacuated after QE2 Runs Aground," *New York Times,* Aug. 9, 1992.

88 **more mass than *Titanic* did.** There are many different forms of floating ice on the ocean. Icebergs are, by definition, the largest. The following definitions are adapted from the May 30, 1912, report of the British inquiry:

"Iceberg—a detached portion of a polar glacier carried out to sea. It is made of fresh water. Only about one-eighth of its mass floats above the surface of sea water.

"Growler—a colloquial term applied to icebergs of smaller mass. It is not infrequently a berg that has turned over and is therefore showing what has been termed *black ice* or, more correctly, *dark blue ice.*

"Pack Ice—floating ice that covers wide areas of the polar seas, broken into large pieces, which are driven ("packed") together by wind and current so as to form a practically continuous sheet. Such ice is generally frozen from seawater and not derived from glaciers.

"Field Ice—a term usually applied to frozen sea water floating in much looser form than pack ice.

"Ice floe—field ice, but in a smaller quantity.

"Floe Berg—stratified mass of floe ice."

89 **iron or steel objects.** From *Assignment Discovery: Icebergs,* a TV classroom documentary that aired on the Discovery Channel. See also Susan Wels, Titanic: *Legacy of the World's Greatest Ocean Liner* (Alexandria, Va.: Time-Life Books, 1997), which is a companion volume to the Discovery Channel cable documentaries.

90 **the average ice cube.** Wayne Curtis, "Peculiar Stuff" in "Ice Never Sleeps," April 8, 1998, *www.discovery.com/exp/icebergs/report3.html.*

90 **ship's bottom paint in 1912.** In *Night to Remember,* in the caption to a photograph (n.p.), Lord referred to "a great scar of red paint" on the iceberg.

90 **Fleet sounded the alarm.** Courses here are given as true. They should not be confused with the compass course, which takes into account variation and deviation.

91 **the underwater ice shelf.** Reade, *Ship That Stood Still,* 46.

91 **after the accident.** "Her Stern Was Swinging Practically Dead South," chapter 4, ibid.

91 **north of the stern.** Ballard, *Discovery of the Titanic,* 91.

92 **50 to 100 feet away.** George Harder, U.S. Senate Hearings, May 3, 1912.

92 **piece was developed.** The full text of Scarrott's article is at the Encyclopedia Titanica Web site, *www.encyclopedia-titanica.org.*

94 **coveralls for the last time.** The Superintendent of Engineering for the White Star Line outlined this emergency procedure in a letter in the April 26, 1912, issue of *The Engineer* (p. 44), a publication of the Institute of Marine Engineers: "When this accident happened and the telegraph rang from the bridge either to stop or reverse the engines a call bell would have rung from the engine room to the engineers' quarters intimating that all engineers were wanted below. At sea and at such a time this

would at once be recognized by the 'watch off' as being an emergency call and they would be down below in a few minutes. F. J. Blake RNR, Engineering Superintendent, White Star Line."

94 **Number 5 section.** Frederick Barrett, U.S. Senate Hearings, May 25, 1912.

94 **forward end," he testified.** Barrett's "third stokehold" refers to the forward half of boiler room #5. Each end of the ship's double-ended boilers was considered a separate stokehold by the crew. In Barrett's reference, the first two stokeholds would have been in boiler room #6. His third stokehold was the forward side of the boilers in boiler room #5. There was no common system of counting boiler rooms and stokeholds on *Titanic.* Boiler rooms were counted from the engine rooms forward, the opposite of how Barrett counted stokeholds.

95 **underneath the water line.** U.S. Senate Hearings, April 25, 1912.

97 **Yes, sir.** Ibid.

97 **were quickly flooded.** Mersey, 32.

97 **seam at its forward end.** "The Flooding in First 10 Minutes," ibid.

97 **no damage above this height.** Mersey, July 30, 1912.

98 **any appreciable amount.** Ibid.

98 **other impurities.** William H. Garzke Jr., et al., "*Titanic,* the Anatomy of a Disaster: A Report from the Marine Forensic Panel (SD-7)," in Society of Naval Architects and Marine Engineers *Transactions,* January 1977, vol. 150: 3–61.

98 **some kind of problem."** Filed by the Associated Press, Boston, December 1, 1998, at 11:45 A.M. The full text is available from Nando Media, *www.news-observer.com/newsroom/ntn, Nov. 1999.*

98 **huge plates of steel together.** According to Parks Stephenson, a member of the Marine Forensic Panel of the Society of Naval Architects and Marine Engineers, hull seams below the superstructure expansion joints were welded on *Titanic* using a new process demonstrated by the Thermite Company in 1907. This new technique was not suited to constructing an entire ship.

99 **joints called *butts*.** Hayler, *American Merchant Seaman's Manual,* 15-1 to 15-5.

100 **faying surfaces of the plates.** Brian Baxter in *Naval Architecture* (London: English Universities Press, 1959; rpt., Hodder & Stoughton, 1976), 174 (rpt. ed.).

101 **like a piece of tin.** Lightoller, in Winocour, *Story of the* Titanic, 286.

102 **from 300 to 200 feet.** At one point in Wilding's testimony, he indicated the damage might have occurred over no more than 200 feet of the hull, although the 300-foot length published in the final British report was based on his estimates.

102 **flooded the different spaces.** Mersey, May 6, 1912.

102 **running into the bottom** "3. A ship strikes when it in any way touches the bottom. To run ashore or aground." Rene de Kerchove, *International Maritime Dictionary,* 2d ed. (New York: Van Nostrand Reinhold, 1983).

103 **negligible listing.** Alf Carver, "Damaged Stability," in *Simple Ship Stability* (Surrey, England: Fairplay Publications, n.d.). This book discusses the impact on stability caused by flooding as the result of an accident. While not specific to *Titanic*, the information is useful in understanding why ships list and loll after an accident.

104 **starboard side forward.** Naval architect Edward Wilding advanced another theory for the immediate starboard list during testimony before the British proceedings. In questions 20,242 through 20,250, he proposes that the starboard list might have been created by water coming up the stairway in the post office and flooding the starboard side of G deck.

105 **Why should I? (laughter).** Mersey, July 30, 1912.

105 **open seams totaling 31 meters,** *Transactions*, Society of Naval Architects and Marine Engineers, vol. 150 (Jan. 1997), 3–62.

105 **where the keel is straight.** Ibid.

106 **struck by the hand.** Capt. John J. Knapp, USN, U.S. Senate Hearings, May 18, 1912.

107 **outside shell plating.** Dan Dietz, "How Did the *Titanic* Sink?", *Mechanical Engineering* (American Society of Mechanical Engineers, 1998), *www.memagazine.org/contents/current/features/titanic/titanic.html.*

107 **starboard side of the hull.** Ballard, *Discovery of the* Titanic, 196–97.

107 **proving how the ship sank.** Bryan Jackson interviewed George Tulloch in March 1998 for WNYT-TV in Albany, New York. Full interview, *http://members.global2000.net/~bjackson/.*

108 **than on the starboard side.** Boyer, "Day 16," Discovery Channel Online.

108 **plowed into the bottom.** "The two large hull sections may have reached a speed of 25 or 30 miles an hour." Ballard, *Discovery of the* Titanic, 206.

108 **almost 60 feet.** Ibid., 168, drawing.

## BLIND FAITH

113 **the London proceedings.** Mersey, 43–45.

114 **back into my bunk.** Lightoller, in Winocour, *Story of the* Titanic, 284.

116 **ostensibly as a passenger,** Ismay made the claim of being only a passenger many times, but never more forcefully than in "Statement Issued by J. Bruce Ismay to a Representative of the Times," *Times* (London), April 21, 1912: "During the voyage I was a passenger and exercised no greater rights or privileges than any other passenger."

117 **became nearly impossible.** "Mr. Lightoller . . . says that the noise of the steam blowing off was so great that his voice could not be heard, and that he had to give directions with his hands." Mersey, 37.

117 **would resume steaming.** "A rather mysterious incident may conveniently be examined here. This is the movement of the *Titanic* after she had stopped as the result of the collision." Reade, *Ship That Stood Still,* 29.

118 **wanting to make way** There is a difference between *under way* and *making way*. Any ship that is not docked, anchored, or aground is considered to be under way. The term *making way* applies when a vessel is

being driven forward by its engines. Thus, a ship can be under way and either not making way or making way.

118 **their social superiority.** Author Roland Huntford explored this aspect of British culture in his epic book, *Scott and Amundsen* (New York: Atheneum, 1984; rpt. *The Last Place on Earth: Scott and Amundsen's Race to the South Pole*, New York: Modern Library, 1999). He places the blame for Scott's failure on his belief that an amateur with heart can overcome all. Amundsen reached the South Pole on December 14, 1911.

118 **during time of war.** *Titanic* lacked the horsepower to win the Atlantic Blue Ribband prize. Its three engines could produce about 45,000 horsepower. Both *Mauritania* and *Lusitania* were smaller ships, but each could produce about 75,000 horsepower.

120 **subdivision of the vessel.** The term *subdivision* refers to dividing a ship into watertight compartments for the purpose of containing flooding in an emergency. It is considered a safety feature equal in importance to lifeboats on passenger vessels.

121 **between 2 ft. 6 in. and 3 ft. . . . .** Mersey, July 30, 1912.

122 **to the tank top deck.** Ibid., 32.

123 **its maiden voyage.** The third and last Olympic-class ship was originally to be named *Gigantic*. White Star changed the name to *Britannic*, apparently to prevent the public from connecting the third ship with its unlucky sister.

123 **beyond all that.** "Disaster at Last Befalls Capt. Smith," *New York Times*, April 16, 1912.

123 **challenged by the accident.** Following *Olympic*'s brush with the warship *Hawke*, Captain Smith told passengers that if either *Olympic* or *Titanic* were cut in half, both sections could float indefinitely. On the night of his last dinner in New York City, the Captain told Mr. and Mrs. W. P. Willie of Flushing, Long Island, that he had no doubt both ships could reach port even if seriously damaged. See George Behe's Titanic Tidbits, *http:// ourworld.compuserve.com/homepages/Carpathia/page2.htm*, "Captain Smith Felt Sure of His Ship."

125 **concerned about his passengers.** The captain's responsibility to the passengers as well as to the ship is still a part of U.S. maritime law. Captains are required to render assistance to others in peril, "so far as the master . . . can do so without serious danger to the master's . . . vessel or to individuals on board." *Title 46, U.S. Code*, chapter 23, secs. 2301–5 (Aug. 26, 1983).

126 **outer shell became damaged.** "Any grounding or similar damage which merely pierces the bottom plating will flood one or more of these tanks instead of allowing water to enter one of the main holds." Felix M. Cornell and Allan C. Hoffman, *American Merchant Seaman's Manual*, 6th ed. (Centreville, Md.: Cornell Maritime Press, 1980), 15-3.

126 **based on scanty information.** The International Regulations for Preventing Collisions at Sea (COLREGS) are specific on this point. Rule 7(c) specifically states, "Assumptions shall not be made on the basis of scanty information."

127 **So I just waited.** Lightoller, in Winocour, *Story of the* Titanic, 284.

127 **jammed open by the blast.** *Britannic* appears to have run over a typical contact mine tethered about 30 feet beneath the surface. Like *Titanic*, the ship's cutaway forefoot protected the forepeak against contact with the deadly device. The mine appears to have exploded beneath the bulkhead between holds #2 and #3, exactly where *Titanic* was damaged on the underwater ice shelf.

127 **replay of *Titanic*.** There is some evidence that the double sides built into *Britannic* might have caused the ship to roll onto its side, increasing the speed with which it sank. Double sides were installed to correct a perceived weakness in *Titanic*, which had only single sides.

## STEAMING TO OBLIVION

130 **Hutchinson blurted out** The expression *making water* is sailor jargon that describes any situation in which unwanted water comes into a vessel.

131 **company's New York office.** This information was brought to light in a written statement to the U.S. Senate investigation by Maurice I. Farrell, managing editor of the Dow Jones News Service. He confirmed it in testimony on May 9, 1912.

132 **that night about *Titanic*.** There is proof that Guglielmo Marconi went to extremes to keep *Titanic*'s surviving radio operator from talking to the press until after a private meeting in New York. Marconi had much to hide in the aftermath of the tragedy. Phillips had rebuffed the first ship to answer his distress call because that vessel was not equipped with a Marconi transmitter. It might have been a simple matter for the inventor of wireless to remove all records of *Titanic*'s Halifax message from his company's files.

132 **nonexistent one about *Virginian*.** Bryceson, Titanic *Disaster*, 95, 96.

132 **Bride recalled the captain's visit** Harold Bride, "Thrilling Tales by *Titanic*'s Surviving Wireless Man," *New York Times*, April 28, 1912.

132 **DON'T WORRY.** The newspaper retracted this story the following day, saying the message had been sent by Phillips's unnamed brother. No mention was made of why the brother would have sent such a message or why he would have mentioned Halifax.

133 **Allan liner Virginian.** "All on Board Safe, Passengers Taken Off," *Daily Mirror*, April 16, 1912.

133 **exclusively from New York.** "London Hears Late of Loss of *Titanic*," *New York Tribune*, April 16, 1912.

134 **anything of that kind.** Philip A.S. Franklin, U.S. Senate Hearings, April 22, 1912.

134 **office in New York.** Maurice I. Farrell, May 4, 1912, statement, U.S. Senate Hearings, April 1912.

135 **sufficient for 710 people.** Ibid.

135 **Tuesday evening.** U.S. Senate Hearings, April 1912.

138 **glad to see this.** Beesley, *Loss of the S.S.* Titanic, 41.

138 **the ship's machinery.** In a true steamship there is little vibration from the engines. Almost all of the vibration comes from the propellers. A "pulse" of water was thrown against the hull by each blade of *Titanic's* three propellers. Since they were four-bladed, that meant twelve pulses per revolution of all three shafts.

138 **engines more noticeable.** Based on the author's personal experience.

139 **an officer anywhere,"** Gracie, in Winocour, *Story of the* Titanic, 124.

139 **gray overcoat and outing cap.** Ibid.

139 **call a "dead calm."** The calm conditions are recorded in at least two sources:

"From 6 P.M. onwards to the time of the collision the weather was perfectly fine and clear." Mersey, 29.

"During the entire voyage the weather was clear . . . and the sea was calm throughout the voyage, with sunshine the whole of each day and bright starlight every night." Senate Subcommittee of the Committee on Commerce, *Investigation into Loss of S.S. "Titanic,"* 62nd Cong., May 28, 1912, final S. Rept.

139 **forward after the accident.** "MR. LIGHTOLLER: We [Lightoller and Murdoch] remarked on the weather, about its being calm, clear." Ibid., April 19, 1912.

140 **keep her afloat.** U.S. Senate Hearings, April 19, 1912.

140 **a major leak.** Opening the automatic watertight doors also indicates there was telephone communication between Captain Smith and Chief Engineer Bell. Once closed from the bridge, the automatic doors were designed so they could not be reopened unless the electric current was shut off from the bridge. Bell and Smith must have discussed the situation before the captain permitted the current to be shut off so Bell could have the doors raised. This discussion might have reinforced the captain's overconfidence in the ability of the ship to float despite major damage.

141 **remained tightly closed.** "Watertight doors . . . should be opened only after making sure that the compartment is dry or so little flooded that no further flooding will be produced by opening the closure."

"Extreme caution is always necessary in opening compartments below the waterline in the vicinity of any damage." *Bluejacket's Manual,* 14th ed., 527.

141 **catastrophic explosion.** "Cold sea water coming into a hot boiler under pressure could also cause an explosion due to thermal stress . . . " Dr. Dennis Griffiths, "The *Titanic's* Engineers," Institute of Marine Engineers, online document, March 27, 1997, *http://newwww.livjm.ac.uk/ ~etmdgril/html_files/titanic1.htm.*

141 **at all times in steamships.** An exploding boiler is a steam engineer's biggest nightmare. Debate continues over whether cold seawater will cause enough thermal shock to force a boiler to explode. Naval architect Edward Wilding of Harland and Wolff told the British inquiry that an explosion could not be caused by ice-cold seawater striking a hot

boiler. Whether an explosion is possible or not, generations of engineers lived in fear of such an event. The actions of Chief Engineer Bell and his men show that they were motivated by that fear as water flooded *Titanic*'s stokeholds.

143 **reported to the Captain.** U.S. Senate Hearings, April 22, 1912.

145 **storeroom is quite dry."** Samuel S. Hemming, ibid., April 25, 1912.

145 **rush of water coming through.** Frederick Clench, ibid.

146 **inspection of the bow was short.** In the aftermath, survivors reported seeing Captain Smith looking for damage as far aft as the second grand stairway and in a variety of passenger accommodations. Many people claimed to have been told privately "by the captain" that the ship was sinking. These stories seem to be embellishments designed to enhance the teller's credibility. There was no reason for Smith to have visited any other portion of the ship than the bow. That is where he knew his ship was damaged.

146 **big reciprocating engines.** "Everything was under pressure of steam of 200 lb.," according to F. J. Blake RNR, the engineering superintendent for the White Star Line. This statement refers to the normal steam pressure when *Titanic* was steaming at 20 knots or better. From Blake's letter to the magazine *The Engineer* (April 26, 1912, 441).

148 **ultimately fill and sink.** Mersey, 34.

148 **not designed to support.** Baxter, "Flooding and Watertight Subdivision" and "The Strength of Ships," in *Naval Architecture*, 174 (rpt. ed.).

149 **becoming aware of the accident.** In Elijah Baker, *Introduction to Steel Shipbuilding* (New York: McGraw-Hill, 1953), there is an excellent drawing and discussion of hull failure caused by hogging (p. 3).

## Time for Us to Leave Her

150 **when Boxhall found him.** In London, Boxhall estimated that he began rousing out the off-watch officers about twenty minutes to half an hour after the accident (Question #15379, Mersey's Inquiry).

152 **to save himself.** Lord, *Night to Remember*, 93.

152 **captain's second visit.** Harold Bride, "Thrilling Story by *Titanic*'s Surviving Wireless Man," *New York Times*, April 19, 1912.

152 **use his sextant.** "It is sometimes difficult to obtain a good star image and a well defined horizon at the same time." G. D. Dunlap and H. H. Shufeldt, *Dutton's Navigation and Piloting* (Annapolis: Naval Institute Press, 1972), section 2211.

152 **called *dead reckoning.*** Dunlap and Shufeldt, "Dead Reckoning and Current Sailing," in *Dutton's Navigation and Piloting.*

152 **cruising around there, sir.** U.S. Senate Hearings, April 27, 1912.

153 **a math error.** Dave Gittins's Web site is part of the South Australian Web site ring. The information about Boxhall's position is at *http://users. senet.com.au/~gittins/sospos.html.*

153 **nearly 13-mile error.** Ibid.

155 **ultimately prove necessary.** Axel Welin, Institute of Naval Architects, March 19, 1912.

156 **only 962 seats.** "The Board of Trade's Administration," in Mersey, 47.

158 **level with the rail.** U.S. Senate Hearings, April 23, 1912.

158 **there was no danger.** Dr. Washington Dodge, *Bulletin*, San Francisco, April 19, 1912.

158 **thought it was going down. . . .** Mrs. J. Stuart White, U.S. Senate Hearings, May 2, 1912.

159 **cracking and splitting.** *Boatswain's Mate 2 & 3*, U.S. Navy Bureau of Naval Personnel, NAVPERS 10121-C (1959).

159 **did give way.** Mersey, June 17, 1912.

161 **affected by the fire.** Ibid.

163 **Bowditch's table 12,** Distance of the Horizon, Bowditch, 673.

164 **guns (signaling cannons).** The firing of a gun at regular intervals (usually one minute) is a distress signal under the International Rules of the Road.

166 **might still have been swamped.** "The most dangerous time in hooking out a boat is THE MOMENT IT BECOMES WATERBORNE" [emphasis in original]. United States Navy, "Boats," in *Boatswain's Mate 2 & 3*, 185.

168 **got there as soon.** British Inquiry, May 14, 1912.

168 **grave responsibility.** Senator William Alden Smith, Michigan, May 28, 1912.

168 **lives that were lost.** Mersey, July 30, 1912.

169 **speed of about 13 knots.** This was Captain Lord's estimate presented during the British inquiry.

170 **spot in full daylight,** This has been the author's experience when rescuing eight people in two separate incidents.

171 **If she moved, yes.** British inquiry, May 14, 1912.

172 **signals if we had done.** Ibid.

## A SHORTAGE OF WOMEN

174 **chances with her afterwards.** U.S. Senate Hearings, April 19, 1912.

175 **put more than 50 in . . .** Ibid., April 24, 1912.

175 **the doomed passengers.** "Most casualties at sea are actually the result of panic. . . . In a life-or-death emergency you are not going to be entirely free of panic." Phil Richards and John J. Banigan, *How to Abandon Ship* (Centreville, Md.: Cornell Maritime Press, 1942; rpt. 1988), 4, 5 (rpt. ed.).

175 **told to don lifebelts,** Although called "lifebelts" under British regulations, these were more like short, cork-filled serapes open at the sides with a hole for the wearer's head.

176 **boats would have held more** U.S. Senate Hearings, April 23, 1912.

176 **there was no response.** Ibid., April 24, 1912.

177 **On the boat deck.** U.S. Senate inquiry.

177 **Lifeboat Loading (table)** Mersey, 38.

179 **class, or nationality, or pedigree.** U.S. Senate Hearings, April 24, 1912.

180 **two men attempted to speak.** "12-53 A.M. . . . 'Caronia' to M.B.C. ('Baltic') and S.O.S., 'M.G.Y.' ('Titanic') C.Q.D. in 41.46 N., 50.14 W. Wants immediate assistance." Mersey, 66.

180 **womenfolk in the receding lifeboats.** Mrs. Ruth Dodge, quoted in *Bulletin*, San Francisco, April 19, 1912.

181 **attempt was unsuccessful.** Ballard's expedition to the wreck found this door still open, awaiting passengers. It might be a monument to the sailors sent to open the gangway because they were lost as the ship sank.

182 **I did not hurt anybody.** U.S. Senate Hearings, April 24, 1912.

182 **launched from the starboard side.** Lord, *Night Lives On*, 128–29.

184 **throw him into the ocean.** U.S. Senate Hearings, May 3, 1912.

185 **in charge of their own departments.** Mersey, May 1912.

186 **they could not go that way.** U.S. Senate Hearings, May 8, 1912.

187 **they have already laid down.** Mersey, June 17, 1912.

188 **Oh, no.** U.S. Senate Hearings, April 23, 1912.

189 **her green light, rather.** Ibid., April 19, 1912.

190 **what actually happened.** Beesley, *Loss of the S.S. Titanic*, 76.

190 **suffered financial difficulties.** Gardiner and van der Vat, Titanic *Conspiracy*, 39.

191 **George Frederick Crowe, Steward** U.S. Senate Hearings, April 25, 1912: Frank Osman, seaman; Edward John Buley, seaman; and George Frederick Crowe, steward.

191 **sank in pieces.** The Discovery Channel claims that the two halves of the ship remained joined at the keel for a short time after the hulk disappeared from the surface. See Wels, Titanic: *Legacy of the Greatest Ocean Liner*, 143–48.

## APPENDIX 2. A TITAN'S WAKE

196 **avoiding certain areas of inquiry.** Mersey.

196 **domination of Europe,** Cynthia Fansler Behrman, *Victorian Myths of the Sea* (Oberlin OH: Oberlin Printing Company, 1977). This slender volume examines how the sea and the navy have influenced England, particularly in a patriotic sense. Although the author does not refer directly to *Titanic*, she presents the background for the particularly British version of jingoism that existed during the last decades of the British empire.

197 **prospect of obtaining damages. . . .** *New York Herald*, Sunday, April 21, 1912.

197 **knowledge of ships and the sea.** Senate Subcommittee of the Committee on Commerce, Titanic *Disaster*, 62nd Cong., 2d sess., pursuant to S. Res. 283, Jan. 1913.

198 **very rapid foundering.** Lord Charles Beresford, "Report: Saving Life at Sea, 1887," quoted in Mersey, 47.

200 **very much appreciated.** Lightoller, in Winocour, *Story of the* Titanic, 305.

200 **I do not believe this.** Mersey, July 30, 1912.

# SELECT BIBLIOGRAPHY

Ballard, Robert D. *The Discovery of the* Titanic. New York: Warner Communications, A Warner/Madison Press Book, 1987.

Beesley, Lawrence. *The Loss of the S.S.* Titanic: *Its Story and Its Lessons.* Boston: Houghton Mifflin, 1912, rpt. 2000. Page citations are to the reprint edition.

Biel, Steven. *Down with the Old Canoe—A Cultural History of the* Titanic *Disaster.* New York: W.W. Norton, 1996.

Brown, Richard. *Voyage of the Iceberg.* New York: Beaufort Books; Toronto: James Lorimer, 1983.

Bryceson, Dave. *The* Titanic *Disaster As Reported in the British National Press April–July, 1912.* New York: W. W. Norton, 1997.

Caren, Eric, and Steve Goldman. *Extra* Titanic, *The Story of the Disaster in the Newspapers of the Day.* Edison, N.J.: Castle Books, 1998.

Eaton, John P., and Charles A. Haas. Titanic: *Triumph and Tragedy.* 2d ed. New York: W.W. Norton, 1995, 1998.

Gardiner, Robin, and Dan van der Vat. *The* Titanic *Conspiracy.* New York: Carol Publishing Group, Birch Lane Press, 1995.

Gracie, Archibald. *The Truth about the* Titanic. N.p.: Mitchell Kennerley, 1913. See also Winocour, *Story of the* Titanic.

Hoffer, William. *Saved! The Story of the* Andrea Doria. New York: Simon & Schuster, Summit Books, 1979.

Huntford, Roland. *Shackleton.* New York: Ballantine, A Fawcett Columbine Book, 1985.

Hyslop, Donald, Alastair Forsyth, and Sheila Jemima. Titanic *Voices, Memories from the Fateful Voyage.* Southhampton, England: Southampton City Council, 1994; reprint, Gloucestershire: Sutton Publishing Ltd., 1998.

Kuntz, Tom, ed. *The* Titanic *Disaster Hearings.* New York: Simon & Schuster, Pocket Books, 1998.

Lightoller, C. H. Titanic *and Other Ships.* London: Nicholson & Watson, 1935. See also Winocour, *Story of the* Titanic.

Lord, Walter. *The Night Lives On.* New York: William Morrow, 1986.

———. *A Night to Remember.* New York: Henry Holt, 1955.

Lynch, Don. Titanic: *An Illustrated History.* Illustrated by Ken Marschall. Toronto: Hyperion, Madison Press, 1992.

Marriott, John. *Disaster at Sea.* New York: Hippocrene Books, 1987.

Marriott, Leo. *Titanic.* London: The Promotional Reprint Book Co., 1997.

Merideth, Lee William. *1912 Facts about* Titanic. Mason City, Iowa: Savas Publishing, 1999.

Newell, Gordon. *Ocean Liners of the 20th Century.* New York: Bonanza Books, 1963.

O'Donnell, E. E. *The Last Days of the* Titanic. Dublin: Wolfhound Press, 1997; reprint, Newot, Colo.: Roberts Rinehart Publishers, 1997.

Pellegrino, Charles. *Her Name* Titanic. New York: Avon Books, 1988.

Quinn, Paul J. Titanic *at Two* A.M: *An Illustrated Narrative with Survivor Accounts.* Hollis, N.H.: Fantail, 1998.

Reade, Leslie. *The Ship That Stood Still.* Edited by Edward P. De Groot. New York: W.W. Norton, 1993.

Stenson, Patrick. *The Odyssey of C. H. Lightoller.* New York: W.W. Norton, 1984.

Tibballs, Geoff. *The* Titanic, *The Extraordinary Story of the "Unsinkable" Ship.* Pleasantville, N.Y.: Carleton Books, A Reader's Digest Book, 1997.

Wade, Wyn Craig. *The* Titanic: *End of a Dream.* New York: Penguin Books, 1979.

Wells, Susan. Titanic, *Legacy of the World's Greatest Ocean Liner.* New York: Time/Life, 1997.

Winocour, Jack, ed. *The Story of the* Titanic, *as Told by Its Survivors.* New York: Dover Publications, 1960. This volume includes Gracie, *Truth about the* Titanic, in entirety, and portions of Lightoller, Titanic *and Other Ships.*

# Acknowledgments

This book would not exist without Jonathan Eaton of International Marine, who believed in the project long before it was ready for publication. Two mariners, Captains Charles B. Weeks Jr. and Thomas C. Wingfield, deserve credit for their considerable effort correcting early versions of the manuscript and suggesting areas for additional research.

Special thanks to historian and editor Roger Long, who helped transform what he termed a "sea-going Russian novel" into coherent prose. Also to Captain Trey Elliott, who provided insightful analysis of both the way ships maneuver and the way the officers who command them respond during emergencies. Finally, thanks to George Behe of the Titanic Historical Society, whose e-mail correspondence helped me understand certain interconnected facts regarding the lookouts.

Every writer on the subject of *Titanic* must acknowledge a debt to Walter Lord, the dean of *Titanic* authors. Without his revival of *Titanic*'s story during the 1950s, there would be little interest today in either the ship itself or in books about its tragic maiden voyage.

# INDEX